EUROPEAN INDUSTRIES

European Industries

Structure, Conduct and Performance

Edited by

Peter Johnson

University of Durham
UK

Edward Elgar

Published by
Edward Elgar Publishing Limited
Gower House
Croft Road
Aldershot
Hants GU11 3HR
England

Edward Elgar Publishing Company
Old Post Road
Brookfield
Vermont 05036
USA

A CIP catalogue record for this book is available from the British Library

Library of Congress Cataloging-in-Publication Data
European industries / edited by Peter Johnson. — 1st
   ed.
     p.   cm.
     1. Europe—Industries.   2. Europe—Economic conditions—1945–
I. Johnson, Peter, 1944– .
   HC240.S765   1993
   338.094—dc20   93–6538
                                                                              CIP

ISBN 1 85278 612 4

Printed and Bound in Great Britain by
Hartnolls Limited, Bodmin, Cornwall.

Contents

Figures

Tables

List of contributors

Anthony Cockerill is Professor and Director of the Management Centre, Manchester Business School, University of Manchester.

Alan Earl-Slater was until recently Junior Research Fellow, Wolfson College, Oxford.

Lynne Evans is Senior Lecturer in Economics, University of Durham.

Michael Fleming is Professor of Economics, Loughborough University.

David Hawdon is Lecturer in Economics, University of Surrey.

Brian Hill is Senior Lecturer in Economics, University of Nottingham.

Nick Hooper is Senior Research Fellow and Deputy Director, Centre for Defence Economics, University of York.

Peter Johnson is Reader in Economics, University of Durham.

Leonie Marks was formerly Lecturer in Economics, University of Durham, and is now at the University of Missouri-Columbia.

Peter Pearson is Senior Lecturer in Economics, University of Surrey, and Director of the Surrey Energy Economics Centre.

Garel Rhys is Professor and Head of the Economics Section, Cardiff Business School, University of Wales, Cardiff.

Barry Thomas is Senior Lecturer in Economics, University of Durham.

Digby Waller is Research Fellow, Centre for Defence Economics, University of York.

Acknowledgements

My first acknowledgement must be to the contributors. It has been a pleasure to work with them, and I am most grateful for the way in which they responded so readily to editorial suggestions and comments.

Julie Bushby, Kathryn Cowton and Lovaine Ord provided efficient secretarial services at the Durham end. Their help is much appreciated. I should also like to thank Edward Elgar and his team for their enthusiastic support of this project. A number of publishers kindly granted permission for material in which they hold the copyright to be reproduced in this book; their assistance is gratefully acknowledged.

Peter Johnson,
Durham

Preface

The purpose of this book is twofold. The first is to provide authoritative chapter-length studies on some important industries in Europe. These studies will be of particular value to those readers seeking an introduction to an industry, but they will also be helpful as a guide to more detailed work. The second purpose is to offer case study material on various aspects of industrial activity. This material will provide empirical illustrations of some of the theoretical issues considered in courses on industrial organization and related subjects.

Each chapter has been written from a European perspective. Although the authors are all based in the UK, they have endeavoured to avoid any specifically UK bias, except where this is justified by the European perspective. 'Europe' has mostly been defined in terms of the current (September 1992) twelve full members of the European Community. However, in a number of chapters it has been recognized that this definition is not the most appropriate, so in these cases a more flexible approach has been adopted.

Several considerations governed the choice of industries although an underlying aim has been to illustrate the wide variety of industrial characteristics and activities within the EC. A starting point for selection was the view that it made sense to include activities that covered the whole industrial classification. The primary, secondary and tertiary sectors are therefore all represented. Secondly, efforts have been made to cover industries that illustrate a range of characteristics. So, for example, both 'science-based' industries (e.g. pharmaceuticals and biotechnology) and more traditional sectors (e.g. steel and construction) are included. Industries with a long history of public ownership (e.g. steel and air transport) as well as those in which private business has played a dominant role (e.g. financial services and tourism) are represented. The industries selected also differ in the extent to which intra-European trade occurs. In construction for example such trade is undertaken by a relatively small number of international firms, whereas in the motor vehicles industry it is the norm for virtually all businesses.

Thirdly, the selection is designed to show the variety of ways in which the European 'dimension' is reflected in industrial activities and development. For some industries, notably non-specialist motor vehicles, production and marketing on a European-wide scale is necessary to achieve economies of scale. In the case of air transport and tourism, a European view of the market is at the heart of many firms' operations. In other industries (such as construction) it is the boundaries of national (or even local) markets that are most relevant for the majority of business operations. EC-level policies have also varied in their nature and impact across industries. In agriculture, for example, such policies have had major implications (for good or ill) for productive activity not only in the industry itself, but also in other sectors, especially manufacturing. In the steel industry too, EC policy has had a significant effect. The *potential* effects in air transport are also considerable. In other industries the impact of EC-level policies has been much more marginal. The very nature of the construction market for example means that for much of the industry's activity, EC policy-making has only limited relevance. Tourism is another sector where policy at the EC level has so far had a relatively insignificant impact.

Productive activities may of course be classified on a variety of bases, and some of the industries included in this volume do not fit easily into a conventional system of industrial classification. This serves to illustrate the fact that there may be several alternative criteria on which it may be valid to group productive units. Tourism, for example, is a 'package' of different components, yet as Barry Thomas points out in Chapter 10 a good case can be made for treating it as a separate industry, given such factors as the complementarities on the demand side and substitutability between some inputs. Again, the defence industries (Chapter 7) cover a very wide range of activities yet the firms concerned have much in common from an analytical point of view: they all face a major government customer who is dominated by political considerations; many of them are also subject to high levels of uncertainty about technological developments. Biotechnology (Chapter 5) inevitably straddles several industries, but the underlying unity of techno-logical interest between firms operating in this field, even if they ultimately serve different final markets, provides a logical basis for grouping produc-tive activities together under this heading. Clearly there is no 'correct' classification system; much will depend on the purpose of the analysis in hand.

It is inevitable, given the way in which the industries covered in this book vary in their characteristics, that the treatment of each chapter differs. Any attempt to impose a detailed common framework on the chapters would have been unsuccessful and, given the diversity of industries, undesirable. However, all the contributions have been written with the overall objectives of the book in mind, and where appropriate a broad structure – conduct – performance – policy framework has been adopted.

Contributors were free to express their own views on the industry about which they were writing. No editorial control was exercised in this respect. As a result, a variety of views on issues such as industrial performance and the effectiveness of policy have been expressed. The views of individual contributors are not necessarily shared by anyone else.

It is a relatively easy task to suggest other industries that might have been included. Yet given the considerations which have been outlined, the constraints on space, and the need to find contributors able and willing to write, the selection provided here offers a reasonably balanced and wide-ranging picture of European industry. The variation in criteria used to define industrial boundaries makes it difficult to estimate the overall coverage of the book, but it is likely that the sectors covered here account for between 40 and 50 per cent of total EC employment.

Note: throughout this book billion refers to one thousand million.

1 Energy

Peter Pearson and David Hawdon

1.1 Introduction

The energy sectors in most European countries differ significantly from other industries in terms of both scale and degree of public ownership and control. Operating units whether in coal mining, electricity generation, oil producing and refining or gas production tend to be large in relation to industry size, characterized by economies of scale and subject to unique pressures due both to their importance as providers of power for the rest of the economy and to the environmental impact of their activities. In most countries, the energy sector has attracted policy intervention because of concern about security of energy supplies in a volatile world market, the significant scale of energy investments in relation to existing capital markets, and the effects of energy on local and national environments. Not surprisingly, significant developments have taken place in the control of the industries included in this sector as, for example, in the United Kingdom's recent privatization programme and in current efforts to extend competition and price transparency to energy throughout the EC. This has often produced policy conflicts such as those between regional and competition policies, or between energy-promoting and environmental protection policies. Following a relatively brief discussion of the development of the sector, this chapter focuses on the evolution of policy and makes an assessment of its economic effects.

The energy industries are a collection of very diverse mining, production and distribution activities involved with primary materials and secondary transformation of such materials into energy forms suitable for the final user. The technologies of electricity generation, gas transmission and petroleum refining are both complex and fundamentally different from one another and are often viewed as the domain of the expert so far as decision-making is concerned. On the supply side actual and potential substitution between factors engaged in these industries is rather limited in the short run. One consequence of restricted substitutability between fuels is that changes in the availability of any one fuel tend to impact on import levels rather than on domestic production. Only in the long run can significant inter-fuel substitution occur through large-scale investment. Opportunities for substitution between fuels at the consumer level are similarly limited to the long run. In the short run, energy consumers are constrained by an existing and fuel-specific set of energy-using appliances – heaters, cookers, lighting and power systems, and so forth. Again with appropriate investment decisions, substitution between fuels is possible for many specific applications. Thus the energy sector is an industry only in a long-run sense, and change in market shares happens slowly and depends upon changes in expected fuel and capital prices. In consequence, official policies are often specific to the fuel concerned and it is, therefore, necessary to look in more detail at energy submarkets than would be necessary for other sectors.

1.2   The European energy market

The contribution of energy to overall employment in Europe is relatively small. In 1988, according to the Commission of the European Communities (CEC, 1991a), employment in energy (1.76 million employees) amounted to 6.6 per cent of total industrial employment in the EC. This share varies both across country and across fuels. Both Belgium and the UK have relatively high energy employment shares (9.8 per cent and 9.4 per cent respectively of total industrial employment), while Italy and France are below average (5.8 per cent and 5.7 per cent). Electricity and gas provide most employment in the sector (63 per cent) while coal mining is still a significant employer (24 per cent). In contrast to its relatively limited role as an employer, energy is an important consumer of investment resources, accounting for around 25 per cent of total industrial gross fixed capital formation in the same period. Again there are substantial inter-country variations with Germany, France, Italy and the UK spending a higher than average proportion of their investment expenditure on energy. Electricity and gas contribute more to total energy investment (72 per cent) than other fuels, so are more important in the investment market than in the labour market. This reflects the relatively high capital intensity of the sector and the importance of electricity and gas within it.

An approximate measure of output in the energy sector may be obtained by aggregating fuels on the basis of gross calorific values, that is, according to the amount of heat that can be derived from each form of energy. A widely used unit is the tonne of oil equivalent (toe) which corresponds to 10 million kilocalories of heat (Shell, 1986). Energy consumption on this basis rose rapidly from 1960 to 1975 from 524 to 950 million tonnes of oil equivalent (mtoe), fell under the impact of the two world oil price shocks (1973–74 and 1979–80) but began to grow again after 1983 as output recovered and oil prices fell. More recent data on energy production and consumption, given in energy balance form in Table 1.1, indicate that while energy production expanded by 12.5 per cent between 1984 and 1992, imports increased by 27 per cent, enabling gross inland consumption to rise by 17.6 per cent. Increased import dependence is due to three factors – reductions in the price of imported crude oil, lack of growth of solid fuel production and decline in the output of North Sea oilfields. Only rapid expansion of natural gas production and nuclear-generated electricity have held back the growth in energy imports.

1.3 Structure and organization of the energy industries

The energy sectors are very diverse in terms of ownership although there is a strong state presence in all sectors, including oil. Some of the main features of energy-producing organizations are the following:

a. They are international in scope, especially in the oil sector. Of the 15 largest companies, five – Royal Dutch Shell, British Petroleum, ELF Aquitaine, Total CFP and British Gas – have significant interests outside Europe.
b. They tend to be either national or local monopolies, especially in coal, gas and electricity. In the electricity industry, the four largest employers (Electricité de France, the former UK Electricity Council, ENEL in Italy, and RWE in Germany) all either are or have been until recently under state ownership.
c. They are large-scale employers. Seven companies (Royal Dutch Shell, British Petroleum, Electricité de France, the former UK Electricity Council, ENEL, INL and Ruhrkohle) each employ over 100 000 people, placing them amongst the largest employers in Europe.

A high degree of concentration characterizes the industry as a whole. Table 1.2 shows turnover, profit and employment data on the 15 largest European energy companies. The top three in terms of turnover account for 19.5 per cent of total energy industry employment, while the top ten account for 58.1 per cent. These levels of concentration understate the true market power of the organizations, which often enjoy national or local monopoly status.

Although the oil industry, including oil exploration, production and distribution, accounts for only 36 per cent of total energy employment, 61 per cent is found in the three largest firms, Shell, BP and ENI. A similar situation existed until 1990 in electricity where 40 per cent of employment in electricity was in the hands of the three largest European firms, EdF, the then UK Electricity Council and ENEL.

The degree of interlinkage between industries differs substantially. Thus the solid fuel industry is dependent on two markets for the bulk of its sales – the electricity sector, which takes around 63 per cent, and the steel industry, which consumes most of the industry's coke production. Other energy industries are less dependent on particular markets although the electricity sector is of growing importance for gas. Interdependence has significant implica-

Table 1.1 Europe 12 Energy Data: Production, Net Imports, Gross and Final Consumption (million tonnes of oil equivalent)

Year	1984	1985	1986	1987	1988	1989	1990	1991	1992
Primary production									
Solid fuels:	143.8	168.4	172.7	166.6	161.8	159.8	152.6	149.6	146.1
Hard coal	106.1	132.5	138.6	134.1	129.7	126.0	119.2	115.8	111.7
Lignite	37.7	35.9	34.0	32.5	32.2	33.8	33.4	33.8	34.1
Oil	146.1	149.8	150.8	148.6	140.7	117.3	117.0	117.4	120.9
Natural gas	119.4	126.7	123.6	128.5	118.4	123.9	129.6	141.0	143.1
Heat:	103.3	125.6	134.0	137.8	147.6	159.2	158.5	163.0	167.6
Nuclear	101.6	123.9	132.2	135.9	145.8	157.3	156.5	161.1	165.6
Geothermal	1.8	1.7	1.7	1.8	1.8	1.9	2.0	2.0	2.0
Primary electricity (hydro)	15.0	14.6	14.2	15.0	16.5	11.3	12.5	13.8	14.9
Other renewable	1.7	1.8	1.7	2.2	2.6	2.5	2.6	2.8	2.9
TOTAL	529.3	586.9	596.9	598.7	587.8	573.9	572.6	587.6	595.4
Net imports									
Solid fuels:	57.9	63.5	60.7	60.5	62.1	66.8	76.5	80.6	85.8
of which hard coal	56.7	63.3	60.3	59.5	61.4	66.6	75.4	79.4	84.5
Oil	350.0	333.5	356.4	357.6	368.8	399.3	409.0	422.2	420.9
Natural gas	57.0	59.1	64.8	71.8	73.0	78.1	80.9	83.5	84.7
Electricity	1.5	1.2	1.2	1.6	1.8	1.6	1.3	1.1	1.3
TOTAL	466.5	457.3	483.1	491.5	505.6	545.8	567.6	587.4	592.7

Gross inland consumption

Solid fuels	219.7	239.0	231.5	231.3	226.8	231.1	234.2	234.8	236.1
Oil	472.0	462.6	474.0	476.7	488.1	491.8	497.4	505.4	511.5
Natural gas	176.7	184.7	186.9	198.1	192.6	201.5	207.7	226.9	230.3
Heat	104.0	125.3	134.0	138.1	148.8	158.9	159.2	163.0	167.6
Primary electricity	16.6	15.8	15.4	16.5	18.3	13.0	13.9	14.9	16.1
Other	1.7	1.8	1.7	2.2	2.6	2.5	2.6	2.8	2.9
TOTAL	990.6	1029.2	1043.6	1062.8	1077.1	1098.7	1115.1	1147.9	1164.5

Net imports as % of consumption

Hard coal	32.0	31.7	30.4	29.9	32.0	34.3	37.8	39.8	42.3
Oil	70.6	68.2	70.7	70.6	71.1	76.5	77.2	78.5	77.4
Natural gas	32.3	32.0	34.7	36.3	37.9	38.7	38.9	36.8	36.8
TOTAL	46.0	43.3	45.0	45.0	45.6	48.3	49.5	49.8	49.5

Oil imports as % of total energy consumption	34.5	31.6	33.2	32.7	33.3	35.4	35.6	35.8	35.2
Estimated final consumption	727.0	744.8	757.7	772.4	777.9	785.0	794.2	822.8	831.1
Energy intensity ratio (Gr. inl. consumption/GDP, 1984=100)	100.0	101.3	99.9	99.2	96.7	95.6	94.5	96.0	95.3
Imported crude oil price cif (US $/bbl)	29.0	27.5	14.5	17.8	14.8	17.6	22.9	19.4	18.0

Note: Figures for 1991 and 1992 are estimates.

Source: *Energy in Europe* (*Annual Energy Review*), special issue, Dec. 1991, Table 1, p. 95, Table 4, p. 112, and authors' calculations.

5

Table 1.2   Principal Energy Companies, 1989

Name	Activity	Country	Turnover (Million ECU)	Employment	Profit (Million ECU)
Royal Dutch Shell	Oil	NL	78 300	135 000	5 884
British Petroleum	Oil	UK	44 500	120 000	3 176
ENI	Oil	I	24 900	83 000	1 022
Veba	Oil	D	21 500	98 000	647
RWE	Electricity	D	22 900	95 000	360
ELF Aquitaine	Oil	F	21 500	72 000	1 028
EdF	Electricity	F	21 100	121 800	−604
The Electricity Council*	Electricity	UK	18 800	130 000	903
Total CFP	Oil	F	15 500	36 000	314
ENEL	Electricity	I	15 100	113 000	103
INI	Oil	E	14 000	151 400	638
British Gas	Gas	UK	12 000	80 500	1 359
Ruhrkohle	Coal	D	11 400	124 800	27
Petrofina	Oil	B	10 300	23 600	503
Repsol	Oil	E	8 900	19 200	494

Note: *privatized from 1990.

Source: CEC (1991a).

tions for any evaluation of the benefits of changes in industry structure and ownership since there are unlikely to be substantial gains from enhanced competition when industries are interdependent.

Changes in ownership have been most marked in the United Kingdom, where both the gas and the electricity industries have been transferred from public to private ownership and the government's intention is to privatize British Coal in 1993.[1] The outcome has been mixed so far as competition is concerned (Robinson, 1992a, 1992b). The gas industry remains a monopoly but in private hands and subject to regulatory control. The electricity sector is split between three large generators and 12 regional distribution companies which retain many local monopoly powers. Prices since privatization have risen significantly in the case of electricity – a result which is inconsistent with the extension of competition to the industry. In most EC countries little attempt at industry reorganization has taken place. France's electricity industry remains entirely centralized and operated by the state monopoly,

EdF. In Germany and the Netherlands a decentralized structure exists which nevertheless has monopoly characteristics deriving from the employment of long-term contractual agreements. In spite of the large number of supply firms in Germany, the sector is tightly controlled. The newly privatized East German power system is to be shared between existing German firms, independent operators and various community producers. Its competitive character is yet to be demonstrated. Belgium has witnessed the merging of its three former private electricity generators into one large organization (Electrabel) in 1990 and the coordination of investment planning and production. Italian electricity is also highly concentrated in the ENEL, a state company responsible for virtually all electricity production. Central coordination is the most important feature of electricity in Portugal and Denmark, as may be seen from Table 1.3

The existence of strong monopoly elements in the energy markets has held back the development of intra-Community trade. Intra-Community trade in crude oil constituted only 7.8 per cent of total input to refineries in 1990, and most of this came from the United Kingdom. The role of intra-Community trade in petroleum products was larger – at 17.8 per cent of total inland deliveries. In the same year trade in gas from the Netherlands amounted to 12.2 per cent of EC consumption. On the other hand, there was much less intra-Community trade in coal (less than 3 per cent of total consumption) and around 6 per cent in the case of electricity (Eurostat, 1991). For gas and electricity, the Commission estimates that removals of barriers to intra-Community trade could lead to economic gains of 50–70 billion ECU for electricity and 625 million ECU for gas by stimulating competition, and lowering average costs (CEC, 1992).

Performance in the energy sectors is quite difficult to measure. Coal, electricity and gas industries have frequently been constrained by public policy to relatively low rates of return. Thus in the case of the UK, financial constraints were set for the nationalized industries at substantially lower levels than prevailing market interest rates, although these were significantly tightened in preparation for the privatization of the electricity industry. In the more international oil market, however, European companies achieved relatively high rates of net profitability in the period 1986 to 1989 in spite of a dramatic reduction in turnover due to the collapse in oil prices. Oil industry net profitability as measured by the Commission (CEC, 1991a) rose from around 2.7 per cent in 1986 to 6 per cent in 1989, and it ranked second highest out of six major industrial groupings. Nevertheless, the importance of individual companies in the energy sector changed during this period. Whilst in 1983, 12 oil companies were amongst the 70 largest firms in Europe (in terms of turnover), only 9 remained in 1989, although Royal Dutch Shell and British Petroleum continued to hold the first two places.

Table 1.3   Structure of Electricity Industry in Europe

Country	Generators	Transmission	Distribution	Private/state
Belgium	Electrabel		Municipality	Coordinated
Denmark	10 private plus 2 municipal firms	Grid used by 28 companies	111 companies	Complex web of private and municipal
France	Electricité de France			
Germany	9 public companies, inc 2 nationalized – first division 60% West German companies	74 regional companies – 2nd division 40% independents + others	Municipal distribution	960 firms coordinated by federal and regional organizations
E. Germany	60% W German companies, 40% independents + others			
Greece	Public Power Corporation			State monopoly

Country	Generation	Transmission	Distribution	
Ireland	Electricity Supply Board			State monopoly
Italy	Ente Nationale per l'Energia + some municipalities and own generation			
Netherlands	4 main regional generators		40 local distribution companies	Centralized through SEP owned by the 4 generators
Portugal	Electricidade de Portugal			State monopoly, although entry possible
Spain	2 groups, Endesa (state) and Iberdrola (private) each have 40% of capacity	REDSA nationalized grid		State and private
United Kingdom	3 generators (National Power, PowerGen and Nuclear Electric (state)) + 3 Scottish companies – but entry possible	National Grid	12 regional electricity companies, but entry possible	Regulation by Office of Electricity Regulator

Source: CEC (1991a) and d'Amonquiz (1991).

9

Productivity in the energy sector has improved only modestly during the last five years due to the decline in international fuel prices. Whilst production of energy increased from 529.3 million toe in 1984 to 573.9 million toe in 1989, employment declined from 1.967 million to 1.725 million, implying a productivity growth of 4.2 per cent per annum. The coal industry, under intense competitive pressure from oil and gas in its major electricity market, produced the highest growth in output per head, of 5.6 per cent per year (using 1983 as a base to avoid the effects of the UK miners' strike). It is likely that further substantial productivity improvements will occur as ownership of the UK mining industry passes into the private sector and as government constraints on electricity producers to purchase indigenous coal are removed. By contrast, crude oil and natural gas productivity in Europe declined by almost 6 per cent per year as North Sea oil production declined and as imported oil grew cheaper to obtain after 1986.

1.4   Energy policy issues

1.4.1   The development of energy policy

The diversity of energy resources in Europe and their uneven distribution between the various member countries of the EC have always constituted major obstacles to agreement on a common energy policy. Indeed the fact that energy is seen as a strategic economic commodity, vital to the economic well-being of individual states, accounts for the continual reluctance to confer central policy-making powers on the Commission. Thus even though the immediate predecessor of the EC was the Coal and Steel Community, energy was specifically excluded from the Treaty of Rome and other founding legislation. The Commission has always encountered vigorous opposition from the member states whenever it has endeavoured to develop a coordinated policy for energy.[2] Only recently, as the powers of the EC *vis-à-vis* the member states have increased, has coordinated energy policy assumed substantial importance.

Since policy always represents a constraint on the free operation of markets, it is perhaps worthwhile to review briefly the perceived benefit of intervention in energy markets in terms of the usual criteria of economic efficiency, distributive equity and macroeconomic impacts. It has already been shown that energy markets possess many characteristics of monopoly and monopolistic competition. The world price of oil, which fundamentally influences local energy prices, is itself partially determined by the activities of OPEC (the Organization of Petroleum Exporting Countries), a formal cartel which uses production quotas in an attempt to maintain price above production costs. Coordinated action by a group of major energy consumers may be justified in terms of bargaining power advantage in this situation. At a more micro level, the maintenance of national monopolies would appear to be hostile to the EC's competition policy. On the distributional side, the fact that energy is relatively more important to poorer members of society has led to government intervention, usually through price subsidization either to consumers or to producers of energy. The EC is concerned where differential subsidies confer advantages to individual countries in terms of trade. Macroeconomic considerations such as the impact of energy price shocks on inflation, growth and employment have given rise to an insurance argument for maintaining otherwise uncompetitive domestic energy production as a premium to be paid for security of energy supplies. Finally, the impact of energy on the environment outside national boundaries has led to the development of EC policies in this area which are sometimes at variance with the drift of energy policy proper.

Early attempts at energy policy formation occurred in 1972 and 1973 when, following heads of state meetings in Paris (1972) and in Copenhagen (1973), the Commission was asked to draw up a coordinated policy in response to the developing world oil crisis. The result was the first EC energy policy statement, which was agreed by ministers in December 1974.³ This early policy initiative focused on the issues of security of supplies, stability of energy prices, and concern over the balance of payments. It emphasized the need for a harmonized community-wide approach. A fixed link was seen between energy input and economic output. Since for the majority of community members, energy consisted of imported oil, the specific policy recommendations of early work by the Commission focused on promoting substitutes for oil. Nuclear energy was to be promoted together with gas to relieve dependence on imported oil. The share of oil in total energy imports was to be reduced from 63 to 40 per cent, while that of oil in total energy supply was to fall from 60 to 40 per cent within ten years. From the outset, however, implementation of the policy was beset with difficulties. The Commission lacked policy instruments. It was concerned with influencing spending on R and D, and its reliance on persuasion failed to prevent national governments from vigorously promoting their own fuel sectors, for example coal production in the UK.

Little had been achieved when the second oil shock of 1979–80 brought about a reappraisal of policy. Massive price increases at a time of relatively high economic growth could not be handled by expansion of nuclear energy alone. So in the policy resolution agreed in June 1980 the role of coal was emphasized,⁴ especially for electricity generation, as well as the importance of energy conservation. Again targets were set but no incentives were provided to encourage the desired shift in production and demand. By the mid-1980s it was clear that the Community's policy had been inappropriate. It had not taken into account the economic effects of high oil prices on energy substitution. On the supply side, new sources of oil outside OPEC had appeared in response to higher rewards. In particular the development of North Sea oil reserves had already reduced overall net import dependence to 30 per cent by 1983. The security of energy supplies had also been much improved by the availability of large-scale Soviet gas exports. Finally, consumers had been able to switch out of energy-intensive uses much more effectively than had been foreseen by the EC planners. Lower oil prices effectively removed the balance of payments constraint on European growth by 1985. Finally, the Chernobyl incident had led to a reappraisal of the role of nuclear generation in future energy provision.

A new energy policy was announced in June 1986.[5] This identified three areas of risk to which the EC was exposed when energy prices were falling – growing demands for energy from the Third World, narrow margins between supply and demand, and lowering of the incentive towards energy conservation. The idea that insurance premiums are necessary as much when prices are falling as when they are rising was not acceptable to all governments and in the end the rigorous targets for reductions in energy intensity were moderated and further emphasis was placed on the role and importance of coal. In all its efforts at policy-making the EC may be seen simply as following the recommendations of the International Energy Agency (IEA) – the body set up by the Organization for Economic Cooperation and Development (OECD) after the first oil price shock of 1973–74. In no cases were effective instruments created for the achievement of objectives.

1.4.2   The Thermie programme

Following the collapse of oil prices in 1986 and the perceived reduction in incentives for further energy-saving measures, the EC adopted the Thermie programme in March 1989. This was intended to provide financial support and to disseminate technical information about energy efficiency, renewable energy sources, clean coal technologies and oil and gas prospecting and development. However, as with most of the EC programmes, little attempt has been made to evaluate the effectiveness of the programme and it is doubtful whether significant benefits have been achieved.

1.4.3   The internal energy market

The aims of the internal energy market   The director responsible for the internal energy market in the European Commission's Directorate-General for Energy, DGXVII, has described the aim of the internal market in the following way (Guibal, 1989, p. 518):

It is to eliminate barriers to the free flow of energy supplies within the European Community, thus increasing internal energy trade and further integrating the national energy economies of the Community. This will lead to increased energy competition inside the Community, both between different energies and between different supplies of the same type of energy. This in turn will lead to a more optimal allocation of energy resources and lower energy consumer prices, benefitting all consumers, but notably European industry, as it competes for markets at home and abroad. It will also improve the structure and increase the flexibility and security of energy supplies.

These are substantial claims, and elsewhere the Commission has estimated (CEC, 1988, p. 8) the cost of 'non-Europe' in the energy sector to be at least 0.5 per cent of Community GDP per year through not realizing: 'a reduction in costs as a result of greater competition and a reduction in certain unit costs as a result of the effects of scale and the optimization of investment or management'.

Considerable scepticism has been expressed about the political feasibility of achieving the desired changes, the size of the economic gains that could be realized and the compatibility of the different objectives involved. This scepticism has been influenced by the problems arising out of the EC's old emphasis on security of supply, the new priority accorded to market mechanisms and the EC's developing concern with environmental objectives.[6]

The history of European attempts to develop a common market for energy
This scepticism relates both to the nature of the energy industries in Europe and to the history of European attempts to develop a common market for energy. McGowan (1989, p. 1) points out that when the 1985 Commission White Paper on completing the internal market in Europe was drawn up, the energy sector was viewed 'as a minefield of monopolistic industrial structures with a high degree of public participation, too intractable for the Commission to tackle. As a result energy was addressed only indirectly....'

Nevertheless, the energy objectives adopted in 1986 did explicitly identify a need for 'greater integration, free from barriers to trade, of the internal energy market with a view to improving security of supply, reducing costs and improving economic competitiveness'.[7] Moreover, by 1988 the Commission had issued a new document (CEC, 1988), in which it outlined the expected results from an internal energy market, drew up a detailed sectoral inventory of the institutional and technical obstacles to its creation and set out the main priorities to be addressed in order to remove unnecessary obstacles. A variety of draft directives concerned with the development of the internal energy market have been circulated since 1988, including several dealing with electricity and gas. A number of the proposals have met with significant opposition,[8] and consequently not all directives survive the consultation process.

The internal market for electricity and gas   The most recent plans are for the internal market for electricity and gas to be completed by 1 January 1996 via a three-phase process. In what the Energy Commissioner, Cardoso e Cunha, calls the 'first phase of liberalisation' (CEC, 1991b, p. 6), three directives have recently come into force relating to electricity and gas transit,[9] and to price transparency. The transit directives are intended to promote competition by ensuring that a grid company whose grid lies between two other grids cannot prevent the other two companies from trading through that grid. The price transparency directive is intended to improve the transparency of natural gas and electricity prices charged to industrial end-users, thus enabling market operators to negotiate prices on the basis of better information.[10] It involves a mandatory system of notification of price data to the Statistical Office of the European Communities (SOEC), at six-monthly intervals, and the publication of prices by the SOEC no later than five months after the surveys.

The proposed 'second phase of liberalisation' of the electricity and gas markets, embodied in a draft directive issued on 17 January 1992, is said to be based on four general principles (CEC, 1991b; d'Amonquiz, 1992).[11] First there should be a gradual, step-by-step approach to the development of the internal market, based on a clear vision of the ultimate goal: 'It is therefore up to the Community to pinpoint now its long-term objectives for the liberalisation of the market.' The second principle is that of 'subsidiarity', implying that, 'the Community must not impose rigid mechanisms but rather should define a framework enabling Member States to opt for the system best suited to their natural resources, the state of their industry and their energy policies.'[12] The third principle is to 'avoid the trap of excessive regulation'. The fourth principle involves the creation of a dialogue between government, industry and the Commission, while reserving the Commission's right to use the powers conferred by the Treaty of Rome in appropriate circumstances.

There are three elements to this second phase of liberalization.[13] The first element has the aim of opening up investment in production and transport to independent operators, especially large industrial users. 'This ... must take account of the vital concerns defined by the national systems for granting licences, relating in particular to energy policy, environmental protection and zoning.' The second element involves the 'unbundling' (i.e. separation) of the management and accounting of production, transmission and distribution operations in vertically integrated utilities: 'to ensure transparency of operations, which is a pre-requisite for the "level playing field", and does not affect ownership structures'. The third element introduces third-party access (TPA) to a limited set of eligible large industrial consumers and some distribution companies: 'whereby the transmission and distribution companies are obliged to offer access to their network to certain eligible entities at reasonable rates, within the limits of available transmission and distribution capacity'.[14] The Commission intended to have these three elements of the second phase of liberalization in force by 1 January 1993, the deadline by which the entire single market, including the internal energy market, was supposed to have been completed.

The third and final phase of liberalization, which will include adapting the criteria for eligibility for TPA, will be 'defined in detail in the light of the experience acquired during the second', and is not expected to be in force until 1 January 1996.[15] It is hardly surprising that not all commentators are enthusiastic about the nature and pace of the developments implied by the draft directive. For example, d'Amonquiz (1992) suggests that the emphasis on 'flexibility' throughout the document is the key to the changes that have occurred since 1985, when the Commission called for a free market across national borders, with almost unlimited TPA:

> There is no hint that the Member States will be forced into radical reorganisations of their electricity or for that matter that anything resembling common carriage will be brought into the EC Members' joint electricity system. ... One of the problems of common carriage – defining the tariffs and connection agreements necessary – is lightly skated over, although it will prove the most contentious element of the new market, if UK experience is anything to go by. It is clear enough, however, that any country which really wants to opt out of the free market – and there are several who do – can do so without too much trouble....
> Although the Directive remains true to its original ideas – if in a much attenuated form – the introduction of subsidiarity, not to mention the delay in the timetable for implementation, suggests that '1992' will never arrive.

In an earlier commentary, d'Amonquiz (1991) also claimed that, 'there are three clear examples of countries which, under the pretence of "preparing for 1992" have managed to go entirely contrary to the EC Commission's wishes'. The first example involves the merging of three large private utilities to form Electrabel in Belgium.[16] The second is the reorganization of the Netherlands' electricity sector into four main regional generators and around 40 local distribution companies, such that it is SEP, whose shareholders are the four generators, which now exercises the central rather than regional control of the system that the government wished to promote.[17] The third example is in Spain, where Endesa, the government generating company, made several acquisitions in 1991, 'to streamline the sector in time for the EC Single Energy Market'.[18]

The coal industry   In comments on the recent activities of the Commission in relation to coal, the Energy Commissioner noted in 1991 (CEC, 1991c, p. 8) that

[The Commission's] actions have been based on the fact that, since 1965, aid to the coal industry has cost the European tax-payer, altogether, more than 70 thousand million ECU and that today, despite these considerable efforts, the industry still remains in a critical situation.

Asserting that some countries have used state aid simply to maintain uneconomic mines, and that there are examples where production costs are from two to five times the world price,[19] the Commissioner questioned whether it was right that high-cost coal should displace low-cost coal. He also criticized the lack of any significant intra-Community coal trade. In his view, a new aid framework is required that simultaneously takes into account both the long-term evolution of the world coal market and a 'reasonable assessment' of the contribution of EC coal to security of supply. Such a framework, along with specific restructuring assistance programmes like RECHAR,[20] might then allow state aid to the coal industry to be limited to a realistic level without prejudicing other Community objectives. However, given the varying status of coal and the divergent objectives of governments in different member countries, the establishment of a new system along these lines is unlikely to be a simple matter.

The European coal industry is not only subject to pressures to reduce subsidies and face increased internal and external competition. It also has to contend with regulatory measures connected with acid deposition. Moreover, in the near future, as the fossil fuel with the largest carbon dioxide emissions per unit of thermal energy released, coal is likely to come under greater pressure when the EC implements policies to address the threat of global warming.[21] These issues of energy and environment are discussed in the next section.

1.5   Energy and European environmental policy

One of the major current issues concerns the compatibility between the objectives of European energy policy and of European environmental policy. Indeed, it has been argued by Owens and Hope (1990, p. 102) that, 'While "Energy" and "Environment" are dealt with by separate Directorates, with different constituencies and a different "world view", we can hardly expect genuine policy integration to be achieved.'

1.5.1   The development of European environmental policy

It has been claimed that environmental concern lies at the heart of the debate about the single European market because the single market will only function successfully if the 12 member states can agree and apply common standards of environmental protection (CEC, 1990a). An official European environmental policy is of relatively recent origin. Before the Single European Act took effect in 1987, there was in fact no explicit legal provision for

Community environmental action.[22] According to the Commission (CEC, 1990a), Article 130R (para. 2) of the Single European Act 'enshrines in the Treaty the Community's underlying philosophy', that:

> Action by the Community relating to the environment shall be based on the principles that preventive action should be taken, that environmental damage should as a priority be rectified at source, and that the polluter should pay. Environmental protection requirements shall be a component of the Community's other policies.

1.5.2   Impacts on the energy sectors

Community regulation in the environmental area has the potential to exert major impact on the energy sectors in the future. Although there are many aspects of EC environmental policy that affect energy, the focus here is on only two of the most significant issues: acid deposition and global warming. While there are agreed Community directives relating to acid deposition, EC action on global warming (and in particular the control of CO_2 emissions) is at the beginning of its life cycle. The discussion of global warming leads fairly naturally into the issue of 'green taxes' and other market-based emissions control instruments, which seem likely to play an increasingly important part in future EC attempts to control energy-related environmental impacts.

Acid deposition and the Large Combustion Plant directive   The history of the 1988 European Community directive on pollutant emissions from large combustion plant (LCP)[23] offers an instructive example of the way European environmental control can evolve (Ramus, 1991; Skea 1991; UK CEED, 1990). The first draft of the directive, produced by the EC in 1983, owed much to domestic West German legislation and proposed a 60 per cent reduction in sulphur dioxide below 1980 levels for all countries by 1995. The next five years saw many proposed amendments and the abandonment not only of equi-proportional reductions but also of a single deadline date for all countries. The situation was also made more complex by the new Community membership of Spain and Portugal, in particular. One example of how the reduction targets evolved is that in early 1988 the proposed target reductions for the UK's LCPs were 26 per cent of 1980 levels for 1993, 46 per cent for 1998 and 70 per cent by 2003; when finally agreed in November 1988, they were set at the less stringent levels of 20 per cent, 40 per cent and 60 per cent, respectively.

It has been suggested that the UK managed to secure comparatively lenient targets because it insisted on its need at that time to continue burning its relatively high-sulphur domestic coal. Higher targets were set for several other countries, including Belgium, France, Germany and the Netherlands, although for two of the countries they were at that time relatively easily met, since France had built up its nuclear electricity capability and Germany had responded to domestic political pressure and was already committed to major reductions, mainly through flue gas desulphurization (FGD). Lower targets, allowing increases in SO_2 emissions, were set for Spain, Greece, Ireland and Portugal, countries which were rapidly developing their electricity supply systems.[24] The UK, with its recently privatized electricity supply industry, now plans to meet the LCP directive and other controls on acid emissions not by relying mainly on a single, fairly expensive method (FGD) but by combining desulphurization equipment, new gas-fired plant and other means such as the use of imported low-sulphur coal.[25]

The stimulus that targets for SO_2 emissions give to gas, in particular through the use of combined-cycle gas turbines (CCGT), is evident. Moreover, CCGT technology has the added advantage that if there were to be a requirement for further reductions in nitrogen oxide (NO_x) emissions, relatively simple modifications and additional technologies could be employed to bring this about (UK CEED, 1990). So meeting European targets for emissions is likely significantly to stimulate an already rising demand for gas in electricity generation. Moreover, there is in the background the presence of the 'joker in the pack' – the central and East European countries, which are likely to focus on gas as a way of making a rapid transition from decades of reliance on poor-quality highly polluting indigenous coal. Their demand for imported gas could add significantly to overall European demand.

Global warming and European carbon dioxide emissions targets   Differential reductions in energy-related emissions for different members of the EC can also be seen in European agreements on carbon dioxide (CO_2) targets, such as that presented to the World Climate Conference in Geneva in November 1990, where the 18 countries in the EC and the European Free Trade Area agreed to a joint statement pledging to peg the continent's emissions at 1990 levels by the year 2000. The agreement was to stabilize CO_2 emissions 'in general' at 1990 levels by the year 2000 in the Community as a whole, but it was noted that 'some member countries ... are not in a position to commit themselves to this objective'. They included Spain, Portugal and Greece, countries 'with as yet relatively low energy requirements', and the UK which at that time did not aim to meet the target until 2005.[26] The agreement implied that efforts would be unevenly distributed: countries that aimed to cut emissions would make the major contribution, while other countries' emissions would grow. The European ministers said that in adopting their targets they assumed that other leading countries would also adopt similar commitments – which meant that they could use this as a reason not to comply if other non-European countries, such as Japan and the US, did not. The mechanisms by which the EC's CO_2 targets were to be achieved were

not determined at the time of the original agreement. Subsequent developments have given some prominence to the potential role of carbon taxes as
the main policy instrument.

*Market-based environmental policy instruments: the European carbon tax
proposals* There has been much emphasis in the EC and elsewhere in the
past couple of years on the adoption of market-based instruments – such as
emissions taxes or tradable emissions permits – to implement the 'polluter
pays' principle, especially in relation to CO_2. Market-based instruments
have been widely advocated by economists on the grounds, among others,
that they may imply lower abatement costs than command-and-control regulations (because with a charge or an emissions permit, each polluter can
choose the appropriate level of abatement, depending on the polluter's own
marginal abatement costs), and they offer the 'dynamic' incentive to continue
to search for ways to reduce emissions and so pay less (Pearson and Smith,
1991). Historically, most EC governments have adopted command-and-control methods to control most forms of pollution, but this is beginning to
change.[27]

In the case of carbon taxes on fossil fuels, it is clear that significant
reductions in carbon emissions are likely to require high carbon taxes, because price elasticities of demand tend to be low (for the UK, long-run
figures of –0.3 have been estimated for aggregate and for domestic energy
demand).[28] Pearson and Smith (1991, p. 51) argue that evidence that a
carbon tax rate would have to be high, and therefore costly, strengthens the
case for using cost-minimizing methods of pollution control, and hence for
selecting market-based instruments. Currently a great deal of activity is
involved in attempting to model the problems and policies associated with
global warming – and there are often wide disparities between the results of
different models. Two significant areas where models tend to differ are in
assumptions about what, if anything, is done to neutralize the impacts of
carbon taxes (e.g. reduce levels of VAT to ensure revenue neutrality), and in
assumptions about the nature and pace of long-term technological change
(especially in energy production and consumption).[29] In terms of the potential impacts of carbon taxes on energy markets, they will tend to reduce the
demand for fossil fuels below what it would otherwise be, and to favour
substitution of gas in particular, in place of coal and oil.

European environment ministers met in Rome in September 1990 to dis-
cuss the use of taxes and other market-based instruments. It is reported that
'the 12 agreed that market forces should be used for environmental ends, but
did not agree on what those ends might be, or whether they should all adopt
the same measures to achieve them'.[30] The European Commission supported
carbon taxes, graduated according to each fuel's carbon content (i.e. the

heaviest tax would fall on coal, then oil and then gas), at the Rome meeting and argued that 'to avoid economic distortions between member states ... a common framework for charging/taxing greenhouse emissions should be agreed at Community level'. While several countries were in favour of this kind of harmonized taxation, the poorer member states opposed it because they feared such taxes would be too high, whereas the Netherlands opposed them because they would be too weak and might interfere with Dutch plans to use market-based instruments.

Subsequently, in a 1991 document focusing on both energy taxation and energy efficiency (including some measures already in the Specific Actions for Vigorous Energy Efficiency (SAVE) programme, and the use of demand-side management), the Commission put forward controversial proposals for a combination tax on the carbon content of fossil fuels and a tax on all non-renewable forms of energy.[31] Carbon-based fuels (coal, oil and gas) would face a two-part tax, one part on the carbon content and the other part on the non-renewable energy content. Non-renewable energy sources, principally nuclear power, would face only the energy-related part of the tax. Overall the tax would be combined in proportions such that the energy component would not exceed 50 per cent (e.g. half of the tax on a typical barrel of oil might be based on the carbon component and half on the energy component). The introduction of the tax would be staged. On its introduction in 1993 it would be at a level equivalent to $3 per barrel of oil; it would then rise by $1 per barrel per year until it reached $10 per barrel by the year 2000. The Commission estimated the following impacts on fuel prices, above 1990 levels, given the existing (uneven) patterns of taxation: (a) for power stations and industry: hard coal (58 per cent), heavy fuel oil (45 per cent), natural gas (34 per cent); (b) for households: light fuel oil (16 per cent), natural gas (14 per cent); (c) for transport: petrol (6 per cent), diesel (11 per cent).

The tax was designed to be revenue neutral, in that the extra tax revenue should be used to offset other taxes that would otherwise be levied. The revenues would be received by the exchequers of each member state, who could decide how to arrange the revenue neutrality. Some exemptions were also mooted for a number of highly energy-intensive sectors, such as the steel, chemicals and cement industries, if energy taxes were not also imposed by the EC's main competitors, because of fears about the impacts of a unilateral carbon tax on international competitiveness.

It has been argued in favour of the EC's proposals (Faross, 1991, p. 27) that:

> There is no doubt that a pure carbon tax would provide the most efficient incentives to cut CO_2 emissions. However this option would put a relatively high

burden on users of solid fuels, the most abundant and secure energy supply world-wide. Furthermore, it would significantly favour nuclear energy, which has advantages in terms of CO_2 reduction but which leads to its own particular problems. ... The mixed energy/CO_2 tax therefore seems to be a compromise reflecting economic and political realities and at the same time stimulating energy efficiency improvements as well as some fuel switching towards less polluting energy sources.

On the other hand, Pearson and Smith (1991) have made a number of critical observations about the 1991 proposals, including the following.

a   The existing structure of energy taxation in the EC produces an uneven pattern of 'implicit carbon taxes', which effectively provide fiscal incentives for the use of high-carbon fuels like coal. However, the carbon/energy basis of the proposals dilutes the incentive to substitute to low-carbon fuels. It would therefore be better to use an explicit nuclear tax if the aim is to avoid the encouragement of nuclear power.
b   Exemption of the six most energy-intensive sectors until similar measures were adopted in other countries would increase the administrative complexity of the tax. A more serious risk is that the exemptions would not prove temporary, implying higher tax levels for other industries and consumers.
c   There are important administrative issues which have received little public attention. They concern the choice between a 'primary' carbon tax, levied on the mining and import of fuels, and a carbon tax on 'final fuel products'.
d   On the positive side, however, the tax revenues could be used to offset other, more distorting taxes, thus yielding a 'double dividend', that is, environmental benefits and a reduction in the economic welfare costs of raising tax revenues (although the tax structure that would maximize this would do little to offset the regressive impacts of higher energy taxes on poorer households).

A recent estimate, by Pariente-David (1992), of the impact of the carbon/energy tax package on EC energy demand, by fuel and by sector, for the years 2000 and 2005 suggests that the major proportional effects would be, not surprisingly, on solid fuels and on the industrial sector.[32]

It was originally hoped by the Commission that the legal texts of these energy tax and energy efficiency proposals would be agreed by the member countries before the United Nations Conference on Environment and Development (UNCED) meeting in Rio in June 1992. In fact, a modified version was discussed but not approved in May 1992 and the future of the carbon/energy tax and its associated energy efficiency measures remains uncertain.

It seems unlikely, however, that the proposal will disappear entirely, and this is why it has been discussed in some detail here.

As the example of the carbon/energy tax makes clear, Europe will have to 'harmonize' its energy and environmental policies (and indeed other areas of policy, such as agriculture and transport) if it is not to frustrate its objectives in the energy-environment area. This is not likely to prove a simple task.

1.6   European Commission scenarios for energy and environment

A study called 'Major Themes in Energy to 2010' has been undertaken by the European Commission. Three scenarios, originally published in 1989 (CEC, 1989), were updated in 1990 with the addition of a new fourth scenario including a form of carbon tax (CEC, 1990b). Scenario 1 ('Conventional Wisdom') is based on a vision of an incomplete internal market for energy, with market forces driving the system within the existing energy policy framework. Scenario 2 ('Driving into Tensions') is intended to demonstrate that rapid economic growth, without policy measures to improve the efficiency of energy production and use, could drive the system into a situation of supply gaps and oil price shocks. Between 1990 and 2010 primary energy demand grows at about 1.4 per cent per year, with final energy demand growing at about 1.1 per cent per year. (The corresponding rates for scenario 1 are 0.9 per cent and 0.6 per cent, respectively.)

Scenario 3 ('Sustaining High Economic Growth'), which also has four sub-scenarios by way of sensitivity analysis, aims to demonstrate that increasing economic growth can be compatible with strict environmental standards, through greater penetration by energy-efficient technologies and a new transport infrastructure. Primary energy demand rises by 2.6 per cent per year until the mid-1990s, after which new policies to reduce demand begin to bite strongly. Between 1990 and 2010 the share of oil falls, while the role of gas rises significantly. Scenario 4 ('High Prices') was prepared after the first three scenarios and, in its recognition of 'the need to internalise the costs associated with environmental externalities' (CEC, 1990b, p. 63), represents the first public attempt by the EC to model the implications of a form of carbon tax on fossil fuels. This scenario combines the moderate economic growth rates of Scenario 1 with higher end-user energy prices. Compared with scenario 3 there are once-and-for-all increases in coal prices of 100 per cent, oil prices of 40 per cent, and gas prices of 30 per cent. Primary energy demand is 9 per cent lower than that of scenario 3. The role of gas and electricity increases in both scenarios 3 and 4, but oil declines in scenario 4. In comparison with the other scenarios, scenario 4 shows the lowest energy import dependency. Total carbon dioxide emissions fall by 19 per cent by 2010, compared with 1987 levels, stabilizing by around 2000.

Scenarios 3 and 4, in particular, make some fairly strong assumptions about the nature and pace of change in energy and other markets – but it is important to remember that such scenarios should be seen as a potential aid to the analysis of energy and environmental issues, not a substitute for it. Viewed with appropriate scepticism (both because the Commission is scarcely a disinterested observer of the policy scene and because the history of energy forecasting shows the need for humility[33]) the reports provide a framework for pondering future developments in the European energy industries.

1.7 Conclusion

In this chapter it has been shown that the energy industries of Europe are large, diverse and the focus of significant public intervention, both at national and European levels. The production and use of energy provokes strategic, economic and environmental concern. Historically, the industries have been subject to high levels of public ownership and control. However, there has been increasing concern over both the efficiency of public owner-ship (reflected in the UK's privatization programme) and the nature and degree of competition within and between the energy industries (reflected in the European Commission's attempts to promote liberalization through the internal energy market and associated directives on transit and price trans-parency). With the added stimuli arising out of growing environmental pres-sures, the next decade seems likely to witness significant change in the energy industries of Europe.

Notes

1. For discussion of the past performance and future prospects of the UK coal industry, see Pearson (1991).
2. See Hawdon (1988) for a detailed discussion of the development of policy in the EC.
3. Resolution dated 17/12/74. OJ C 153 1975.
4. See OJ C 149 1980 for details.
5. See OJ C 241 1986. See also Jones (1989).
6. See, for example, d'Amonquiz (1991, 1992), Finon (1990), Hancher (1990), RIIA/ SPRU (1989), Surrey (1990).
7. OJ C 241, 25.9.86, quoted in CEC (1988, p. 6).
8. For example, the proposal for a regulation notifying the Commission of investment projects of interest to the Community in the petroleum, natural gas and electricity sectors (Document: COM (89) 335 – 15 September 1989). See the discussion in CEC (1991b, p. 6).
9. Council Directive for electricity (90/547/EEC), OJ L 313/13.11.90. Council Directive for gas (91/296/EEC), OJ L 147/12.6.91.
10. Council Directive concerning a Community procedure to improve the transparency of gas and electricity prices charged to industrial end-users (Council Directive (90/377/ EEC), OJ L 185/17.7.90).
11. The quotations in this paragraph are from CEC (1991a, p. 6).
12. D'Amonquiz (1992, p. 7) suggests that this new emphasis on subsidiarity in this context

is the most notable feature of the draft directive's explanatory memorandum. The Energy Commissioner has explained its implications in detail (CEC, 1991a, pp. 7–8).

13.   All the quotations in this paragraph are from CEC (1991a, pp. 6–7).

14.   Cardoso e Cunha (CEC, 1991a, p. 7) has noted that: 'I want to ensure that there are enough "players" to create a market but not so many as to risk creating chaos. We need to prove the system.' See also d'Amonquiz (1992, p. 7).

15.   CEC (1991a, p. 7).

16.   According to d'Amonquiz (1991, p. 6), the board chairman of Tractebel, the energy-holding group that was the driving force behind the merger, said: 'We must anticipate the creation of the single European energy market. Separately, each of these companies is too small to withstand international competition. The new share structure will bring stability and security against takeovers.'

17.   Thus d'Amonquiz (1991, p. 8) argues that: 'The threat of 1992 has, in Holland, led to the setting up of a series of prospective internal trade barriers, and has served to centralise, through the SEP, what was once one of the most disaggregated power systems in Europe.'

18.   'The programme which was meant to loosen the hold of the big utilities has in fact helped to give Spain two of the ten biggest utilities in Europe [Endesa and Iberdrola] ... and turn the state company from a generator into a semi-integrated utility' (d'Amonquiz, 1991, p. 9).

19.   In Germany more than 80 per cent of coal burned in electricity generation had to be domestic coal, while the difference between the German coal price (around £89 per tonne) and the world price (around £24 per tonne) has been funded by an electricity tax (Pearson and Smith, 1991, p. 13).

20.   The decision to implement the RECHAR programme for the 'economic conversion' (including environmental improvements and the renovation and modernization of social and economic infrastructures) of eligible coal-mining areas was published in the official Journal of the European Communities on 27 January 1990. The RECHAR initiative is the counterpart to similar programmes for the steel and shipbuilding sectors (RESIDER, RENAVAL).

21.   For discussion of the issues raised in this paragraph, in the context of the UK coal industry, see the contributions in Pearson (1991).

22.   Nevertheless, more than 100 instruments, mostly directives, were adopted in the 15 years after the Paris Summit of 1972.

23.   Council Directive on the limitation of emissions of certain pollutants into the air from large combustion plants (88/609/EEC), OJ L 336, 7/12/88.

24.   A table showing the SO_2 reduction requirements, based on 1980 levels, for existing LCPs for the Europe 12 countries for 1993, 1998 and 2003 can be found in Skea (1991, p. 21). The LCP Directive sets SO_2 nitrogen oxide (NO_x) and particulate emission limits for 'new' (post-July 1987) plant, as well as the ceilings for SO_2 and NO_x from existing plant.

25.   UK CEED (1990). For the future, Skea (1991) has suggested that there may be further pressures on UK emissions levels, both from the European Commission (given that less FGD than originally envisaged is likely to be used) and from the UNECE Long Range Transboundary Air Pollution (LRTAP) Convention and its application of the 'critical load' concept as a basis for future agreements.

26.   The UK agreed to adopt the 2000 target shortly before the UNCED meeting in Rio in June 1992.

27.   It has, however, been argued that with the Single European Act, the Commission's proposals for harmonization of indirect taxes could even introduce constraints on the appropriate use of taxes for environmental policy, if they cut down the range of taxable products and excluded national and regional differences in tax rates (Folmer, 1990).

28.   See Pearson and Smith (1991, pp. 14–17). See also Nordhaus (1991) and Pearce (1991).

29.   For a review of recent models, see Boero *et al.* (1991).

30.   *New Scientist*, 29 September 1990.

31.   'Communication from the Commission to the Council. A Community strategy to limit

carbon dioxide emissions and to improve energy efficiency.' SEC/91/1744 final, 14/10.91. For an outline of the proposals, see Faross (1991). For a valuable assessment, see Pearson and Smith (1991).

32. The OPEC Secretariat also prepared a number of carbon tax scenarios, including one EC-style scenario implemented in all OECD areas (MEES, 1991). In all their scenarios, oil remains the dominant fuel, because the major substitution effect is between coal and gas. See also CEC (1990b).

33. 'It is sometimes argued that energy forecasters were created to make economic forecasters look good'. (This statement, attributed to a former US Deputy Energy Secretary, is quoted and discussed by Stelzer, 1989).

References

Boero, G., Clarke, R. and Winters, L.A. (1991), *The Macroeconomic Consequences of Controlling Greenhouse Gases: A Survey*, London: HMSO.

CEC (Commission of the European Communities) (1988), 'The Internal Energy Market', *Energy in Europe*, special issue, 1–59.

CEC (Commission of the European Communities) (1989), 'Major Themes in Energy', *Energy in Europe*, special issue, September, 1–62.

CEC (Commission of the European Communities (1990a), *Environmental Policy in the European Community*, Luxembourg: CEC.

CEC (Commission of the European Communities) (1990b), 'Major Themes in Energy Revisited', *Energy in Europe*, special issue, July, 31–90 (Report), 131–237 (Technical Annex).

CEC (Commission of the European Communities (1991a), *Panorama of EC Industry*, Luxembourg: Office for Official Publications of the European Communities.

CEC (Commission of the European Communities) (1991b), 'Interview with Commissioner Cardoso e Cunha', *Energy in Europe*, **18**, (December), 5–9.

CEC (Commission of the European Communities) (1991c), *Information Energy Europe*, (EIE Feb/91), Brussels: Directorate General for Energy.

CEC (Commission of the European Communities) (1992), 'Transit of Electricity and Gas', *Information Energy Europe* (EIE Jan 92.5 – Rev.4), Brussels: Directorate General for Energy.

d'Amonquiz, C. (1991), 'New Markets, Old Hands', *Energy Economist*, **122**, 5–9.

d'Amonquiz, C. (1992), 'The Subsidiarity Principle', *Energy Economist*, **124**, 6–9.

Eurostat (1991), *Energy: Monthly Statistics*, 1990 Supplement, Luxembourg: Office for Official Publications of the European Communities.

Faross, P. (1991), 'Community CO_2 Stabilization by the Year 2000', *Energy in Europe*, **18**, (December), 26–8.

Finon, D. (1990), 'Opening Access to European Grids', *Energy Policy*, **18**, (5), June, 428–42.

Folmer, H. (1990), *Environmental Impacts of the Single European Market* (Key Environmental Issues, 2), London: British Gas.

Guibal, J.C. (1989), 'The 1992 European Internal Energy Market', *Energy Policy*, **17**, (5), October, 518–21.

Hancher, L. (1990), 'Towards a Free Market for Energy? A Legal Perspective', *Energy Policy*, **18**, (3), April, 233–45.

Hawdon, D. (1988), 'Energy Policy', in Peter Coffey (ed.), *Main Economic Policy Areas of the EEC – Topwards 1992*, Dordrecht: Kluwer Academic Publishers.

Jones, C. (1989), 'Energy Policies and Strategies in the European Community', Ch. 3 in Peter Pearson (ed.), *Energy Policies in an Uncertain World*, London: Macmillan.

McGowan, E. (1989), 'The EC Proposals and their Context', Ch. 1 in RIIA/SPRU (Royal Institute of International Affairs/Science Policy Research Unit), *A Single European Market in Energy*, London: Royal Institute of International Affairs.

MEES (Middle East Economic Survey) (1991), 'Opec Secretariat Assesses Impact of Proposed New Carbon and Energy Taxes', *MEES*, **35**, (12/13), D1–D8.

Nordhaus, W.D. (1991), 'To Slow or Not to Slow: the Economics of the Greenhouse Effect', *Economic Journal*, **101**, (407), 920–37.

Owens, S. and Hope, C. (1990), 'Energy and Environment: the Challenge of Integrating European Policies', *Energy Policy*, **17**, (2), April 97–102.

Pariente-David, S. (1992), *The Energy, Economic and Industrial Impact of CO_2 Control Policies*, 15th Annual International Conference of the International Association for Energy Economics (IAEE), Tours (mimeo).

Pearce, D. (1991), 'The Role of Carbon Taxes in Adjusting to Global Warming', *Economic Journal*, **101**, (407), 938–48.

Pearson, P.J.G. (ed.) (1991), *Prospects for British Coal*, London: Macmillan.

Pearson, M. and Smith, S. (1991), *The European Carbon Tax: An Assessment of the Commission's Proposals*, London: Institute for Fiscal Studies.

Ramus, C.A. (1991), *The Large Combustion Plant Directive: An Analysis of European Environmental Policy*, Oxford: Oxford Institute for Energy Studies.

RIIA/SPRU (Royal Institute of International Affairs/Science Policy Research Unit) (1989), *A Single European Market in Energy*, London: Royal Institute of International Affairs.

Robinson, C. (1992a), *Energy Trends and the Development of Energy Policy in the United Kingdom*, Surrey Energy Economics Centre Discussion Paper (SEEDS 61), University of Surrey, Guildford.

Robinson, C. (1992b), *The Results of UK Electricity Privatisation*, Surrey Energy Economics Centre Discussion Paper (SEEDS 62), University of Surrey, Guildford.

Shell (1986), *Information Handbook*, London: Shell International Petroleum Company.

Skea, J. (1991), 'The EC Large Combustion Plant Directive: Implications for the UK Electricity Supply Industry', *ENER Bulletin*, **9–91**, 19–35.

Stelzer, I. (1989), 'A Market-Based Energy Policy', Ch. 4 in Peter Pearson (ed.), *Energy Policies in an Uncertain World*, London: Macmillan.

Surrey, J. (1990), 'Beyond 1992 – the Single Market and EC Energy Issues', *Energy Policy*, **18**, (1), January/February, 42–54.

UK CEED (1990), *UK CEED*, Bulletin 29.

Further reading

CEC (Commission of the European Communities), *Energy in Europe*, Luxembourg: Office for Official Publications of the European Communities [3 issues per year].

CEC (Commission of the European Communities) (1992), *Panorama of EC Industries 1991–92*, Luxembourg: Office for Official Publications of the European Communities [annual publication].

Eurostat (1992), *Energy: Yearly Statistics*, Luxembourg: Office for Official Publications of the European Communities [see also *Energy: Monthly Statistics* and *Rapid Reports: Energy*, both from the same source].

IEA (International Energy Agency), *Energy Policies and Programmes of IEA Countries*, Paris: OECD Publications [annual publication].

Pearson, M. and Smith, S. (1991), *The European Carbon Tax: An Assessment of the Commission's Proposals*, London: Institute for Fiscal Studies.

Surrey, J. (1990), 'Beyond 1992 – the Single Market and EC Energy Issues', *Energy Policy*, **18**, (1), January/February, 42–54.

2 Agriculture

Brian Hill

2.1 Introduction

Community agriculture accounts for 3.1 per cent of GDP but 6.6 per cent of employment, with much variation between member states, as Table 2.1 shows. The fact that employment shares exceed GDP shares on average by a factor of more than two suggests that incomes in agriculture are very low. To some extent this is true, but the margin is not as large as suggested by these data because they ignore the non-agricultural sources of income enjoyed by many farmers; indeed for 23 per cent of farmers, farming is not their main

Table 2.1   Agriculture in the EC Economy (percentages)

	Share of GDP (1989)	Share of labour (1990)	Share of investment (1989)
Belgium	2.4	2.8	1.7
Denmark	4.2	6.0	4.0
Germany	1.7	3.4	2.3
Greece	16.5	25.3	6.5
Spain	4.7	11.8	3.0
France	3.3	6.1	2.5
Ireland	10.5	15.0	11.7
Italy	4.0	9.0	6.3
Luxembourg	2.4	3.3	2.7
Netherlands	4.6	4.6	5.5
Portugal	5.5	17.8	3.5
United Kingdom	1.5	2.2	1.2
EC 12	3.1	6.6	3.2

Notes: Column 1 is measured as gross value-added/GDP; col. 2 is numbers employed in agriculture, forestry, fishing and hunting as a percentage of the employed civilian working population; col. 3 is investment as gross fixed capital formation.

Source: ECC (1992), pp. T/20–1.

employment and a further 7.1 per cent have other secondary employment (see Table 2.5). These data also ignore income from non-agricultural investments and pensions, on which very little EC information is available, although such categories are important in the UK (Hill, 1988).

Agriculture has important links with other industries. Those with the food industry are obvious, but it is also a major client of firms in other sectors. In 1990, in producing an output of 202 billion ECU, agriculture purchased inputs from other sectors to the value of 43 billion ECU; the main components are fertilizers and crop protection chemicals (14.6 billion ECU), energy (8.6 billion ECU) and machinery (10.5 billion ECU) (ECC, 1992 p. T/27).

Agriculture is often described as being perfectly competitive because its various products are homogeneous and there are many producers and purchasers. It does not, however, have perfect factor mobility, and the occupational immobility of farmers is at the root of its major problems, as discussed below. Within each of the Community states, output is dominated by a minority of farmers who have large farms, the remaining majority having small farms and concomitantly low incomes. Even large farms are small businesses when compared to firms in other sectors. Most farm businesses are family based; indeed the farm is also the family home. Employment is dominated by family labour, with only 28.1 per cent of employment being undertaken by non-family paid employees (ECC, 1992 p. T/96).

Farms are invariably multi-product firms, for four main reasons. First, production of any product inevitably results in the output of some joint products even if the latter are not wanted, for example grain producers necessarily produce straw. Secondly, many products are interrelated, notably through rotation – the process of moving crops from field to field over the years to prevent a build-up of pests and diseases, and to benefit from the soil-improving effects of certain crops. Thirdly, a mix of different activities enables the farmer to keep himself, any employed labour, and the machinery more fully occupied during the different seasons. Finally, uncertainty is a major problem in farming, because the production processes are peculiarly subject to the vagaries of weather, pests and diseases; market prices are also variable. So farmers attempt to reduce income variance by combining several activities, although there are some products where price and output variance are relatively low, giving rise to specialization; dairying is the best example. Of course there are other types of farming where the physical constraints enforce specialization despite the risks – thus hill sheep are the only possibility on some land.

The price elasticity of demand of most foods is low at the retail level, and because marketing margins tend to be fixed, these elasticities are even lower for unprocessed foods which is the form in which foods leave the farm. Output is very variable due to the weather, pests and diseases, but once

Table 2.2   Demand Elasticities for Selected Foods in the UK, 1989

	Income elasticity	Price elasticity
Milk	−0.40	−0.29
Beef	0.08	−1.25
Pork	-0.05	−1.73
Chicken	0.24	−0.13
Sugar	−0.54	−0.24
Potatoes	−0.48	−0.21
Fresh green vegetables	0.13	−0.58
Bread	−0.25	−0.09

Source: MAFF (1990), *Household Food Consumption and Expenditure 1989*, London: HMSO.

harvested, output is in almost fixed supply. This results in often wild year to year price fluctuations in a free market. In the long run the income elasticity of demand is also low and declines with increasing income – the Engel effect. Table 2.2 gives some illustrative elasticities for the UK, as EC data are unavailable. With low income elasticities and little population growth, demand is static, but supplies increase under the spur of technological change. Gradually, supplies have outstripped demand, exerting a downward pressure on product prices and resource returns. Perfect competition theory suggests that reduced resource returns should lead to their reallocation to other uses. But neither land nor labour, particularly farmers themselves, are perfectly mobile, so farm incomes tend to remain relatively depressed. This slow adjustment of farmers to changing economic circumstances arises because their skills are not applicable to other forms of employment. Their specialized knowledge and inclinations leave them trapped in agriculture; they generally leave only when forced to do so by advancing age, ill-health, retirement or death. As a result, there are more older farmers, 30.5 per cent being over the age of 55 years (1989) contrasting with only 9.3 per cent and 10.7 per cent in this age category in the industrial and service sectors respectively (ECC, 1992, p. T/98).

   Low incomes in the agricultural sector, regarded as undesirable in the twentieth century, have attracted government intervention in all developed countries. In the Community, as in most other countries, the policy instrument selected to raise farmers' incomes is market intervention to raise prices above their free market levels. The policy is essentially social, not economic, but clearly has major economic consequences. First, price stabilization is usually included with price raising, resulting in less uncertainty and thus enhancing economic efficiency. Secondly, artificially raised prices, if much above free market levels, distort the allocation of resources both nationally and, for major trading countries, internationally. Thirdly, price intervention redistributes incomes between farmers, consumers and taxpayers. In the Community the most visible result of artificially high prices has been to encourage output to expand whilst demand has remained static, resulting in growing surpluses, disposal of which has proved extremely expensive, as large quantities are exported with the aid of export subsidies. High surplus disposal costs and the anger of competing world market suppliers has put great pressure on the Community to reform its agricultural policy.

2.2 Production

The Community has over 8 million farms. Details of their distribution and average size in terms of land area, are given in Table 2.4 (see p. 32). Differing historical developments have bequeathed very different farm sizes to the different member states. Thus UK farms are on average much larger than farms elsewhere, being double the average size for Denmark – the second largest – and more than fifteen times the average for the country with the lowest average size, Greece.

2.2.1 Structure of output

The value and structure of output are detailed in Table 2.3 Whilst most products are produced in all countries, there are marked regional differences. Most obviously, wine is not statistically significant in the north-west of Europe. Fruit and vegetables are of particular importance in the Mediterranean regions. Cattle is the most important sector for the Community as a whole, milk, beef and veal adding up to 31.2 per cent of the total output. Both Ireland and Luxembourg are very heavily dependent on cattle, which are evidently of great importance in north-west Europe where the climate favours grass growth. Physical land and climatic characteristics are obviously of considerable significance in influencing the geographical distribution of production, but taste and other factors are also important. Thus sheep meat is almost absent from some regions where production conditions are suitable, because it is not liked by consumers. Denmark's pig industry is an outstanding example of comparative advantage acquired by experience. In the last quarter of the nineteenth century cereals imported from North America became very cheap. This stimulated protection in many European countries but Denmark processed cheap grain imports into much higher-value pigmeat, and this still shows up in the current data.

Table 2.3 Value and Structure of Agricultural Output, 1990

	Value mn ECU	Cereals	Other crops	Fruit & vegetables	Wine	Milk	Beef & veal	Pigs	Eggs & poultry	Sheep & goats
						percentage shares				
Belgium	6 081	4.4	17.0	17.4	0	15.1	20.2	19.6	6.1	0.2
Denmark	6 851	14.9	18.7	3.7	0	24.4	8.4	27.1	2.7	0.
Germany	27 681	8.7	16.3	8.0	3.6	25.3	15.9	16.7	5.2	0.3
Greece	8 117	9.9	36.9	23.7	1.5	9.7	3.4	3.2	5.0	6.7
Spain	25 215	9.8	19.9	26.6	4.4	9.1	6.8	11.5	7.6	4.3
France	48 323	17.4	13.6	10.9	14.1	15.7	14.2	6.1	6.9	1.1
Ireland	4 187	5.2	7.0	3.0	0	32.4	38.5	5.5	3.9	4.5
Italy	36 308	9.3	18.6	27.2	8.4	11.8	9.6	6.4	8.0	0.7
Luxembourg	190	4.5	3.3	1.9	7.5	48.7	25.4	7.9	0.8	0
Netherlands	15 632	1.2	28.8	13.7	0	21.7	9.7	17.5	6.8	0.6
Portugal	3 535	10.8	14.9	16.3	8.9	12.0	10.2	13.1	10.1	3.7
United Kingdom	18 769	16.1	15.1	10.5	0	21.3	13.5	7.8	11.0	4.7
EC 12	202 012	11.4	17.9	14.4	6.3	18.1	13.1	10.3	7.0	1.5

Source: ECC (1992), pp. T/22–3.

31

2.2.2   Structure of farming

Diversity of land quality and climate is suggested by the wide variation in the percentages of agricultural land irrigated (see Table 2.4). Table 2.4 also gives the numbers of farms in 'less favoured areas'. Such areas are officially designated and farmers there receive special subsidies to compensate them for the natural disadvantages of their land. These include high altitude, poor and thin soils, steep terrain and remoteness from markets. Combinations of such problems make labour productivity low, and without extra assistance to farmers, such regions would have become depopulated even more rapidly than they have. Traditional farming systems based largely on extensive livestock grazing are necessary in these areas to preserve the traditional landscapes which urban dwellers wish to visit. The survival of farming is essential to both the landscape and the economic infrastructure of many regions.

Table 2.4   Agricultural Land, Number and Size of Farms, Various Years

	Farm land (000 ha) (1990)	Percentage irrigated (1988)	No. Farms (000s) (1987)	No. Farms in less favoured areas (000s) (1989)	Average size of Farm (ha) (1987)
Belgium	1 363	0.8	93	8.1	14.8
Denmark	2 799	15.1	87	0	32.2
Germany	11 868	2.7	705	245.7	16.8
Greece	5 741	20.6	953	215.5	4.0
Spain	27 110	12.2	1 792	224.3	13.8
France	30 581	4.5	982	1 549	28.6
Ireland	5 697	0	217	96.1	22.7
Italy	17 215	17.8	2 784	56.5	5.6
Luxembourg	127	0.8	4	3.0	30.2
Netherlands	2 019	27.0	132	1.2	15.3
Portugal	4 532	14.0	636	96.2	5.2
United Kingdom	18 447	0.9	260	56.1	64.4
EC 12	127 499	8.6	8 644	11 576	13.3

Source: ECC (1992), pp. T/20, T/122–6, T/129.

Fundamental to any understanding of the problems of agriculture is an appreciation of the size structure of farms; this is shown in Table 2.5. The most striking feature is that almost half of the Community farms are in the smallest size category. Apart from some very labour-intensive forms of production, small farms produce little and do not keep the farmer fully

Table 2.5   Distribution of Farms by Land-area Size Groups, 1987

Size group (ha)	Percentage of farms in each member state				
	1<5	5<10	10<20	20<50	50 & over
Belgium	27.7	18.1	24.5	23.9	5.8
Denmark	1.7	16.3	25.3	39.4	17.2
Germany	29.4	17.6	22.1	24.0	6.1
Greece	69.4	20.0	7.6	2.5	0.5
Spain	53.3	19.0	12.3	9.4	6.6
France	18.2	11.7	19.1	32.8	18.1
Ireland	16.1	15.2	29.2	30.5	9.0
Italy	67.9	16.9	8.7	4.6	1.9
Luxembourg	18.9	9.9	12.4	32.5	26.2
Netherlands	24.9	18.4	25.0	27.3	4.4
Portugal	72.5	15.0	7.2	3.4	1.9
United Kingdom	13.5	12.4	15.3	25.4	33.3
EC 12	49.2	16.8	13.5	13.7	6.8

Source: Eurostat (1992).

occupied. In stark contrast, the large farms (50 hectares and over) dominate output in most countries. The paradox to note is that most farms are small but most land is on large farms; this structure has obvious implications for income and employment which are examined below.

Many of the Community's small farms do not provide enough work for one person. Table 2.6 shows that 72.5 per cent of farms are in this category, with 56 per cent having too little work to occupy one person for half their time, yet two full-time workers is the minimum efficient size for most types of farming (Britton and Hill, 1975). As would be expected from the data on farm size distributions in Table 2.4, there is huge variation between member states. If the majority of farms provide so little employment it must be expected that many farmers would have additional non-farm employment. Whilst this is shown in Table 2.6 off-farm employment figures are much lower than the farm data suggest. Clearly there are far fewer part-time farmers than part-time farms. There are two reasons for this. First, the part-time farms data have been calculated on the assumption that all farmers use the same modern production techniques – but small farmers tend not to use the same modern production methods as the large farmers because they cannot afford to buy the equipment involved. Secondly, even if a farmer of

Table 2.6   Importance of Part-time Farms and Farmers, 1987

	Farms		Farmers	
	work provided as % of full-time farm		non-farm employment	
	50 to 99	<50	secondary	main
Belgium	6.5	28.3	3.0	29.2
Denmark	16.5*	20.1*	22.5	9.3
Germany	8.5	47.5	4.7	38.3
Greece	21.4	69.2	6.5	26.9
Spain	13.0	60.9	6.4	23.2
France	14.3	27.8	19.9	11.8
Ireland	24.3	32.4	10.5	26.0
Italy	17.9	69.3	3.4	20.5
Luxembourg	25.0	25.0	4.4	14.4
Netherlands	14.0	11.6	8.1	15.5
Portugal	24.0	46.9	6.4	31.8
United Kingdom	13.2	26.0	10.0	13.9
EC 12	16.5	56.0	7.1	23.0

Notes: *1985; part-time farmers are based on data from farm structures survey data indicating the proportion of holdings on which the farmer worked for 100%, 50 to 100% and less than 50% of the annual working hours of a full-time worker.

Source: ECC (1992), pp. T/102–3.

what appears to be a part-time holding has enough time to work off the farm, he may be too distant from alternative sources of employment to do so. The structure of agriculture may be characterized as predominantly small farms and fewer, though many, part-time farmers with a minority of large farms operated by full-time farmers.

2.2.3   Tenure of agricultural land
On an individual farm the land may be wholly owned by the farmer, wholly rented, or partly owned and partly rented. Table 2.7 shows the areas owned and tenanted in 1977 and 1987. The total for 1977 relates to EC 10 as data for Portugal and Spain are not available. The two years given represent opposing trends in various member states. In the Netherlands and UK the area owned by farmers has been expanding, with a contraction in the area tenanted. Data for Greece appear to be inconsistent, with figures for both

Table 2.7 Mode of Tenure of Agricultural Land in 1977 and 1987

	Area owner-farmed (000 hectares)		Area tenant farmed (000 hectares)	
	1977	1987	1977	1987
Belgium	406	434	1 043	936
Denmark	2 502	2 287	426	511
Germany	8 519	7 534	3 688	4 309
Greece	2 801	2 954	654	876
Spain		17 256		7 462
France	15 352	13 099	13 954	14 959
Ireland	4 882	4 710	186	198
Italy	13 028	12 418	3 489	3 098
Luxembourg	75	65	57	61
Netherlands	1 185	1 305	876	719
Portugal		2 204		1 121
United Kingdom	9 880	10 485	7 266	6 261
EC 10	58 629	55 290	31 640	31 930
EC 12		74 751		40 513

Source: Eurostat (1991a).

categories increasing; an examination of other years shows huge and still inconsistent swings in the Greek data. As all these data arise from surveys it is easier to believe that there have been problems with data collection and analysis than that wild changes have been occurring. Loss of agricultural land to roads and urban developments and the abandonment of some land – particularly poor land in remote areas – means that the totals for 1987 are lower than those for 1977. In Belgium for example the area farmed in 1987 (owned plus tenanted) declined to 1370 from 1449 hectares in 1977. For other member states there has been a steady decline in area owner-occupied, with increases in area tenanted. The explanation is that as the owners of many small farms have died or retired they have not been replaced as farmers by the next generation. Inheritors of land are often reluctant to sell, preferring instead to rent to neighbouring farmers. This attachment to land is not entirely emotional since land is an exceptionally durable asset. For example during the inter-war years of German hyperinflation it proved to be one of the best stores of wealth.

Table 2.8 *Agricultural Products Sold through Cooperatives, 1989 (%)*

	Pigmeat	Beef	Poultrymeat	Eggs	Milk	Sugarbeet	Cereals	Fruit	Vegetables
Belgium	15	–	–	–	65	–	25–30	60–65	70–75
Denmark	98	44	0	60	91	17	47	90	90
Germany	..	..	..	..	65	..	49	51	12
Greece	5	6	30	3	20	–	49	51	12
Spain	2	5	4	18	10	14	10	26	12
France	78	30	40	25	50	16	75	45	35
Ireland	65	5	26	0	95	0	50	..	2
Italy	15	6	–	5	32	–	35	31	10
Luxembourg	±25	±25	–	–	85	–	79	10	–
Netherlands	23	16	23	15	84	63	65	75	82
United Kingdom	16.6	5.1	0.3	17.5	4.3	0.5	19.0	21.1	24.9

Notes:
nil: –
no information: ..
Spanish data are for 1985, Ireland 1990 and Italy 1987; no data for Portugal.

Source: ECC (1992), p. T/127.

Table 2.9 Agricultural Products Sold under Contracts Concluded in Advance, 1989 (%)

	Pigmeat	Calves	Poultrymeat	Eggs	Milk	Sugarbeet	Potatoes	Peas	Canning tomatoes
Belgium	55	90	90	70	–	100	20–25	98	–
Denmark	0	0	–	–	–	100	40	100	–
Germany	14–15	14–15	73	20–25	99	100	50	95	–
Greece	..	..	..	..	2	100	2	80	–
Spain	..	..	..	..	..	100	..	..	–
France	30–32	30–35	45–50	15–20	1	100	8–10	90	–
Ireland	..	..	90	25	10	100	8–10	100	–
Italy	..	..	..	..	..	100	..	..	100
Luxembourg	15	–	–	–	–	–	–	–	–
Netherlands	40	85	90	50	90	100	50	85	–
United Kingdom	70	1	95	70	98	100	14	100	–

Notes: nil: –

no information: ..

German data are for 1979, France 1981, Ireland 1987, Italy 1985. There are no data for Portugal.

Source: ECC (1992), p. T/127.

2.3   Marketing

Brand images are virtually absent from farmers' sales because of the small size, in relation to the total market, of individuals' outputs, and the homogeneity of products. The wholesale marketing firms with which farmers deal, either directly or via produce auctions, are generally much larger businesses than are the farms. Farmers have traditionally complained about their relatively weak marketing position and one method of improving their situation is to combine in cooperatives. These may also enable farmers to benefit from economies of size in matters such as cleaning and pre-packaging vegetables, thus adding considerable value to products in ways which would be uneconomic for individuals. Because of the larger volumes of output they handle, cooperatives are able to supply supermarket chains, obtaining higher and more stable returns than would otherwise be available. Table 2.8 shows that the significance of cooperative marketing varies considerably between products and member states. Another method of reducing uncertainty is for farmers to sell by contract. Table 2.9 indicates that for sugarbeet this is the only way of selling. The beet is processed into sugar in factories which can undertake no other activity. Their specialized processing is capital intensive, so they need a guaranteed supply of beet to keep them fully occupied during the beet harvesting season. As the crop has only limited storability, excess supplies cannot be handled. The rather rigid requirements of the beet factories are mirrored at the farm level. From the farmers' point of view beet is only of value for sale to processors – it could be used as animal feed but cheaper alternatives are used. Finally, beet is heavy in relation to its value. In combination, these unusual features result in all beet being produced by farmers on contract with their local factory. Vegetables destined for freezing are also subject to contracts: they have to be produced close to the freeze-processors to avoid loss of freshness and hence quality, but of course not all vegetables enter this sector of the market. In interpreting Tables 2.8 and 2.9, note that sales through cooperatives and by contract are not mutually exclusive categories.

2.4   Farm incomes

It was noted in the introduction that little is known about farmers' total incomes, but there is information about their incomes from farming. Table 2.10 gives data for 'commercial' farms, that is, farms which market the bulk of their production. Approximately half of Community farms fall into this category – very little is known of the incomes of the other half. The table shows that more than one-third of commercial farms generated an average income of 800 ECU in 1989–90 – a reasonably typical year. At the other extreme a little over 10 per cent of farms provided an average income of 37 800 ECU, a relatively high income. The table suggests that average

Table 2.10   Incomes from Farming on Commercial Farms in EC, 1989–90

Class of income (000 ECUs)	Percentage of farms	Average area (ha)	Income, ECU per full-time family member
<0 – 4	34.4	10.7	800
4 – 8	23.2	13.6	5 200
8 – 12	13.3	21.3	9 000
12 – 24	18.2	35.4	15 500
>24	10.8	52.9	37 800
All farms	99.9	21.9	9 400

Notes: Based on farm accountancy data network surveys of 'commercial' farms.

Source: ECC (1992), p. T/54.

incomes are strongly correlated with farm size. The data illustrate the points made earlier: that the majority of farmers have low or very low incomes, whilst a minority are relatively wealthy.

2.5   Consumption
Table 2.11 illustrates Engel's Law: that as incomes rise a decreasing proportion of income is spent on food. It follows that as incomes rise, price and income elasticities of demand for food fall, with consequences for the stability and level of food prices (in a free market) which were noted earlier. Food expenditure's share of total consumer expenditure is of major significance to the distributional effects of raising prices through policy measures, as will be discussed in section 2.7. Table 2.11 gives national averages which demonstrate the strong relationship between income and food expenditure. The poorest countries, in terms of income per head, have incomes rather less than half of those of the richest members, but in percentage terms they spend about twice as much on food.

2.6   Trade
The Community is the world's second largest exporter of agricultural products, accounting for 13.9 per cent of world agricultural exports in 1990. This compares with 15.8 per cent of world agricultural exports supplied by the US. The Community is by far the major importer of agricultural commodities, having a 22 per cent share in 1990. The imports and exports are of fundamentally different commodities. Imports are mainly tropical fruits and beverages, rubber, timber and cork, skins and furs, and oilseeds (used largely

Table 2.11   Average Incomes and Expenditure on Food

	GDP per head ECU (1990)	Food expenditure as percentage of total consumer expenditure (1989)
Belgium	19 089	15.7
Denmark	19 809	14.8
Germany	21 074	12.3
Greece	9 850	30.4
Spain	14 557	20.2
France	24 301	12.1
Netherlands	19 093	14.5
Portugal	10 373	32.7
United Kingdom	19 528	11.6
EC 12	18 622	16.5

Note: GDP is at purchasing power standard.

Source: ECC (1992), pp. T/20–1, T/155.

Table 2.12   Trade in Agricultural and Food Products, 1990 (Mn ECU)

	Imports		Exports	
	EC states	Non-EC countries	EC states	Non-EC countries
Belgium	8 281	2 903	8 444	1 263
Denmark	1 667	2 038	5 158	2 993
Germany	20 892	11 652	11 273	5 448
Greece	1 904	866	1 379	622
Spain	3 763	4 892	4 747	2 391
France	13 796	7 267	20 389	7 874
Ireland	1 534	423	3 317	1 072
Italy	14 479	8 434	6 011	3 039
Netherlands	9 101	6 605	19 948	5 544
Portugal	1 267	1 619	822	344
United Kingdom	12 459	9 190	6 184	4 596
EC 12	89 144	55 889	87 671	35 186

Source: ECC (1992), p. T/152.

as animal feedstuffs). Many of these commodities are ill suited to the European climate. The exports are principally surpluses of temperate zone products which have been generated by the support system discussed in the next section. Export of these products is thus a residual, the difference between EC consumption and production.

Table 2.12 summarizes the value of trade in agricultural and food products of the member states. Trade flows within the Community, though distorted in the past by non-tariff barriers and different excise taxes, are to some extent governed by comparative advantage; distortions should be reduced by the 1992 single market programme.

2.7   The Common Agricultural Policy (CAP)

2.7.1   Objectives and instruments

When the EC was formed each of its six original members had their own policy. To permit the free movement of food within the Community and at the same time support farmers, it was necessary to devise a common policy. The objectives are set out in Article 39 of the Treaty of Rome and may be summarized as:

(a)   to increase productivity
(b)   to raise farm incomes
(c)   to stabilize markets
(d)   to assure the availability of supplies
(e)   to ensure reasonable prices to consumers

Raising farm incomes was regarded as the primary objective and the instrument chosen was market intervention to raise prices. This is outlined in principle in Figure 2.1 with reference to wheat. The target price was selected to be much above the 'low' world price. To prevent imports pushing prices below this level they were made subject to a variable import levy, this being the difference between the lowest price of wheat delivered to EC ports and the target price less transport costs. Immediately after harvest a seasonal surplus would have resulted in prices falling below the target level even in the absence of imports. So intervention agencies were set up in each member state to purchase wheat if it fell significantly below the target level. In theory the seasonal wheat surpluses could be bought and stored until later in the year when the post-harvest glut was over. This policy raised prices to farmers, who therefore moved up their supply curves (compared to the free trade position) and enjoyed higher incomes. As the policy also raised prices to consumers it effected an income transfer from them to producers. The increase in price – compared to the free trade world price – is considered to be an

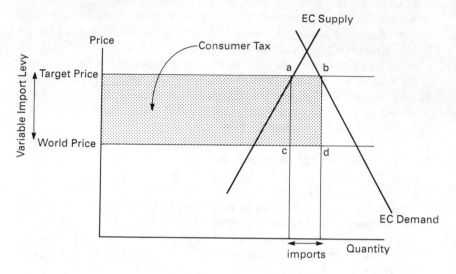

Figure 2.1   Price Raising Using a Variable Import Levy

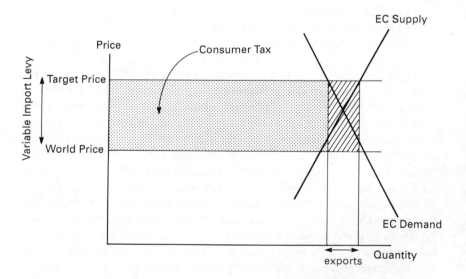

Figure 2.2   Operation of a Variable Import Levy when Supply Exceeds Demand

implicit consumer tax, and this is shaded in the figure. The variable import levy times the quantity imported (area abcd) was a contribution to EC revenues – reducing the need for other forms of taxation to finance EC policies. Of course the expansion of Community supplies which the policy induced reduced food imports and damaged the interests of third-country suppliers. Cereal prices were the first to be set. As cereals are inputs to livestock production and compete for the use of land with other crops, once high prices had been set for them, high prices had to follow for other products. Although there are substantial differences in the detailed implementation of the policy for different products, raising prices above free market levels is the basic method of support.

When the CAP was devised the Community was a major importer of many agricultural commodities so no limits to the extent of intervention buying were considered necessary. The intervention system was 'open ended' so that the industry demand curves, as well as those facing individual farmers, were in effect perfectly elastic. However, the actual market demand for food was both inelastic and static because consumers were already well fed and the rate of population growth was insignificant. In sharp contrast, technological advances resulted in an inexorable expansion of supplies. Inevitably, the Community's supply of almost every product eventually surpassed Community demand, and occasional or seasonal surpluses became chronic surpluses. Had the market been free to adjust, the inelastic demand for agricultural products would rapidly have reduced prices enough to restore equilibrium, and many farmers would have become impoverished or bankrupt. In practice, the CAP-manipulated market kept prices high for the benefit of farmers, and structural surpluses became the norm. The intervention agencies were obliged to purchase surpluses and to store them despite the fact that they would not later be saleable on the internal market. Storage facilities are finite and society regards the destruction of food as immoral, so some method of surplus disposal had to be found. In the decade following the Second World War the US, for similar reasons, had ended up with excessive food stocks, particularly of cereals. A popular solution had been to use them as food aid and the US passed Public Law 480 in 1954 to regularize this procedure. By the time the Community surpluses became a problem, large-scale food aid was no longer regarded as an acceptable method of disposing of surpluses because of its undesirable effects on recipient countries. Briefly, these arise because Third World countries have agriculture as their main economic activity, typically occupying more than half the population. Food aid necessarily reduces food prices in such countries, thus making farming unprofitable. Farmers therefore fail to invest, and *inter alia*, this reduces the ability of the countries to feed themselves. Of course humanitarian famine relief remains an important destination of some food surpluses. If surpluses cannot be used as food aid or destroyed the next obvious outlet is the world market.

When the free world's trading system was reorganized after the Second World War under the General Agreement on Tariffs and Trade (GATT) agricultural products were deliberately excluded. So it was possible for the Community to purchase agricultural surpluses at high prices within the Community and then to export them at much lower world market prices with the aid of export subsidies. Figure 2.2 depicts this situation. Consumers are still subject to artificially high prices – an implicit food tax – but now taxpayers have to finance surplus disposals (the hatched area) instead of benefiting from levies on imports.

It is appropriate at this point to examine in more detail the income transfers from consumers to producers. From Table 2.1 it seems probable that consumers are on average richer than producers. But it is in the nature of averages to hide disparities. In section 2.4, on farm incomes, it was argued that most farms are small and provide low incomes whilst a minority of farms are large and their occupiers enjoy high incomes. Section 2.5 showed that poor consumers spend a higher proportion of income on food than do rich consumers. So to a significant extent the CAP transfers income from poor consumers to richer farmers. Large farmers benefit disproportionately because the support system operates through raised prices – clearly those who produce most will gain most. The poorer farmers, for whom the CAP was intended, are left relatively poor despite enormous income transfers and huge budgetary expenditures, which are considered below.

As the CAP affords a much higher level of protection to agriculture than is given to other industries, resource allocation must be distorted. Resources are used in agriculture which would be more productive in other sectors. Resource misallocation is not confined to the Community: by dumping cheap food on world markets comparative advantages are overruled by subsidies and other trading countries are harmed. Their reduced wealth results in them importing less from the Community than they otherwise would. Thus the CAP is indirectly responsible for extra unemployment in some Community export industries. Stoeckel (1985) estimated that between 1973 and 1983 the CAP caused manufacturing exports to be reduced by 4 per cent and manufacturing imports to be increased by 5 per cent. As a consequence the output of this sector was reduced by 1.5 per cent, representing about half a million jobs. More up-to-date figures are not available, but the situation has probably worsened since 1983.

2.7.2   Financial and consumer costs of the CAP
Table 2.13 details the Community budget since 1971. It can be seen that the European Agricultural Guarantee and Guidance Fund (EAGGF) has domi-

Table 2.13   EC Budgetary Expenditure, 1971–92

	EAGGF	Social Fund	Regional Fund	Industry energy research	Administration	Other	Total
			Mn UA/EUA/ECU*				
1971	1 883.6	56.5	–	65.0	132.1	152.2	2 289.3
1972	2 477.6	97.5	–	75.1	177.2	247.1	3 074.5
1973	3 768.8	269.2	–	69.1	239.4	294.4	4 641.0
1974	3 651.3	292.1	–	82.8	336.7	675.2	5 038.2
1975	4 586.6	360.2	150.0	99.0	375.0	642.8	6 213.6
1976	6 033.3	176.7	300.0	113.3	419.7	909.5	7 952.6
1977	6 463.5	325.2	372.5	163.3	497.0	883.4	8 704.9
1978	9 602.2	284.8	254.9	227.2	676.7	1 302.4	12 348.2
1979	10 735.5	595.7	671.5	288.0	863.9	1 447.9	14 602.5
1980	11 596.1	502.0	751.8	212.8	938.8	2 056.1	16 057.5
1981	11 446.0	547.0	2 264.0	217.6	1 035.4	3 024.6	18 546.0
1982	12 792.0	910.0	2 766.0	346.0	1 103.3	3 509.7	21 427.0
1983	16 331.3	801.0	2 265.5	1 216.2	1 161.6	2 989.9	24 765.5
1984	18 985.8	1 116.4	1 283.3	1 346.4	1 236.6	2 150.8	26 119.3
1985	20 546.4	1 413.0	1 624.3	706.9	1 332.6	2 599.8	28 223.0
1986	23 067.7	2 533.0	2 373.0	760.1	1 603.2	4 526.2	34 863.2
1987	23 939.4	2 542.2	2 562.3	964.8	1 740.0	3 720.5	35 469.2
1988	27 531.9	2 298.8	3 092.8	1 203.7	1 947.0	6 186.8	42 261.0
1989	25 868.8	2 676.1	3 920.0	1 353.0	2 063.0	9 978.9	45 899.8
1990	29 525.5	3 677.4	5 007.5	1 763.5	2 362.1	4 341.3	46 677.3
1991	35 458.0	4 069.0	6 309.0	2 077.1	2 827.7	6 681.2	57 422.0
1992**	36 008.0	4 872.2	7 702.8	2 154.3	2 932.0	8 738.0	62 407.3

Notes: *currency units have changed from Units of Account to European Units of Accounts to ECUs; **draft budget.

Source: Eurostat (1991c), p. 267.

nated the budget for many years. Consequently little has been left to finance other policies and so other developments have been stifled.

Figures 2.1 and 2.2 suggested that in addition to the known financial costs of the CAP there were major (implicit) consumer tax transfers. These have been estimated by OECD (1992) to total 50 billion ECU for 1991. So the budgetary costs and consumer taxes totalled 85 billion ECU for 1991, equivalent to about 266 ECU (£185) per head in that year. In fact OECD estimates of the value of assistance to farmers including national subsidies in addition to EC budgetary costs and consumer taxes came to 118 billion ECU, or 369 ECU (£257) per head. For comparison, the OECD also esti-mated the costs of agricultural support in the US to be 182 ECU per head in 1991, approximately half the cost level in the Community.

Table 2.14   EC Budgetary Receipts, 1971–92

	Mn UA/EUA/ECU*				
	Miscellaneous	Agricultural levies	Import duties	GNP or VAT	Total
1971	69.5	713.8	582.2	923.8	2 289.3
1972	80.9	799.6	957.4	1 236.6	3 074.5
1973	511.0	478.0	1 564.7	2 087.3	4 641.0
1974	65.3	323.6	2 684.4	1 964.8	5 038.2
1975	320.5	590.0	3 151.0	2 152.0	6 213.6
1976	282.8	1 163.7	4 064.6	2 482.1	7 993.1
1977	504.7	1 778.5	3 927.2	2 494.5	8 704.9
1978	344.4	2 283.3	4 390.9	5 329.7	12 348.2
1979	230.2	2 143.4	5 189.1	7 039.8	14 602.5
1980	1 055.9	2 002.3	5 905.8	7 093.5	16 057.5
1981	1 219.0	1 747.0	6 392.0	9 188.0	18 546.0
1982	187.0	2 228.0	6 815.0	12 197.0	21 427.0
1983	1 565.0	2 295.0	6 988.7	13 916.8	24 765.5
1984	1 060.7	2 436.3	7 960.8	14 594.6	26 052.4
1985	2 491.0	2 179.0	8 310.0	15 218.0	28 198.0
1986	396.5	2 287.0	8 172.9	22 810.8	33 667.2
1987	74.8	3 097.9	8 936.5	23 674.1	35 783.3
1988	1 377.0	2 606.0	9 310.0	28 968.0	42 261.0
1989	4 018.4	2 397.9	10 312.9	29 170.6	45 899.8
1990	5 419.0	2 283.2	11 349.9	27 652.2	46 677.3
1991	4 356.0	2 295.4	11 949.7	38 821.8	57 420.0
1992 draft budget	413.2	2 328.6	11 599.9	48 065.6	62 407.3

Note: * see note to Table 2.13.

Source: Eurostat (1991c), p. 268.

EC budgetary receipts are detailed in Table 2.14. National contributions to the Community budget fall into three major categories. A GNP or VAT element is at the same rate for each member, but the other two elements – levies on agricultural imports and import duties on all other goods – vary considerably between countries. As agricultural surpluses are the main cause of budgetary expenditures, national receipts vary according to national contributions to surpluses. This arrangement is particularly unfavourable for the UK, which is a major importer but whose agricultural exports are relatively small, resulting in UK contributions greatly exceeding receipts. Throughout the 1980s the UK has received some repayments after tough negotiations but is still a substantial net contributor. Between 1973 and 1988 the UK's cumulative net contributions to the budget exceeded 14 billion ECU (more than £10 billion) at current market prices. Obviously at constant 1992 prices the total would be much higher. The net contribution is currently estimated to be of the order of 2.8 billion ECU (£2 billion) annually. No other member state is disadvantaged to such an extent.

2.7.3 'Green' money

Because agricultural prices are determined by the Community they are denominated in ECU, but of course they are applied in national currencies. To provide stability to food prices and thus to farmers, a system of green currencies has developed whereby farm product prices are denominated in ECUs at constant rates of exchange which differ from those operating in the relatively free and therefore variable market for national currencies. These artificial 'green' rates have diverged from market rates of exchange by considerable amounts since they were introduced in 1969 (Hill, 1984). One consequence has been that prices actually received by farmers in different countries may differ considerably when actual market rates of exchange are used. In the past, national price differences often greatly exceeded transport costs, yet the illusion of a common policy with common prices and free trade has been preserved by a system of monetary compensatory amounts (MCAs): when an agricultural commodity travels from one member country to another the real price difference is adjusted at the border by a compensating tax or subsidy. These MCAs are manipulated through EAGGF. Over the years the green exchange rates have diverged from market rates, constituting a hidden price subsidy to agriculture. Under the single market the national divergencies are supposed to be phased out and then each national green currency will differ from the true market rate by the same amount. The situation in 1991 is shown in Table 2.15.

2.7.4 CAP reform

Before examining policy reform a summary of CAP problems is advisable. Summarizing the above sections, the CAP raises prices to help poor farmers, resulting in: surpluses which are dumped on world markets; transfers of income from consumers to farmers – often inequitably, from poor consumers to richer farmers; inequitable national transfers; the misallocation of resources within the EC and between the EC and the rest of the world.

For more than a decade the Community has tinkered with the CAP and pretended that the effects were reforms. In 1985 a new round of GATT trade negotiations – known as the Uruguay round, since this is where the first meeting was held – began with the objective of reducing barriers to international trade. Some of the major participants, notably US and the Cairns Group (a group of fourteen food-exporting countries including both devel-

Table 2.15   Exchange Rates of the ECU – National Green and Market Currency Rates, 1991

	Market rate	Green rate	Difference (%)
Belgium	42.2812	48.5563	14.8
Denmark	7.90295	8.97989	13.6
Germany	2.05399	2.35418	14.6
Greece	222.801	257.895	15.8
Spain	128.096	145.756	13.9
France	6.97281	7.89563	13.2
Ireland	0.768948	0.878776	14.3
Italy	1532.09	1761.45	15.0
Netherlands	2.31460	2.65256	14.6
Portugal	179.096	205.190	14.6
United Kingdom	0.698480	0.795423	13.9

Notes: Market rates are January to August averages, green rates are at 1 July.

Sources: Eurostat (1991b), p. 126 and ECC (1992), p. 17.

oped and developing) were determined to include agriculture. Clearly the data given earlier on costs of agricultural support in the EC and US indicate that the former is not the only source of food trade distortions – though it is certainly the major offender. The EC refused to make any significant changes to the CAP, and the Uruguay round, which should have been completed by the end of 1990, kept being extended. In July 1991 the Commission, under the twin pressures of excessive budgetary expenditures on agriculture and the anger of other participants in world trade, came up with a CAP reform proposal ECC (1991). The 'MacSharry Plan' (named after the Commissioner for Agriculture, Ray MacSharry) proposed that EC prices should be reduced, bringing them nearer to world levels, and that farmers should be compensated with some form of direct income payment. In essence the plan would reduce output and surpluses – and hence disposal costs and trade problems with other countries. At the same time the direct income payments could be targeted at poor farmers, instead of the main beneficiaries being, as previously, the relatively rich farmers. Consumers would be better off and inequitable consumer transfers would be greatly reduced – as a greater share of the burden of support would fall on taxpayers. Finally, resources would be more efficiently allocated.

After prolonged debate, the MacSharry Plan was eventually modified, and in May 1992 was agreed by the Council of Agriculture Ministers (see *Agra Europe*, 1992). Its main decision is to reduce cereal prices gradually, the cumulative reduction to be 29 per cent by 1997. Farmers are to receive compensatory payments equal to the difference between current supported prices and the new reduced prices on condition that 15 per cent of their arable land is set aside, that is, not used to produce a CAP-supported product. Set-aside was introduced as part of a 1988 'reform' package. It offered compensation to farmers who volunteered to remove land from arable production. Farmers were not enthusiastic and the measure reduced the area cultivated by about 1 per cent only. Clearly the new version of set-aside, which is compulsory if farmers wish to receive compensation for lower prices, will be more effective. The rate of subsidy for set-aside land is likely to give farmers a return similar to that which would have been achieved if a crop had been produced.

In the livestock sector, support prices are to be reduced to reflect the lower prices of feeding-stuffs consequent upon the cereal price reduction. There are no changes in milk quotas, which were introduced in 1984 to limit the budgetary expenditure on milk and milk products.

This reform package is notable because it is switching some support from market prices to direct payments to farmers. Concomitantly some of the burden of support passes from consumers to taxpayers. If the reduction in support prices and the set-aside reduction in arable land succeed in cutting the production and export of surpluses there should be worthwhile improvements in resource allocation and indirect trade benefits. However, it is not certain that the reforms will achieve major reductions in cereal surpluses. The 15 per cent set-aside is to be rotational, that is the land will be 'rested' for a time and then brought back into cultivation whilst another equal area is rested. Inevitably this will enhance yields, which are already increasing at significant rates. The concentration of farmers' resources on smaller areas of land is also likely to be yield enhancing. The reaction of farmers to their receipts in the form of compensatory payments is unknown. Although the payments break the link between output and receipts, farmers might nevertheless regard them as just an addition to profit to be invested in the farm. Thus the reduction in cultivated area could be negated by higher yields within a few years. This problem arises because set-aside applies to the area of land, not the quantity of output produced. A quota on output would have been more effective in theory but extremely difficult to implement in practice. A major criticism of the reform is that it fails to address the inequitable income distribution within agriculture: the Commission's original proposal had been to limit the amount of compensation paid to individual farmers, but the agreement is to compensate all farmers, regardless of size.

2.8 Efficiency

2.8.1 Pricing efficiency

The operation of price support mechanisms and the resultant residual nature of trade has kept prices stable to an excessive degree. As noted earlier, the CAP has provided the industry with an almost perfectly elastic demand curve. Thus consumer requirements both within and outside the Community have not been transmitted to producers: the corollary has been that prices have not adequately guided resource allocation. Clearly pricing efficiency is a concept which is alien to the CAP.

2.8.2 Technical efficiency

The physical output of agriculture has been rising throughout the existence of the Community (as it has in other countries also). National diversities and the growing membership of the Community make precise measurement difficult, but the growth in output as land (slightly) and labour (substantially) have declined, indicates substantial improvements. Increases in crop yields are still occurring, for example over the years 1985–89 the yield of cereals increased by 0.8 per cent per year. A considerable part of the rising productivities of land and labour is due to the use of extra capital in both chemical (fertilizer and crop protection) and mechanical guises.

2.8.3 Economic efficiency

There is no doubt that the vast majority of farms are far too small to exploit the available economies of size. It is not surprising that agriculture's share of GDP is less than half its share of the employed labour force. However, agriculture has a major impact on the environment and the contributions to welfare of externalities such as landscape and wildlife have not been taken into account. It is likely that the environmental contributions of small farms compare favourably with those of bigger (and usually more modern) farms. Unfortunately measurement of these externalities has not proceeded far enough to permit an assessment to be made.

Ignoring environmental considerations, the evidence suggests that agriculture is very inefficient. The total value of agricultural output in 1990 was 202 billion ECU, but no less than 118 billion ECU was contributed by EC and national taxpayers and consumers (67.8 billion ECU and an implicit consumer food tax of 49.9 billion ECU respectively: see OECD, 1992). The very existence and nature of the CAP indicates the extreme inefficiency of this industry. Only a modest or temporary amelioration seems likely to proceed from the reforms of 1992 even though they are relatively radical. These reforms do not seem to address the greatest problem of agriculture, that it encompasses enough poverty to inspire expensive policy intervention, but the main beneficiaries are usually the relatively wealthy large farmers.

2.9 Concluding remarks
EC agriculture adjusts very slowly to changing economic circumstances, so that there are far too many small farms, providing their farmers with relatively low incomes. The social problem of agricultural poverty has given rise to a policy of raising agricultural product prices. This has proved to be a multifaceted economic disaster which has not brought about the desired distribution of incomes. The MacSharry reforms of 1992 are relatively radical, but their effects are very uncertain.

References
Agra Europe (1992), **1492**, 22 May.
Britton, D.K. and Hill, B. (1975), *Size and Efficiency in Farming*, Farnborough, Hants: Saxon House; and Lexington, Mass.: Lexington Books.
European Communities Commission (ECC) (1991), *Development and Future of the CAP* (COM (91) 258), Luxembourg: Office for Official Publications of the European Communities.
ECC (1992), *The Agricultural Situation in the Community 1991*, Luxembourg: Office for Official Publications of the European Communities.
Eurostat (1991a), *Agricultural Statistical Yearbook 1990*, Luxembourg: Office for Official Publications of the European Communities.
Eurostat (1991b), *European Economy 48*, Luxembourg: Office for Official Publications of the European Communities.
Eurostat (1991c), *European Economy 50*, Luxembourg: Office for Official Publications of the European Communities.
Eurostat (1992), *Basic Statistics of the Community 1991*, Luxembourg: Office for Official Publications of the European Communities.
Hill, Brian E. (1984), *The Common Agricultural Policy, Past Present and Future*, London: Methuen.
Hill, Brian, E. (1988), 'Agriculture', in Peter Johnson (ed.), *The Structure of British Industry*, London: Unwin Hyman, pp. 20–1.
OECD (1992), quoted in *Financial Times*, 22 May, 4.
Stoeckel, A. (1985), *Intersectoral Effects of the CAP: Growth, Trade and Unemployment*, (Occasional Paper 95), Canberra: Australian Government Publishing Service, Bureau of Agricultural Economics.

Further reading
Harris, S., Swinbank, A. and Wilkinson, G. (1983), *The Food and Farm Policies of the European Community*, Chichester: Wiley. A detailed analysis of the CAP and its influence on the food industry and trade.
Johnson, D. Gale (1991), *World Agriculture in Disarray*, 2nd edn, London: Macmillan. A perceptive analysis giving an excellent world perspective.
Tracy, Michael (1989), *Government and Agriculture in Western Europe 1880–1988*, 3rd edn. Brighton: Harvester-Wheatsheaf. Detailed coverage of West European countries.

3   Steel

Anthony Cockerill

3.1   Introduction

Steel, like coal, is at the heart of the European Community. As well as being an engine of industrialization, steel has also been a vital requirement for war. Recognizing these two facets of steel, the Treaty of Paris, signed in 1951, set up the European Coal and Steel Community (ECSC) to form a common market in the two commodities. The initiative, which was a forerunner of the other Community activities that were to merge eventually in 1972, was intended to bind closely together, both economically and politically, the founder member states (West Germany, France, Belgium, Luxembourg, Italy and the Netherlands) and, in particular, France and Germany, so as to make a resurgence of hostilities in Western Europe less likely.

The structure of the industry had been devastated by war, so major investment schemes to restore and expand capacity to meet the needs of postwar reconstruction and development were necessary. Liquid steel-making capacity in the original six member states was 34.8 million tonnes in 1951, two-thirds of which was in Germany and France. Between 1951 and 1960, capacity more than doubled to 76.5 million tonnes. Output grew by 112 per cent over the same period, from 34.5 to 73.1 million tonnes.

Expansion continued to be driven by industrial growth throughout the 1960s until, in 1974, annual output (for the then nine members) reached an historic peak of 132.6 million tonnes, close to the sector's capacity of 150.4 million tonnes.

The economic importance of steel during this period was reflected in its share in value of the ECSC's products in total trade of the Community countries, which varied between 4.7 and 5.9 per cent from 1951 to 1970. In the 1970s, however, as the economies of the member states matured and final demand shifted towards services and away from manufactures, the steel intensity began to fall and a more tenuous relationship developed between movements in overall economic activity and the demand for steel. This, when associated with the two energy price-related recessions of the mid and late 1970s, led to a reversal in the growth trend in output and to the emergence of a chronic overhang of surplus capacity. The balance of the Community's steel demand and supply was affected by the enlargement of the Community in 1973, which brought, in particular, the manufacturing capacity of the UK within the terms of the Treaty of Paris. Weak demand and excess capacity continued to characterize the sector in the first half of the 1980s, but stronger economic activity and the effects of rationalization improved prices and margins in the second half of the decade. These improvements were, however, partially undermined subsequently by the slowdown in activity in the early 1990s. The Community was widened again in 1984, and also in 1986, to include in particular Spain as a steel-producing nation of growing importance. Figure 3.1 shows the composition of steel production by member state in 1990.

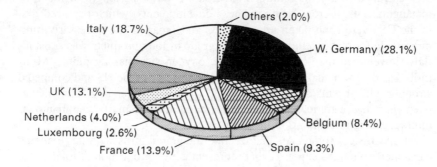

Italy (18.7%)
Others (2.0%)
W. Germany (28.1%)
UK (13.1%)
Netherlands (4.0%)
Luxembourg (2.6%)
France (13.9%)
Spain (9.3%)
Belgium (8.4%)

Source: Eurostat, *Iron and Steel Statistical Yearbook 1991.*

Figure 3.1   Share of EC Steel Output, 1990

Steel is a molecularly reconstructed form of iron, manufactured by reducing the carbon content of iron. The resulting metal is both stronger and more malleable than iron. Steel can be alloyed with other metals (e.g. chromium, tungsten, vanadium) to produce special steels with particular physical and chemical characteristics (e.g. rust resistance, cutting edges). Volume production is, in essence, large scale, carried out typically in mills that bring together ironmaking from the metal ore, steel melting, casting, rolling and finishing. With the exception of the last, each of these stages requires the metal to be hot in order for it to be worked, and the opportunities to conserve heat and to maintain quality standards are important factors that explain the development of large-scale integrated steelworks.

Special steels (high-quality alloys for particular uses) are made by melting common steel and the alloys in an electric arc furnace, removing impurities, and then casting. Typically, manufacture is carried out at much smaller volumes than for common grades of steel, in part because the economies of scale are less and in part because demand is smaller. In the 1960s electric arc furnaces began to be used to make common grades of steel. Three factors made this possible; first, higher industrial activity and replacement of capital equipment and buildings increased the supply (and cut the price) of scrap steel. Scrap steelmaking is energy intensive as the scrap is melted and purified in an electric furnace. Secondly, the real price of electricity was reduced as primary fuel costs fell and generating scale grew bigger. Lastly, the cost and complexity of casting was reduced by the development and introduction of the continuous caster, into which molten steel is poured and then extruded in a semi-solidified state as a continuous length of metal of rectangular lateral cross-section. These developments, which occurred first in the US, were soon taken up in the EC and Japan as the necessary minimum scale for manufacture of common grade of long products was substantially lower than the conventional basic oxygen steelmaking plant. 'Mini-mills' (as they were called) were established quickly in the US and competed strongly with the major steel producers. Generally, their development has been much less significant in the EC, although in Italy small-scale manufacturers are a significant part of the industry.

European steel companies that operate integrated mills with large annual capacities have fixed expenses that represent a high proportion of total costs. Figure 3.2 shows a typical distribution of the items that make up the price of a tonne of steel in West Germany (as it was) and the UK. A substantial proportion of labour costs (those relating to indirect labour, sales and marketing, management and administration) are relatively fixed. The same is true of financial charges (depreciation and interest). Those fixed costs that are specific to the steelworks (e.g. past capital expenditures and their associated financial costs) are also sunk costs, that is, they cannot be recovered by the sale of the plant because it has no alternative use. These two features have important consequences for the behaviour of steel prices (see section 3.3). In the short run, when most costs are fixed, average costs rise in relation to decreases in capacity utilization, and profit margins are eroded quickly. Because of the importance of fixed costs, average variable costs are a small part of average total costs over most of the range of output in a steelworks. As a result, adjustments to lower demand are made both by reducing output and by cutting price. In firms that operate more than one works, increases in demand are met by raising output according to the plants' relative production costs and the types of products they are capable of manufacturing. This suggests that the industry's short-run supply curve

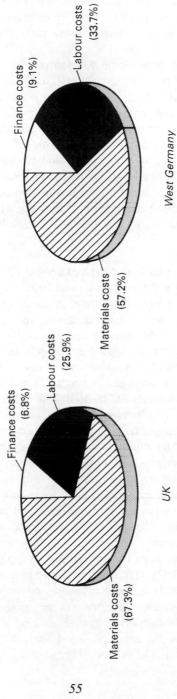

Source: Drawn from data in Howell *et al.* (1988) (by permission of Westview Press, Boulder Colorado).

Figure 3.2 Structure of Costs of One Tonne of Steel: UK and West Germany, November 1987

rises quite sharply with increased output. Over the long term, the industry benefits from the economies of scale derived from large volumes of annual output, indicating that the long-run supply curve is declining over an extensive range of output.

Steel consumption depends on the demand for steel-using products and activities: consumer products (e.g. coins), durables (e.g. cars, domestic appliances), capital goods (e.g. machinery, ships) and construction. Steel demand is, therefore, a derived demand and depends mainly on the level of overall economic activity (income). In consequence, considering the industry as a whole, the elasticity of demand with respect to income is high but overall demand is insensitive to price variations, so that the price elasticity of demand is low (typically –0.3). However, because steel from one producer is hard to differentiate from steel from another, the cross-elasticity of demand with respect to price is high: thus if one firm lowers its price in an effort to maintain sales in a weak market, others will quickly match the cut.

3.2   Market structure

The Community steel industry produces around 137 million tonnes of liquid steel a year, making it the world's second largest by output after the former Soviet Union. Output from the founder members of the EC represents more than two-thirds of Community output, the industries of Germany, France and Italy being the largest. EC enlargement since 1973 brought in first Britain and later Spain as significant producers. Despite its overall size, the structure of the industry within the Community is nationalistic, undiversified and fragmented. Each producer nation supplies the bulk of domestic demand from its own sources. Intra-EC trade has increased with the Community's economic growth and wider membership, but represents less than one-third of overall steel consumption. With few exceptions, enterprises are registered for ownership in the country in which they mainly operate; cross-shareholdings with enterprises in other member states are rare; and government involvement in the ownership, financing and strategic direction of enterprises is common. Enterprises have remained, in the main, devoted to the manufacture and distribution of iron and steel products and, so far, have not sought to diversify. Undoubtedly government involvement in the industry has been an important factor in this. The industry in Germany is the main exception; the leading firms of Thyssen and Krupp (and Hoesch, with which Krupp merged in 1992) have been engineering companies for a long time and during the 1980s these interests became more widespread.

Some of the Community's steelmakers are among the largest in the world. For example, Usinor-Sacilor of France, the EC's largest producer, ranks second in the world, in terms of liquid steel output, after Nippon Steel Corporation of Japan. The degree of large seller concentration within the

EC's internal market is comparable to that of the US but low with respect to Japan. The combined outputs of the largest five Community producers in 1990 represented 46 per cent of the total, as compared with 63 and 45 per cent respectively in Japan and the USA.

This low level of overall market concentration contrasts sharply with high output concentration levels within national markets. In each major producing nation, the four largest firms (or fewer) account for at least 80 per cent of total output. The presence of (relatively) large firms in EC countries is the outcome in the main of mergers and acquisitions intended to consolidate production in each market in a small number of enterprises. In most cases, national governments encouraged and frequently financed the rationalization process.

The industry's structure is yet more fragmented when the size of plants (steelworks) is considered. Table 3.1 compares the average size of plants by capacity in each producing country and shows also the average size of enterprises (firms). This table shows that the industry in each country is characterized by multi-plant operation: firms control on average between one and four plants each.

Table 3.1   Average Size of Firm and Plant by Capacity, 1987 (million tonnes)

	Firm	Plant
West Germany	2.4	1.6
France	3.4	1.2
Italy	3.0	2.0
Netherlands	4.0	4.0
Belgium	2.0	1.5
Luxembourg	5.5	1.8
United Kingdom	2.1	1.0
Ireland	0.4	0.4
Denmark	0.9	0.9
Greece	1.4	1.4
EC(10)	2.5	1.5

Source: Author's calculations based on data from Cordero *et al.* (1987).

Earlier work (Cockerill, 1974) has shown a close and systematic positive relationship in the EC between national steel output and the average sizes of firms and plants. This reflects the lack of integration within the internal market and suggests that, if economies of scale are important, the existing structure fails to achieve to the full the potential cost benefits offered by size. The implication is that restructuring and rationalization will lead to fewer, and larger, firms and plants, organized on a cross-national basis within the Community. Firms' product ranges typically increase with size as gauged by annual output. The larger firms offer a full complement of products, including flat and long products and special steels. The breadth of the product range reflects economies of scope for the big firm: large-scale iron refining and steel melting can feed specialized rolling mills to provide a mixture of products to meet the needs of the market. The variety also gives production flexibility as the pattern of demand changes, in both the long run and the short. Large firms are also highly integrated vertically, combining the manufacture of liquid steel from (mainly) iron with its casting, rolling and finishing, usually in a single plant. This organization yields production economies by conserving energy, reducing transport charges and improving quality control.

On the same basis, smaller firms are more specialized in their products and control fewer stages of production. Where this has not been the case, smaller vertically integrated enterprises producing a variety of products have generally been absorbed by acquisition. The smaller firm in each country now tends to specialize in the manufacture of special steels, or common grades of long products (billets, reinforcing bars and wire) derived from recycled scrap. In both cases, cold steel is melted in electric arc furnaces and cast into the required form, enabling high-quality alloys to be manufactured in the case of special steels, and the overhead costs of large-scale ironmaking and steel melting to be avoided in the case of long products. A general trend has been for the share of output taken by smaller firms to increase. But probably because of the importance in the EC market of large integrated firms supported directly or indirectly by their national governments, independent mini-mills (scrap-based electric arc steel melters making common grades of steel) have not expanded in terms of market share to the same degree as in the USA, where, by the early 1990s, they took about one-quarter of the market.

In the period of the industry's output and capacity growth between 1960 and 1973, investment strategies concentrated on iron and steelmaking facilities, rather than on rolling, finishing, stockholding and distribution. With the subsequent fall in demand and the emergence in certain parts of the market of large, powerful and knowledgeable customers (vehicle manufacturers, for example), firms have placed increasing emphasis on customer service and on capturing as much as possible of the value-added to their product of the finishing and distribution process. It remains true, however, that the industry's customers are diverse, each accounting typically for only a small part of a producer's total output and being supplied through the intermediary of a stockholder rather than by direct sales. Save in particular cases, therefore, buyers are sensitive to price and lack loyalty to individual steelmakers.

Government ownership and control of enterprises is a distinctive feature of the structure of the EC steel industry. With the exception of Germany, Britain and the Netherlands, governments are directly or indirectly responsible for the greater part of steel output in the principal producer nations of the Community. This involvement has developed because governments have considered the industry to be of strategic importance as a supplier of an intermediate product essential for the industrial base. The industry has also made a vital contribution to output, employment and the trade balance, and influenced the general level of prices. Moreover, the preference for industrial intervention on the part of governments in several EC member states has been fostered by the perceived need, from time to time, for action to increase capital expenditure, to reduce excess capacity, to encourage rationalization and to support financial losses. The amount of state aids to the industry reached a peak in the late 1970s and because that was generally seen to have been insupportable, since then governments have retreated from their involvement with the industry and in several countries assets have been transferred, in whole or in part, to the private sector. The privatization of British Steel plc in 1988, which returned more than 70 per cent of liquid steel output to the private sector, is the best example of this policy in operation. Increased amounts of private capital have also been introduced into the industry in France, Italy and Spain. Direct government involvement has not been a feature of the German steel industry but support has been given indirectly through transport and coal subsidies.

Apart from the actions of individual member states, European Community policy has influenced the structure of the steel industry in two main ways. First, the promotion of the internal market and the provision of the common external tariff has increased competition and cross-trading among the community's steel firms, but has protected them from external import competition. Secondly, during the period of falling output, excess capacity and weak prices, the European Commission has taken steps to stabilize the market and then rationalize the structure of the industry.

3.3 Market behaviour

Competition in the steel industry is driven mainly by price. Prices and profits tend to move cyclically with variations in the level of economic activity, rising at times of increasing demand and declining as consumption falls. The reasons for this pattern are embedded in the structural characteristics of the industry, which together result in very long lags in the sector's adjustment to changes in demand. These conditions suggest that the industry contains the fundamental element that may bring about chronic market failure – the inability of a sector to make timely adaptations to changes in the environment in which it operates.

One element is the nature of demand. Consumption levels for steel depend more on overall economic activity levels (income) than on price. At the same time, steel has commodity characteristics that make it hard to differentiate, so that price differences between competing suppliers are difficult to sustain. For these reasons, overall demand exhibits a high income elasticity of demand, while the cross-elasticity of demand between producers is high, reflecting the sensitivity of individual producers' sales volumes to price differences between them. Price differences between producers, therefore, are typically narrow and the overall price level is governed by the state of demand in relation to capacity.

Secondly, the optimal size of individual steelworks, as influenced by economies of scale, is large in relation to the total output and capacity of most markets (minimum efficient scale of a typical basic oxygen furnace plant is about 5 million tonnes per annum). If capacity additions lag behind demand, steel supplies will be scarce and prices will rise. Alternatively, if capacity additions precede consumption growth, excess capacity will develop and prices will weaken.

The structure of costs is a third factor. As section 3.1 indicated, fixed charges typically form a significant part of total costs and, in turn, part of those charges are sunk costs. Under these cost conditions, and associated with the high cross-elasticity of demand, any weakening of the market will drive suppliers to cut prices in an attempt to maintain or increase their sales volume. In theory, the floor price in the short run will be set by the amount of variable costs per unit of output, which must be covered by average revenue (price) if production is to be worthwhile.

Fourthly, entry and exit barriers prevent capacity adjusting swiftly to permanent (as distinct from cyclical) variations in consumption and output. The capital required, the existence of excess capacity and uncertainty about the long-term path of demand are the main factors that deter entry. The principal exit barriers are sunk costs, exit expenses, and interdependencies among producers.

Sunk costs are a particular type of fixed costs; they refer to past expenditures on specific assets which have no alternative use and which can be amortized (or recouped), wholly or in part, only by trading. The presence of such costs will encourage firms to maintain capacity for so long as price yields some contribution to overhead costs and decisions to retire surplus capacity will be considered only when price has fallen below unit variable cost or (which amounts to the same thing) when the operating efficiency of the plant has deteriorated, driving unit variable cost above price.

Exit costs include redundancy charges and other cash costs associated with plant closures. They are incurred by enterprises that rationalize their operations whilst continuing as trading entities, so are not suffered by enterprises that file for bankruptcy. The costs associated with rationalization may delay action to reduce capacity, in particular if net cash flows are already strained as a consequence of weak demand. Interdependencies refer to the recognition of mutual interests that may develop in industries with a small number of producers of similar size. There are likely to be restraints on firms considering being a first mover in the industry by closing capacity, because the effect will be to offer sales volume and market share to a competitor. Firms are likely to delay rationalization decisions until implicit or explicit understandings can be reached with competitors or a further significant deterioration occurs in profitability.

Lastly, externalities (or social costs and benefits) associated with the industry's output, pricing and investment decisions which are, in conventional economic theory, not taken into account by private decision-makers when framing policies, are likely to give opportunities for governments to become involved, directly or indirectly, in the industry. The forms of involvement include ownership, financial support and exhortation. Although each may be presented as a means of equating private and social net benefits and assisting adjustment to changed market circumstances, in reality they usually give rise to delays in adaptation, whilst the actions of other firms and their governments are studied, and policies are agreed. In consequence, in weak markets, excess capacity and financial losses are likely to continue for longer than would otherwise be the case.

Adjustment lags arising from the steel industry's built-in market imperfections are lengthy and are a significant factor in explaining its market behaviour and performance. From time to time, adjustments will be triggered by factors that include: a stabilization of demand; mutual recognition by major producers of the need for capacity reductions or increases; and steps taken by governments or trade associations to reduce or compensate for exit costs.

In the absence of official measures by governments to stabilize markets, weak price discipline and long adjustment lags have, from time to time, encouraged steel producers to look for concerted efforts to maintain prices at profitable levels and to regulate capacity and output. The obvious way to do this is through a cartel, although this formal means of rigging the market is illegal in individual EC member states (as it is in most countries) and within the Community as a whole. Cartels maximize joint profits by setting market price and output at levels that equate (aggregated) marginal costs and marginal revenue and then equate each individual producer's price and marginal cost to determine its output. Output quotas are then set for each member of the cartel. As a single price is set for the market, the demand curve faced by each individual producer is perfectly elastic. There is then a strong temptation for cartel members to make secret price reductions (by such means as discounts, rebates or mis-classification of product quality) because the cross-elasticity of demand is very high: market share and sales volume will both increase rapidly. Such actions on a significant scale, if undetected or if sanctions are not applied effectively, will undermine the discipline of the cartel and eventually cause it to collapse. When this happens, trading conditions in the market will become volatile once again.

Near-cartel conditions can develop from close mutual recognition between producers: a price leader may emerge, encouraging price discipline, and individual capacity expansion or reduction decisions will be taken in the context of the likely reactions of competitors and the implications for the overall profitability of the industry.

Before the creation of a single internal market for steel in the Community, the market of each member state was protected from import competition by tariffs and quotas which raised prices above the free market level and protected relatively inefficient producers in each country. Typically, prices were similar for the leading producers in each country, suggesting at least recognition of mutual self-interest and oligopolistic pricing and possibly *de facto* cartelization. The single market has increased competition within the EC's steel industry and has encouraged cross-penetration of domestic markets by exports. This has led prices expressed in a common currency (dollars for example) to converge. However, the common external tariff protects EC producers from external competition and supports Community steel prices at levels above the world market price.

Increased competition and price convergence between the leading EC producers have been associated with the emergence of the German industry as a low-cost, powerful producer that has, in consequence, become the price leader. Exchange rate movements have become a major factor in competitiveness and profitability: all else equal, a fall in the value of a country's currency against the Deutschmark (DM) will raise its steel industry's profitability and boost exports (because price expressed in DM will fall). Conversely, currency appreciation will squeeze profits and drive up export prices. During the 1980s exchange rate movements were connected more with interest rate differentials and financial capital flows than with trade balances. These variations became an important and unpredictable factor in price behaviour, competitiveness and financial performance.

In efforts to contend with the risks and uncertainties of the market and to achieve such differentiation of the products and services as is possible, steel producers have recognized the importance of building and maintaining effective long-term relationships with their principal customers. This has involved close attention to quality standards, investment in new processing equipment, movement forward into steel stockholding and distribution, and close contact with customers.

3.4   Performance

3.4.1   Output and trade

The formation of the ECSC in 1951 was the basis for the reconstruction and growth of the steel industry after the Second World War, and in the first phase of the European community between 1952 and 1973 the sector grew strongly as the rate of expansion of economic activity increased and heavy investment in new capacity took place. The world recession that followed the energy crisis of 1973 hit the European industry hard as demand fell both within the Community and in its principal export markets, most notably the United States, and imports increased. Output fell more sharply than demand as the net export position of the industry worsened, leaving a substantial amount of surplus capacity. The adjustment of output to reduced demand was more severe than in either the US or Japan.

Since then, the industry's net output has grown more slowly than the Community's overall gross domestic product, between 1974 and 1990. This reflects the reducing importance of steel in the structure of the EC's economic output, declining net external trade, and an increase in indirect imports of steel, in the form of finished products (such as cars and electrical appliances). These trends indicate, at first sight, a deterioration in the industry's international competitiveness.

While the external trade position has deteriorated, steel trade between the member states (intra-trade) has increased strongly, from 13 per cent of total output volume in 1973 to 26 per cent in 1990. This has reflected, generally, the relative competitiveness of the industries of the member states within the Community: the former West Germany and Spain have gained shares in intra-trade within the internal market. Intra-trade has also been encouraged by the removal of tariff and quota barriers within the internal market and by protection against imports from outside the Community by means of the common external tariff and by specific bilateral import restraint agreements with exporting countries, in particular Japan and several countries in South America and eastern Europe. Important non-tariff barriers to intra-trade still remain, in particular the difficulty faced by a producer in one country in obtaining access to distribution channels in another, other than by acquisition, which often proves difficult to achieve.

Market interpenetration so far has taken place mainly by means of direct trade flows rather than by cross-border investments and, at the start of the 1990s, the European industry was still organized on a national basis. Reorganization on a European scale, giving potential for increases in efficiency, is hampered because of barriers to cross-border acquisitions. Such barriers include differences in the forms of corporate ownership and control, government participation and long-term financing by banks, which make outright transfers of ownership difficult and in some instances impossible. Production in each major steelmaking nation continues to be concentrated in a small number of large, vertically integrated enterprises using the basic oxygen steelmaking technique. Alternative techniques that offer lower-cost production, in particular mini-mills, have not developed in relation to the size of the industry to the same degree as in Japan or the US, suggesting that the adaptation of the European industry has been slowed down by the fragmented nature of its internal market and by the influence of the major producers.

3.4.2   Productivity and costs

Comparisons of labour productivity provide a useful, if partial, initial indication of the relative efficiency of steel production. Figure 3.3 compares man-hours per tonne of steel produced in 1987 in the steel industries of

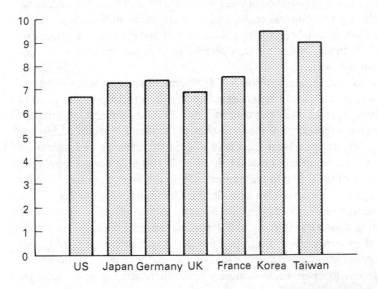

Source: Drawn from data in Howell *et al.* (1988) (by permission of Westview Press, Boulder, Colorado).

Figure 3.3   Man-hours per Tonne of Steel Produced, 1987

some major producers. The UK has the highest level of productivity of the three EC countries. This may be explained by the substantial adjustment programme undertaken in the 1980s and by tight managerial control, which have ensured efficient operation. The West German industry was widely regarded during the early 1980s as the comparator for technical efficiency. However, as the figure shows, it had lost its productivity advantage in Europe by the second half of the 1980s.

International competitiveness depends more on relative unit costs than on productivity. Labour costs per tonne can be taken as a rough proxy for total unit costs because employment costs are a significant fraction of total costs, and raw material expenses and (to a lesser degree) the cost of capital are similar between the major steel-producing regions. Unit labour costs are a function of output per worker (productivity) and employment costs per worker. Table 3.2 shows unit labour costs, man-hours per tonne and hourly employment costs in the steel industries of the EC in 1987. Wide variations in productivity and employment costs can be seen among the various countries. Employment cost inflation in terms of national currencies has been particularly marked in Italy and Britain.

Table 3.2   Unit Labour Costs (ULC)[1], Hourly Employment Costs (HEC)[2] and Man-hours per Tonne of Steel Produced (MHPT), 1987

	ULC	HEC	MHPT
West Germany	127.3	23.8	7.4
France	132.0	19.4	7.5
Italy	90.9	–	–
Luxembourg	113.2	19.2	–
Denmark	90.0	17.3	–
Portugal	81.4	6.3	–
United Kingdom	72.0	14.3	6.9

Notes:
1.   ULC – $/tonne.
2.   HEC – $/hour.

Source: As for Figure 3.2.

The unit labour cost comparisons in Table 3.2 show that by 1987 Britain had achieved the lowest costs. It had done this by combining low relative hourly employment costs with productivity rates that had increased substantially during the 1980s. It had also had the benefit of a fall in the exchange rate of the pound against other major Community currencies during much of the period. Indeed, for several countries – Italy and Spain, in addition to Britain – currency devaluations played an important part in maintaining the international competitiveness of the steel industry during a time in which cost inflation was high in relation to other countries, in particular West Germany. In Britain in the 1980s, downward adjustments in the exchange rate of the pound were more important than subsidies in offsetting reductions in competitiveness from inflation and low productivity.

Wider membership of the exchange rate mechanism (ERM) of the European Monetary System (EMS) now means that this avenue for offsetting relative deterioration in cost competitiveness has become closed to most of the main steel-producing nations of the EC, with the consequence that increased emphasis is being put on productivity improvements through higher operating efficiency and increased investment. Job losses, in the face of slow demand growth, are an inevitable outcome of this process.

In addition to efficiency improvements and exchange rate movements, various forms of subsidy payments from national governments have been significant in supporting output and employment in the Community's steel industry and, more importantly, in affecting the relative cost advantages of Community partners. Because of this, subsidy given to the industry in one country has led from time to time to matching assistance being provided in another whose sales and profits are thought to have been damaged. This in turn has led to escalations of subsidies. Subsidy as part of public policy towards the EC steel industry will be considered in more detail in Section 3.5.

3.4.3   Prices

Steel prices are set in the short run mainly by operating costs and the strength of international competition. Since the development of a single integrated market in steel with the Community's enlargement in 1973, West Germany has been the benchmark for costs while persistent over-capacity has led enterprises to cut prices competitively as they have tried to keep up sales volumes. As a result, price-cost margins have been poor, even after taking account of subsidies. In spite of this, steel prices inside the EC have remained high by world standards; only American prices are higher on average. Protection of the internal market from outside competition has been the main reason for this. The Community's common external tariff limits imports from outside the EC within the terms of the General Agreement on Tariffs and Trade (GATT). In addition, bilateral deals have been made between the EC and major steel-exporting countries to control the volume of imports – the so-called voluntary restraint agreements (VRAs).

While internal prices are high, the Community has from time to time been accused of supporting its own exports to third markets by pricing unfairly (dumping). This allegation has been made most frequently and strongly in America. Dumping is hard to define and even more difficult to prove. It is usually taken to refer to pricing in the export market below cost or realized price in the home market. Marginal costs that are low in relation to full costs are a feature of the steel industry and price discrimination between a protected internal market, where the price demand elasticities are relatively low, and a highly competitive export market where elasticities are high, is an understandable tactic for firms to follow. But it is difficult for aggrieved parties to measure home costs or prices and to prove dumping so, in practice, the threat of anti-dumping suits under US trade law has most often been used as a bargaining counter with the EC in negotiating VRAs.

3.4.4 *Profitability*
Slow growth, surplus capacity, high costs and strong price competition in the internal market imply a poor profitability record for the EC steel industry. Table 3.3, which shows the annual return on sales for the industry between

Table 3.3 Profitability in the EC Steel Industry (Net Income over Sales, %)

	1981	1984	1987	1988	1989	1990
Thyssen[1] (Germany)	–0.2	0.5	2.1	–	5.9	4.4
BSC[2] (UK)	–34.1	–7.6	10.2	12.1	14.6	–
Hoesch (Germany)	–	1.3	1.1	2.5	2.8	–
Hoogovens (Netherlands)	–	2.8	2.9	5.8	11.7	8.9
Usinor-Sacilor (France)	–16.8	21.1	3.7	12.8	10.6	–
Cockerill Sambre (Belgium)	–11.8	2.4	–	7.6	11.2	–
Arbed (Luxembourg)	–7.4	1.1	–	10.3	13.2	–

Notes:
1. Financial year August to September.
2. Financial year April to March.

Sources: 1987–90 reproduced from *The Times 1000*, 1987/88, 1988/89, 1989/90 and 1990/91, published by Times Books, a division of Harper Collins Publishing; other figures from Keeling (1988).

1981 and 1990, confirms this. In addition to relatively low prices and efficiency, profitability has been reduced further by the high social costs to firms of employment in the EC (mainly pension, welfare and severance fund contributions), by financial charges associated with the capacity growth that was widespread in the 1970s and early 1980s, and by obligations set by governments to maintain employment for social reasons.

The industry in the former West Germany has been the most consistently profitable since 1973, but during the 1980s steel producers and their governments in each of the main EC steelmaking countries confronted the need to reduce subsidies, cut costs and increase efficiency through restructuring, and profitability improved as a result. British Steel, which was privatized in 1988, made one of the most impressive recoveries, returning to profit in 1985 for the first time for more than twenty years and then maintaining five years' profit growth until affected by the recession of the early 1990s. Among others, Usinor-Sacilor in France also achieved marked improvements.

The figures in Table 3.3 reflect the overall activities of the enterprises. Some of the differences between them are due to variations in the extent of non-steel activities. German companies have for some time been more diversified into engineering and allied activities than firms elsewhere in the EC, but widening the range of activities – including strengthening links in steel distribution, where profit margins are higher – has now become part of the strategy of most large steelmakers.

3.4.5   Economic efficiency

In terms of overall economic efficiency, the performance of the EC steel industry has been poor. Costs are high, productivity is low relative to Japan and America, surplus capacity remains a chronic feature as a result of imprudent investments, and markets are weak despite protection from imports. Adoption of new technologies with lower capital and operating costs that may be more suited to the changed conditions in the market has been very limited. Several factors explain the slow pace of adjustment. First, the influence of the governments of the member states, through the supply of finance and less direct pressures, has imposed social obligations on firms and, at the same time, has prevented cross-national mergers and rationalization. Secondly, sunk investments and high closure costs have delayed restructuring. Lastly, the common external tariff and other devices have protected the industry from the full force of international competition. The consequences of the industry's inefficiency have been borne by steel users and final consumers in the form of higher prices, lower sales, and probably also in the form of higher employment than would have been possible in an internationally competitive industry.

3.5 Public policy

For many years, the economic importance of the steel industry and the anticipated unregulated conduct of its firms have made the sector a prime target for government intervention. Governments usually justify their involvement on one or more of three grounds: market failure (discussed in section 3.3), macroeconomic policy and political considerations. Macroeconomic concerns have included the transmission of inflationary pressures through the economy at times of strong steel demand and high prices; the direct and indirect employment effects of cuts in steel output and capacity in an industry that is highly concentrated regionally; and the impact on the balance of trade of a fall in exports or a reduction in the share of the home market supplied. Political considerations are closely connected with these issues and are reflected in the concerns of elected representatives about employment opportunities and regional activity rates.

Interventions by the governments of member states in support of their national steel industries are in theory prohibited by the Treaty of Paris unless they form part of a Community initiative, that is, unless they are in line with the goals of the single market. Government ownership of all or a substantial part of the industry has been a feature of each national industry except in the former West Germany, where the Federal Government had until quite recently a majority holding only in Salzgitter, the fourth largest manufacturer.

Although state ownership does not in itself represent assistance, it is in practice likely to be associated with the supply of finance in volume or at rates that are not available in the market. Financial assistance in preferential terms has been given in various forms. Direct operating subsidies have been paid, even though these are prohibited by the Treaty. Provision of capital from public funds has been more usual and is harder to detect as a subsidy. Governments have supplied share capital, with the option to waive dividend payments.

In addition, loans have been made at below-market interest rates which, in some cases, have later been converted into share capital. Although strictly intended for investment in machinery and buildings, much of this money has been used to meet current expenses and in effect has been a concealed operating subsidy. Capital write-downs have also been used to reduce the burden of interest and dividend charges on enterprises and to improve their financial operating ratios. In some cases assistance to steelmakers has been given indirectly by subsidy payments to cut the costs of energy, transport of raw materials and the finished product, and research and development.

The financial assistance given to British Steel during the period of nationalization from 1967 to 1988 – calculated as the difference between the amounts of interest that would have been payable if the capital had been supplied at market rates and the interest and dividends that were actually paid – represented, on average, more than two-thirds of the cost of a tonne of steel produced.

Tariffs and quotas have not been important forms of assistance for member states in the internal EC steel market except as transitional measures to smooth the entry of new member states, but non-tariff barriers, such as access to distribution networks and restrictions on cross-border acquisitions, have given significant protection to Community producers' sales volumes and prices and, in some cases, continue to do so.

State aids to steel producers have been given for several, sometimes contradictory, reasons. These include support for enterprises' operating cash flows at times of weak demand; provision of funds for capital projects that would not otherwise have gone ahead; maintenance of regional employment and incomes; full or partial compensation for the financial consequences of government impositions such as price controls intended to counter inflation; matching assistance given by other governments; and inducements to rationalize. The role of the most efficient producers in setting price levels and the strength of competition in the European market imply that it has been the weaker enterprises and producing regions that have needed the greater subsidies.

The overall policy aim at Community level as intended by the Treaty of Paris has been to encourage the integration and efficiency of the steel industry in the internal market by dismantling trade barriers between member states, thereby increasing competition. Protection against disruption by imports from outside the Community is given by the common external tariff. Although until the present time the EC steel industry has remained nationalistic in structure and ownership, internal competition through cross-border trading has increased substantially.

State subsidies distort the operation of the internal market by reducing the effect of price as an instrument of resource allocation: output, employment and capital investment will be higher, and redundant capacity will remain in operation for longer than would otherwise be the case. Until the early 1970s the European Commission's policy was to encourage the withdrawal of state aids to steel, but the combination of the effects of the first oil shock and a sustained increase in world supply resulted in a fall in demand, low prices, strong competition from imports and persistent surplus capacity. The structural crisis that followed obliged the Commission to intervene in an attempt to stabilize the market.

Article 58 of the Treaty of Paris enables the Commission, with the assent of the Council of Ministers, to declare a state of 'manifest crisis' and to arrange stabilization measures. The provisions of the Treaty in this respect, which apply only to coal and steel and allow, in effect, an official cartel to be set up, are much stronger than those in the Treaty of Rome applying to other industrial sectors. The Commission is empowered to set output quotas and minimum prices and to impose penalties on enterprises that can be shown not to have complied. Under provisions elsewhere in the Treaty, the Commission can set limits to imports from outside the Community, can authorize subsidy payments and relate them, if necessary, to restructuring requirements.

The Commission's first market stabilization initiative, which did not involve the use of Article 58, was in 1977, following the collapse of demand after the first oil shock. Minimum prices were set for concrete reinforcing bars, a part of the market that is sensitive to severe price competition in times of weak demand, and guideline prices were indicated for other products. The following year, as market conditions continued to deteriorate, minimum prices were set for merchant bars and hot-rolled wide strip. These measures helped limit the deterioration in the main Community steelmakers' financial position but it soon became apparent that stronger measures would be needed, in view of the long-term nature of the imbalance of demand and supply.

In 1980 the European Commission, with the assent of the Council of Ministers, published the first of a series of decisions setting market-wide production quotas for a range of products taken under the 'manifest crisis' provisions of Article 58. As well as setting production quotas, the Commission also specified the proportions of output to be delivered to the Community's home market; by so doing it circumvented the strict wording of Article 58, which seeks to limit the Commission to control of overall production levels. Quota controls continued until 1988, when some improvement in market conditions coupled with agreement among the member states on restructuring and the withdrawal of subsidies allowed a return to freer market conditions.

The process of quota setting is complex. First the Commission fixes an annual reference tonnage for each firm for each class of product covered by the decision. Next, after consulting with representatives of consumers, employees' associations and governments, an assessment is made by the Commission of the appropriate output levels for the relevant products in the market as a whole for the following quarter, taking account of the desired balance between supply and expected demand. The assessment includes provision for a reserve, from which supplementary quota allowances can be made. The quarterly assessment is then related to the total of the annual reference tonnages ascribed to each firm so as to determine the 'abatement rate' – the percentage by which the forecast for the following quarter is greater or less than the pro rata total of the annual reference tonnages. Firms are then notified of their individual quotas.

Quotas may be exchanged with, or sold to, other Community producers; this does not, of course, increase the total of the provision made for output.

The Commission monitors output in relation to quota and can impose sanctions, including fines, on firms that do not comply. As with cartels generally, policing members' output and pricing actions is important because individual producers have a strong incentive to undercut the agreed price so as to increase sales volume and market share, provided that their actions go undetected. A number of devices have been used to achieve this, including secret rebates and the mis-classification of products.

To be effective, the quota mechanism had of necessity to be supported with price controls, provision for which is made elsewhere in the Treaty, and as well as setting quotas, the Commission also announced minimum prices. These measures were, in turn, incorporated by the steelmakers' association Eurofer into its plans for coordinating the market. An official cartel was thus linked to a producers' price ring.

The depressed market conditions in much of the late 1970s caused the Commission to begin to link production quotas and price control more and more with efforts to restore balance between supply and demand in the longer term. Its permission for subsidy payments increasingly became tied to undertakings on the part of producers and their governments to reduce effective capacity and to close redundant plant. The quota system together with the associated measures helped to stabilize prices and outputs during a period of low demand. It also gave time for longer-term trends in the market to be assessed and for plans to be drawn up for rationalization. By supporting output and employment it sustained regional economies and reduced the burden of welfare payments on public expenditure.

To set against these benefits, the quota system maintained inefficiency in the industry and reduced its flexibility of response to changing market conditions. In effect it froze the pattern of supply by basing each firm's permitted tonnage in the quota period on the proportion of total output it had supplied over the previous two years. As a result, any changes in relative efficiency would not be reflected in changes in market share, so cost reduction and rationalization were discouraged. Moreover, the attractiveness of entry was reduced as prospective new suppliers needed to obtain quotas. In turn, this reduced the rate of innovation by keeping production in the hands of the established integrated producers and excluding alternative technology in the form of mini-mills. Costs and prices were therefore higher than they would otherwise have been, to the detriment both of consumers and export sales.

By the mid-1980s the costs of supporting steel production had become a heavy burden on the public finances of member states, and the long-term problem of surplus capacity was plain. Having achieved a degree of stability in the market, the Commission began to emphasize the need for a phased withdrawal of subsidies and for plant closures. It was helped in this by a recovery in demand; by the end of the decade nearly 40 million tonnes of capacity had been removed or decommissioned (in the Community of ten). However, this still left more than 30 million annual tonnes of surplus capacity in the industry of the twelve, the excess being a problem particularly in the flat-rolled products sector, where demand depends heavily on sales to the automotive industry.

On balance, it seems that the Commission's interventions to deal with the structural crisis in the steel industry that began to emerge in the mid-1970s delayed adaptation longer than was necessary for a smooth reduction in the size of the industry to be assured. The delay was brought about by the Commission's desire to protect the interests of the main steelmakers and to recognize the social and political impact of plant closures and job losses in regions of heavy industry. The high costs of production by international standards have been damaging to the long-term prospects of the industry in the Community, to its export opportunities and to its customers.

3.6 Conclusion and review

The original long-run economic goal of the European common market in steel was to build an industry of international scale and competitiveness. So far, that goal has not been achieved. Steel consumption is cyclical and the economics of the industry means that prices and profitability are very sensitive to movements in demand. Producers are likely to coordinate their actions so as to stabilize the market in their favour. This, together with the net social benefits that have conventionally been ascribed to the industry, has led governments to suppress the operation of market forces by regulation and protection. Removal of tariff barriers to trade in steel has limited the extent to which producers can cartelize and has increased pressures of competition in the internal market. Coupled with the imbalance of supply and demand, these have damaged the financial position of the industry, leading member states to provide subsidies to their own producers and the Commission to take steps to stabilize prices and outputs and to regulate imports from outside the Community. The effect of these measures has been to protect inefficient producers and to slow down the rate of rationalization.

Steel production is expensive by international standards and the industry has lost world market share in both output and exports. Although cross-border trade within the EC has increased, the structure of the industry remains fragmented, limited in scope and nationalistic: plant sizes are small and enterprises still make the greater part of their sales in their home markets.

Meeting the challenge of the global market in steel will require extensive restructuring by means of cross-border mergers, acquisitions and joint ventures; closing redundant capacity; increasing the efficiency of operations by improving working practices and investment in cost-saving techniques; and movement into adjacent sectors so as to assure effective communication between producers, their suppliers and their customers. The appropriate role in this for public policy on the part of the Community and its member states will be to seek to provide a robust macroeconomic environment in which industrial activity can flourish, assuring strong internal demand for steel, and to take no steps either to shield Community steel producers from international competitive pressures or to inhibit strategic initiatives intended to strengthen efficiency rather than market power.

References

Cockerill, A. (1974), *The Steel Industry: International Comparisons of Industrial Structure and Performance*, Cambridge: Cambridge University Press.

Cordero, R., Serjeanston, R. and Cook, H. (eds) (1987), *Iron and Steel Works of the World*, London: Metal Bulletin.

Howell, R.H., Noellert, W.A., Kreier, J.G. and Wolff, A.W. (1988), *Steel and the State: Government Intervention and Steel's Structural Crisis*, Boulder and London: Westview Press.

Keeling, B. (1988), *World Steel: A New Assessment of Trends and Prospects*, London: EIU.

Further reading

Cockerill, A. (1974), *The Steel Industry: International Comparisons of Industrial Structure and Performance*, Cambridge, Cambridge University Press.

Commission of the European Communities (CEC) (1978), 'The Social Aspects of Steel Policy', *Official Journal*, (SEC 78) **3205**, Brussels: CEC.

Cordero, R., Serjeanston, R. and Cook, H. (eds) (1987), *Iron and Steel Works of the World*, London: Metal Bulletin.

CEC (1985), *General Objectives for Steel 1990*, (COM (85) 208 Final), Brussels: CEC.

Communication from the Commission to the Council on Steel Policy (COM (87) 388 Final), Brussels: CEC.

Federal Trade Commission (1976), *Staff Report on the US Steel Industry and its International Rivals: Trends and Factors determining International Competitiveness*, Washington, DC: Bureau of Economics, November.

Goldberg, W.H. (ed.) (1986), *Ailing Steel: The Transoceanic Quarrel*, New York: St Martin's Press.

Howell, R.H., Noellert, W.A., Kreier, J.G. and Wolff, A.W., (1988), *Steel and the State: Government Intervention and Steel's Structural Crisis*, Boulder and London: Westview Press.

Organization for Economic Co-operation and Development (OECD) (1991), *The Steel Market in 1990 and the Outlook for 1991*, Paris: OECD.

Useful statistical sources are Eurostat's *Iron and Steel Statistical Yearbook* and the International Iron and Steel Institute's *Statistical Yearbook*.

Acknowledgement

The research on which this chapter is based has been supported by a personal award from the Economic and Social Research Council.

4 Pharmaceuticals
Alan Earl-Slater

4.1 Introduction
The pharmaceutical industry is probably one of the most highly regulated industries in the world in addition to being one of the most important. This chapter examines some of the complex issues involved in the operation of such an important industry. The rest of section 4.1 provides a brief historical sketch of the industry's development and outlines some of the characteristic features of the health care market and of the industry's products. Some basic statistics on the industry are also provided. Section 4.2, on industrial structure, offers an appraisal of barriers to entry and market concentration. Sections 4.3 and 4.4 look, respectively, at key elements in the industry's behaviour and performance. Policy matters are considered in Section 4.5, which offers an insight into the evolving nature and extent of regulation in the EC. The concluding section brings the analysis together and offers some pointers to ways ahead for fruitful research on the industry.

4.1.1 A brief historical sketch
Until the early twentieth century many products were derived from natural sources such as vegetables and plants. These yielded products such as atrophine, morphine, aspirin, digitalis and strychnine; vaccines for smallpox, cholera and typhoid; anaesthetics such as chloroform and ether; sedatives such as chloral; and pain- and fever-relieving agents such as acetanilide and antipyrine.

Crucial breakthroughs in pharmaceutical knowledge came from the efforts of Ehrlich, Fleming and some French scientists. Paul Ehrlich, a medical student working on coal-tar derivatives at Strasbourg University around the turn of the twentieth century, developed the idea that it might be possible to selectively stain organisms. Furthermore, if staining dyes could carry chemicals, diseased areas could not only be identified but also be attacked by the chemical, leaving the host area undamaged. Then in the test of compound number 606 (Salvarsan), Ehrlich found that he had cured a syphilitic rabbit: the search for the 'magic bullet' had truly begun.

In the late 1920s Scottish bacteriologist Alexander Fleming started to discover the antibiotic powers of penicillin: the therapeutic potential of penicillin was developed by Florey and Chain, with large-scale production initially taking place in the USA by chemical corporations with expertise in fermentation techniques.

In the early 1930s a dye called prontosil rubrum was tested by French scientists and found to kill streptocci bacteria *in vitro*. Further research found that it did not kill animals. The product was administered to a dying child, who then recovered her health. These developments in turn led to the discovery in 1935 of the relevant active ingredient: sulphanilamide. The research on sulphanilamide demonstrated that pharmaceuticals could destroy germs in the body. Practical uses soon followed; for example the mortality rate for women who had childbed fever was significantly reduced.

Dye companies around European textile mills, for example in Basle, were some of the first to develop pharmaceutical interests. Chemical companies and their ancillary firms also diversified into pharmaceuticals, as shown for example by the production in Germany of the anti-syphilitic substance, Salvarsan. The growth of synthetic organic chemistry from the 1940s made it possible to synthesize molecules previously unknown in nature and led to the appearance of a new form of business: the research-intensive pharmaceutical manufacturer.

Developments in legislation – for example in relation to patent protection – also played a major part in the evolution of the pharmaceutical industry. Legislative changes have also helped companies to perform certain activities; for example changes in French legislation allowed chemical companies with expertise in fermentation techniques to diversify into pharmaceuticals in the mid-1940s.

Today's pharmaceutical companies have varied origins. Some can be traced back to the business of selling cures and tonics through pharmaceutical houses or in pharmacies and chemists. Areas technologically akin to pharmaceuticals, such as dyes, chemicals or animal health products, are the source of other firms. There are also some specialist vertically integrated companies who have developed from a pedigree of R and D to manufacturing, formulating and marketing. Some firms, however, engage only in one of these activities, such as manufacturing or research. Some of the firms have as their principal activity the business of manufacturing pharmaceutical products for human consumption, whilst others are also engaged in activities such as chemicals, transport, metals, domestic hygiene products, cosmetics and agribusiness.

4.1.2   Characteristic features of the health care market and of pharmaceutical products

The financing, organization and administration of health care services differ across nations but there is at least one common element: the finance of health care is characterized by 'insurance'. There is uncertainty on the timing, severity and costs of ill-health: insurance may be conceived as the pooling of resources to finance health care services. Health care financing is either private or public in nature. The former includes voluntary insurance and direct payments by the consumers as well as charities and some religious houses; the latter includes sources such as general taxation (central, regional or local) and compulsory 'state' insurance.

The distribution of pharmaceutical products takes place along a path from the manufacturer to one or more of five types of outlet: wholesalers; dispensing pharmacies and dispensing physicians; drug stores; mail-order companies; and hospitals. From one of these five outlets consumers receive their product. Paths of supply may sometimes be complex: for example wholesalers in country X may export the product to wholesalers in country Y, who in turn re-export the product to pharmacists or wholesalers back in country X. (This 'loop' phenomenon of parallel imports takes place because there are margins to be made on such trade and because, in some countries, there is positive encouragement from the health insurance system.) Some companies may miss out the wholesaler and supply direct to the dispensing pharmacists. Not only does the actual path of supply vary across nations but the scale of the trade along each path differs. In Italy almost all of the hospital supplies of pharmaceutical products comes from the manufacturers; in the UK around half of hospital supplies is obtained from industry and half from pharmacies; and in Ireland, France and Germany over 80 per cent of hospital supplies come via pharmacies who procure from the industry and wholesalers.

Pharmaceutical products have some special characteristics. First, the demand for pharmaceuticals is a *derived* demand, that is, pharmaceuticals are demanded because health or health care is demanded. In this context, it is worth noting that few people actually *like* to be in the position of having to consume the product. Secondly, the consumer does not know which product is the best available and generally delegates the decision on products to his or her 'agent', usually the prescribing physician. Thirdly, few patients have to pay the full cost of their consumption although many have to make some form of financial contribution. Finally, most pharmaceutical products need some form of marketing licence before they are allowed on to a health care market in Europe.

The output of the industry can be divided into three broad categories. The first consists of pharmaceuticals which are available to the public only on prescription (prescription-only medicines: PoMs) and dispensed by an authorized dispensing unit. Another group of products is available only through pharmacists. The third general group of products is often referred to as 'over the counter' drugs (OTCs), for which no prescription is required. A distinction may also be made between patented and non-patented pharmaceuticals, and between branded, commodity and corporate products. Branded products refers to products sold under a brand name; commodity products refers to those products sold under the generic name of the basic active chemical ingredient; and corporate products are those where the company name, or an abbreviation of it and/or a company logo play a conspicuous part in identifying the product.

4.1.3   The scale of the industry

Table 4.1 gives the number of pharmaceutical firms operating in each EC country and in Switzerland, Japan and the US. The table shows wide variations across countries. This variation is also shown in the data on market

Table 4.1   Number of Pharmaceutical Companies,[1] 1990

Country	Number
Belgium[2]	250
Denmark[3]	164
France	362
Germany	1 009
Greece	54
Ireland[4]	400
Italy	303
Luxembourg	–
Netherlands	78
Portugal	306
Spain	351
UK	352
Total: EC	3 629
Switzerland	387
Japan	1 315
US	790

Notes:
1. The companies are those engaged in the production of pharmaceuticals for human use. The data exclude wholesalers, retail or dispensing units and specialist, research-only companies.
2. 1989.
3. 1988.
4. 1987.

Sources: Eurostat, and industry sources (details available from the author).

Table 4.2 National Pharmaceutical Market Value[1] and Output[2] of the
Pharmaceutical Industry, 1990 (millions of ECUs)

Country	Market value	Output
Belgium	1 298	1 589
Denmark	420	1 053
France	9 670	12 446
Germany	10 032	12 512
Greece	523	404
Ireland	233	662
Italy	8 897	10 271
Luxembourg	53	
Netherlands	1 135	1 455
Portugal	734	581
Spain	3 603	4 881
United Kingdom	4 414	9 433
Total: EC	41 012	55 287
Japan	23 248	
US	40 581	
World	132 154	132 154

Notes:
1. The value of the pharmaceutical market of each country is calculated on ex-industry prices, which represents income to the industry. Wholesaler's margins, retailer's margins and purchase tax (e.g. VAT) are excluded.
2. Output from the industry located in a country, regardless of corporate nationality.

Sources: Industry sources (details available from the author).

value and output (Table 4.2). It is interesting to note that, in terms of market value, the EC and US are broadly similar in size.

In the interpretation of these and other data in this chapter it should be borne in mind that each nation produces statistics that in part reflect the finance, organization and delivery of its own particular health care services; a certain amount of prudence is required when making comparisons across nations or over time.

4.1.4   Employment

The EC pharmaceutical industry directly employs nearly half a million people. Table 4.3 shows how direct employment varied across member states in
1990. The two extremes are Germany, which employed well over 100 000
people in 1990 and Luxembourg, which has no indigenous industry and is
mainly reliant on the Belgian pharmaceutical industry. France, Germany,
Italy and the UK accounted for over three-quarters of total direct employment. The relative dominance by these four nations in Europe is long-
standing. Around half as many again are *indirectly* employed by the pharmaceutical industry.

Table 4.3   Direct Employment in the Pharmaceutical Industry, 1990

Country	Number directly employed
Belgium	17 603
Denmark	11 514
France	91 000
Germany	107 825
Greece	8 000
Ireland	6 300
Italy	69 950
Luxembourg	–
Netherlands	12 900
Portugal	11 000
Spain	39 326
United Kingdom	87 800
Total: EC	463 218

Sources: Industry sources (details available from the author).

The quality of the industry's labour force has increased over time. A
significant proportion of this labour force is of a relatively high quality, with
many employees being of graduate calibre. New recruits are frequently
graduates: for example, over half the 500 or so new recruits into the industry
in Ireland in 1989–90 were of university graduate or postgraduate status, and
this is a feature likely to be emulated elsewhere in Europe. The high level of
human capital engaged in the industry should come as no surprise: it is
inherent in the science-based nature of the business. The skills employed in
the industry are wide-ranging; the labour force includes personnel trained in

engineering, pharmacy, chemistry, medicine, statistics, computer sciences, law, economics, business studies, and management research.

Quality is likely to be further increased as a result of market pressures. These include the increased sophistication and articulation of purchasers' requirements, and the (now ubiquitous) health care cost containment programmes which are increasingly imposing binding financial constraints on health care budgets.

A further stimulus to increased quality in the labour force is more stringent regulatory requirements. Such a stimulus may be generated if for example the regulators and purchasers in Europe follow the Australian moves of the early 1990s in requiring evidence of a fuller economic appraisal, for example a cost-effectiveness analysis of a product, as part of the submission dossier for marketing approval and reimbursement by the health care insurance system.

So far the overall trend in employment has been upward (although there have been fluctuations across nations and over time). The rate of increase in numbers employed may, however, be checked by the rationalization of plant operations, one of the consequences of the harmonization process now under way in Europe. On the other hand, new market opportunities are likely to remain extensive: there are many ill-health conditions yet to be overcome, and there are opportunities for markets to be better served, for example in eastern Europe. Even if the labour force stabilizes at the turn of the century the industry will still be a significant employer in Europe.

Clearly then the pharmaceutical industry is an important source of employment in the EC in both quality and quantity terms. Yet this employment depends on the continued success of the industry, which in turn is determined not only by its own efforts but also by the legislature, regulators, education policies and especially the health care policies of nations.

4.2 Industrial structure

4.2.1 Barriers to entry

Barriers to entry in the pharmaceutical industry and health care markets are of at least three different types: legal, administrative and economic. The standard framework of analysis usually treats barriers in the negative sense: they are seen as having adverse effects on competition and welfare. However, some barriers may positively benefit society. For instance, before a pharmaceutical product can be launched on to a market in Europe, it must have satisfied the requirements of a lengthy and expensive period of *in vitro* trials, clinical trials and regulatory review. Since the mid-1960s products have had to meet an increasingly sophisticated set of requirements on safety, efficacy and quality; and the firms supplying these products have themselves been subject to multifarious licensing requirements. These barriers have been erected in response to and in continuous fear of inferior-quality products. Such barriers can significantly reduce the opportunities for 'inferiors' getting on to health care markets, so in this sense they can be considered beneficial.

One example of a legal barrier to entry is the current requirements of safety, efficacy and quality just referred to. Another may arise from the protection of intellectual property. If such property is not protected by law, then there is no recourse against people who copy a firm's product. If there is also no protection of copyright on the dossier submitted to the authorities for marketing approval, there would be little incentive to engage in the costly R and D programmes necessary to generate new or better products. There may indeed be a perverse incentive to be at best second: second to make the product and second to apply for marketing authorization. But then who goes first? Who searches for new products? Who is first to submit a detailed application for marketing approval with the knowledge that all and sundry can not only copy the new product instantly and exactly but can also use, without charge, the information contained in the dossiers. With no legislative barriers to such action, markets could collapse.

Administrative barriers come in various guises. For example firms may face considerable difficulties in becoming familiar with, and meeting, the regulatory requirements of foreign countries. In Europe, as in the US and Japan, specialist firms may be used to aid entry to health care markets. These contract firms or 'caretakers' carry out some or all of the necessary administration and registration process locally, using local experts with a local language and local contacts. The very existence of these 'enabling' firms makes markets much more contestable. Such 'caretaker' systems do of course need an element of vertical control: control by the producer on the 'caretaker'; and control by the regulatory system on the holder(s) of the certificate to market.

The third category of barrier to entry is 'economic' in character. An incumbent firm may for example have an absolute cost advantage over all other firms. Such an advantage exists where a firm can produce any amount of the product at a lower cost than any other firm.

Where the unit cost of a product is lower the greater the volume of output, then economies of scale in production exist. Some economists have argued that economies of scale also constitute a barrier, since an incumbent may as a result be able to take a lower price on the product. A lower price could increase market share and dominance if purchasers are price sensitive.

Product differentiation is often considered an economic barrier to entry. One argument is that if the incumbent firms have, collectively, a product portfolio which completely covers all therapeutic needs, then there is no space for others to enter. But this implicitly assumes that all therapeutic needs are being satisfactorily met, an assumption patently not tenable in the markets for pharmaceuticals. Furthermore, the product space satiation argument ignores a fundamental feature of the health care market: even people with the same ill-health condition may differ in their response or tolerance to any given pharmaceutical product. People are different; how different is often not known until they are on a particular medication. Patients' different reactions to a product is due in part to variations in their metabolism and in the workings of their immune defence systems. So product differentiation can actually increase the efficiency of health care markets: if the patient's condition does not improve on one regimen, another product can be prescribed, for example a capsule, liquid or transdermal patch, or a once-a-day slow-release product rather than a three-times-a-day quick-release product. Differentiation may enable a closer matching of the product to the patient, which in turn can lead to a more efficient treatment regimen and less waste of the already scarce resources in health care markets.

Product differentiation involving the use of brand names cannot strictly be considered a barrier to entry in pharmaceutical markets if those who write the prescription for products use the generic name and not the brand name of that product. Even if the brand name is written on the prescription there are opportunities, and indeed financial incentives, for the dispensing pharmacist in Europe to substitute a generic equivalent.

Advertising is frequently regarded as another type of economic entry barrier, with potential entrants having to engage in such activity to gain a market share. However, advertising may raise the incumbent's unit cost and hence prices. These higher prices may act to encourage entry by firms who think they can compete effectively by adopting a strategy of lower (or zero) advertising and lower prices. Advertising may also have other positive effects: it can diffuse information on a new product or a new use for an existing product, or provide revenues for medical journals that might not otherwise be viable.

It should be noted that there is a wide range of restrictions on pharmaceutical advertising, including statutory and self-regulatory rules and codes of conduct. In many health care markets controls are exercised (for example by the purchasers or marketing approval authorities) not just on the amount of advertising expenditure but also on the medium, frequency and content of advertisements. In addition, there are controls on exactly what can be advertised and to whom; for example PoMs in Europe are generally advertised only to those who write the prescriptions.

In few industries do advertisements have to say what the product may do in terms both of its positive benefits for the consumer and of its negative effects (contra-indications and side-effects). Many PoM advertisements in

Europe have to do so. Financial penalties for companies that breach codes on advertising also exist. For example under the UK system in the early 1990s any excess expenditure above the 'allowable' advertising expenditure constraint may be counted as profit, and taxed accordingly. A fine may also be imposed on the offending company, and there could also be a loss of patronage from purchasers.

All three categories of barrier overlap in the patent field. Patents are one form of intellectual property right that are considered by some to be a barrier to entry in pharmaceuticals markets. However, it should be remembered that a patent is at best valid only for a tightly defined specified product, process or method in the patent authority's jurisdiction for a limited and specified period of time. About half this time is usually taken up by the pre-market approval regulatory review. In many countries there is also a provision that if a patent is not worked then others can operate it. If it is worked but not 'sufficiently', licences may be available to others who want to produce the product. Furthermore, in many health care systems purchasers may procure from outside the relevant jurisdiction or regardless of the patent if it is deemed to be in the 'public interest' to do so. Finally, any grant of patent can be legally tested.

The important question for health care markets is not whether barriers exist but whether some barriers may be considered excessive. There is much more analysis to be done before it will be possible to identify any barriers which, if dismantled, would make markets more competitive and more beneficial to society.

4.2.2 Concentration

The assumption is sometimes made that a higher level of concentration in a market is symptomatic of greater barriers to entry and therefore generates higher profits for incumbent firms. These profits are then seen as indicative of greater market power and as acting against the consumer's interest. There is, however, no satisfactory evidence to show that pharmaceutical markets are concentrated to any significant level in terms of product, therapeutic class of products, company or corporate nationality at the level of either the EC or the individual country. Furthermore, there are also good grounds for arguing that the industry's profits do not derive either from concentration or from barriers to entry.

Very few pharmaceutical manufacturers compete on all therapeutic classes of products: most companies focus their efforts on a small number of such classes. One reason for this is the sheer scale of the resources that would be needed to cover more than four or five therapeutic classes successfully. The majority of a company's revenue from a given therapeutic class is on average accounted for by no more than two or three products in that class. This dependence on a few products increases the sensitivity of the company to product obsolescence, patent infringement and the perennial problems associated with public policy measures.

Concentration in health care markets may be considered in a variety of ways, each of which provides different information. One way is to look at the share of the total market held by the product with the biggest sales. In 1991 the top-selling product in terms of EC sales excluding hospital sales (about 15 per cent of the market), accounted for less than 2 per cent of the total. The top two products accounted for less than 3 per cent of total sales and the top five for just over 5 per cent. Clearly no single product can be said to have dominated the EC market in 1991.

If the share of EC sales held by therapeutic *classes* of products is considered, the largest – for the twelve months to June 1991 – was anti-peptic ulcerants, which had only 4.5 per cent of the market. The second largest class was central nervous system and peripheral vasotherapeutics products, which had 4.1 per cent. The next four classes, (anti-rheumatics; non-narcotic analgesics; calcium antagonists; and angiotensin-converting enzyme inhibitors) accounted for less than 4 per cent each. In total, less than a quarter (21.4 per cent) of the EC market was taken up by the six largest therapeutic classes. From these data it is evident that the EC pharmaceutical market is certainly not concentrated to a significant degree along therapeutic class lines.

A third way to look at market concentration is in terms of corporate holding. The corporation selling the greatest amount in the EC pharmaceutical market for the year ending June 1991 held only a 4 per cent share. The second and third largest corporate holdings were only marginally smaller. These three corporations together held less than 12 per cent (11.7 per cent) of the EC market. The top ten accounted for under a third (31.2 per cent).

It may also be of interest to look at market share by corporate nationality. The EC market is not of course the preserve of EC nationals. The corporate nationalities of companies holding the top ten market shares (by sales) in the EC in 1991 were: US (two); Swiss (three); German (two); and British (one); plus two joint-nationality corporations, one US/French and one US/British. The top three market shareholders were all of different nationality. The smallest of these had a joint nationality (US/French), thus ensuring that four nationalities were represented by the top three corporate entities.

The above data suggest that on a range of statistical criteria the EC market is not significantly concentrated in sales terms. However, it may be more appropriate to look at concentration in terms of *national* market shares. Data on the market shares held by the leading corporate groups in twelve nations are presented in Table 4.4. This table shows that even in the most concentrated market (France) the holding was less than one-third of the market. The

Table 4.4   Market Shares by Leading Corporate Groups,* 1990 (%)

Country	The five leading corporate groups
Belgium	22.93
France	30.48
Germany	19.07
Italy	21.06
Luxembourg	27.54
Netherlands	27.83
Spain	18.21
United Kingdom	29.57
Australia	27.54
Canada	29.38
Japan	22.75
US	28.70

Notes: *The leading corporate groups in each country are determined by their sales in that country. The concept of 'corporate group' is superior to that of 'company' as the former also captures corporate affiliations. Shares are calculated on an historic basis, so that sales of a newly acquired unit are attributed to the acquiring corporate group in the year of acquisition.

Source: I.M.S. International Inc.

unweighted average market share held by the leading five corporate groups in each of the twelve nations was just 25.4 per cent. (For the European nations only, the figure was 24.6.) Thus the data do not offer much support for the idea that national pharmaceutical markets are significantly concentrated.

The above data are only illustrative, yet they may serve to undermine the common misperception that pharmaceutical markets are seriously concentrated. Of course a frame of reference which defines a market more narrowly (for example in terms of a product in a particular nation at a particular time) might generate different results.

4.3   Aspects of behaviour

4.3.1   Prices

The pricing of pharmaceutical products seems to be one of the more controversial issues associated with the industry: if a price is considered too high in market A, then the industry is said to be at fault; if a price is thought to be low in market B, the industry is blamed for 'dumping' low-priced products; and when both hold there is argument about cross-subsidization.

It is sometimes argued that health care insurance makes consumers less sensitive to the price and costs of the health care services and products that they consume. Furthermore, if the patient's physician does not have to consider the cost of the product, but only the medical need of the patient, it may be thought that he or she will not be price sensitive. Yet it should be noted that in many nations across Europe at least some patients have to make a direct financial contribution to the cost of their consumption. These payments are on either a flat rate or an *ad valorem* basis. Physicians in Europe are also now being subject to prescription audit as well as measures such as 'drug budgets' which aim to contain if not reduce pharmaceutical consumption costs.

In some European countries the price of a product is intrinsically linked to the authorities' approval for marketing: if there is no agreement on price between the company and the authorities then there is no marketing approval. Interestingly, most pharmaceutical companies are in fact price-takers in Europe: the purchasers determine the price they are willing to pay, for example, through a reference pricing system such as now exists in Germany, whereby the price of a product is based on existing prices of products in the same therapeutic class.

Some data on prices are presented in Table 4.5, which is based on a basket of pharmaceutical products across nations and over time. As can be seen, half of the national price indices are moving towards the EC average. Further price convergence is expected, with the relatively high-price countries, such as Denmark, Germany, Ireland and the Netherlands, coming down towards the EC average, and the relatively low-price countries, such as France, Greece, Portugal and Spain, moving up towards it. This convergence is due to a number of factors. For instance in Germany it is just one of the results of the new reference pricing scheme. In Ireland a new pricing scheme came into force in August 1991 under which the price of new products is to be related to the lesser of the UK price, or the average price of the product in five EC nations (Denmark, France, Germany, the Netherlands, the UK). Levelling up will happen in Portugal as a result of the lifting of a price freeze in 1990 and changes in VAT rates, while in France the upward movement towards the EC average will reflect the price premiums that have been introduced in order to encourage R and D.

A whole range of factors are pertinent to the consideration of pharmaceutical prices. These include the existence of reimbursement lists (lists of products the health insurance system will or will not pay a contribution towards); the incidence of the ill-health condition treated; the number of dispensing pharmacists and physicians per capita; and the incentives and

Table 4.5[1]   Price Indices for a Basket of Pharmaceutical Products[2]

Country	Index 1988	Index 1991
Belgium	88.6	100.5
Denmark	128.1	143.4
France	71.5	63.8
Germany	128.4	110.5
Greece	73.8	85.5
Ireland	130.5	129.8
Italy	79.1	96.1
Luxembourg	97.1	94.5
Netherlands	131.9	134.1
Portugal	67.5	57.7
Spain	71.6	83.7
United Kingdom	115.9	124.6

Notes:
1. The figures come from a recent update in *Pharmazeutische Zeiting* on the original data which was co-authored by Dr Frank Diener and the late Hannelore Sitzius-Zehender, both of the German pharmacist association Arbeitsgemeinschaft Bundesvereinigung Deutscher Apothekerverbämde (ABDA). The ABDA update, which took into consideration various factors such as purchase taxes, health insurance discounts and exchange rates, was itself an update on the pioneering work done by the Bureau Européen des Unions de Consommateurs (BEUC) in comparing the price of a basket of pharmaceutical products across the EC in the late 1980s.

    The 'basket' totalled 125 products, with the selection sample being the 25 largest-selling products in terms of sales value in each country plus any product not so included in the 25 but in the nation's top ten products by volume. This 'basket', which varies across countries, is said to have had a minimum representativeness of 20% in terms of total value of sales for each country. Just as importantly, only proprietary medicinal products were included and the initial prices were those that a private individual would have had to pay for the product. In view of these procedures, too much weight should not be placed on the data.
2. EC = 100.

Source: ABDA update on BEUC.

propensity to prescribe. In connection with the last point it should be noted that according to industry sources (details of which are available from the author) the percentage of diagnoses by general practitioners/specialists involving the prescription of drugs varied in 1990 from 95 per cent in Italy to 56 per cent in the Netherlands (the US rate was 65 per cent).

Monitoring costs or prices alone is a useful, but not the best, exercise: the public would be much better served if authorities fashioning health care cost containment policies also considered the *benefits* of the products. It is also important to bear in mind that the drug bill is not a major component in health care budgets: in the EC (excluding Luxembourg) it averaged only 17 per cent of the total health care budget in 1990; most health care expenditure is on labour.

4.3.2 Research and development
Employment, output and exports are only three of the beneficial factors which the pharmaceutical industry can bring to a nation. Another source of gain is the industry's investment in R and D. Since the pharmaceutical industry is pushing forward the frontiers of knowledge, such investment often has spin-offs for ancillary industries, the medical profession and the education/training services associated with the industry. For example some of the basic research comes from the work of industry-sponsored academics in medical schools. Again, most of the necessary clinical trials of a new

Table 4.6   *R and D Expenditure: Total[1] and as % of National Sales,[2] 1990*

Country	R and D (millions of ECU)	R and D (% of national sales)
Belgium	141.9	14.8
Denmark	125.7	35.8
France	1 426.2	17.6
Germany	2 008.8	25.9
Italy	1 426.2	11.2
Netherlands	213.2	22.6
Spain	83.6	2.8
United Kingdom	1 560.4	40.8
Total EC	6 986.0	20.0
Switzerland	1 567.5	–
Japan	2 235.6	11.0
US	5 124.4	20.7

Notes:
1. R and D expenditure includes funding of projects to enhance quality, safety and efficacy of products, but excludes physical capital and staff training expenditure.
2. National sales excludes export sales.

Sources: Industry sources (details available from the author).

product are overseen and run by professionals in the health care market, working in collaboration with personnel in industry.

The industry finds most of the funding for its R and D from its own resources and without recourse to capital markets. Table 4.6 shows the R and D expenditure incurred in eleven countries in 1990. The table also shows, for each country, R and D expenditure as a percentage of sales. It can be seen that the total amount of R and D expenditure in France, Italy, Germany and the UK makes up over 90 per cent of the EC total, and that countries varied widely in their R and D/sales ratios. One interesting feature of the data is that the EC average is very close to that for the US.

Another way of looking at the composition of R and D expenditure is by the nationality of the firms involved rather than the amount per nation. In 1989 40 per cent of the world's top 60 firms in terms of R and D expenditure were of European nationality (24 firms), 35 per cent (21) were US and 25 per cent (15) were of Japanese nationality.

Expenditure on R and D is an input measure and as such it says little about how productively the activity is carried out. Nevertheless it does offer an indication of the magnitude of the commitment that companies make to the search for new products. Some of this expenditure is on pure research, from which a greater understanding of particular conditions could lead to the identification of the factor, e.g. a gene, which is responsible for triggering a health defect. Once the problem is identified and its cause established, a company is in a much better position to proceed towards designing products not only for alleviating the symptoms and containing the condition, but also for reducing its incidence and prevalence and maybe even preventing and curing it. When one new chemical entity is formulated to deal with a condition, computer simulations of its chemical structure can help in formulating derivatives to identify other possible products.

Long-term commitment to R and D may, however, be seriously weakened by many factors, most of which are avoidable. Such factors include uncertainty in the health care market about regulation, price controls by the purchasers, erosion of intellectual property rights and unnecessary delays in marketing approval for products.

4.4 Performance

4.4.1 Innovation
The performance of the pharmaceutical industry can be viewed in a variety of ways. One possibility is to look at the number of new products developed by the industry over a period of time. This number runs into thousands each year, but only some of these products may be classified as new chemical entities (NCEs). Table 4.7 gives an indication of the number of NCEs intro-

duced by pharmaceutical industry into health care markets over nearly half a century, by country of origin.

Table 4.7 shows that the total number of NCEs introduced in the 1980s was around a third of the number introduced in the previous 20-year period. As the total amount of expenditure on R and D in the pharmaceutical industry has been rising in real terms for over 40 years now, it may seem that the industry is becoming less productive in this activity. However, this may reflect the existence of an R and D 'plateau', where the knowledge necessary for a new generation of products is not yet sufficiently advanced. Other explanations might be increasing regulatory stringency and the concomitant increasing costs.

Table 4.7   Number of New Chemical Entities (NCEs) Introduced to Health Care Markets,[1] 1941–89[2]

Country	1941–63	1961–80	1981–89
Belgium	3	36	6
France	21	272	31
Italy	1	112	42
Germany	32	191	37
Spain	na	na	10
Netherlands	6	na	2
United Kingdom	27	73	21
Switzerland	44	106	34
US	355	348	106
Japan	3	154	117
World Total	587	1 498	522

Notes:
na: not available
1.   Introduction is by nation of origin of NCE.
2.   Note that two of the time periods overlap: 1941–63, 1961–80.

Sources: Industry sources (details available from the author).

The exact causes of the fall in the number of innovations still requires thorough empirical testing, but this fall should not detract from the importance of innovations that have taken place: penicillin and streptomycin by the 1940s; corticosteroids and tetracyclines in the 1950s; diuretics and the polio vaccine in the 1960s; beta-blockers, H-2 antagonists, calcium channel blockers in the 1970s; and ACE inhibitors and antivirals in the 1980s. One important feature of innovation in the pharmaceutical industry reflects the Schumpeterian view that new products do in fact open up new markets, e.g. anti-malarials or cardiovasculars, and new opportunities for resource allocation in health care markets.

4.4.2   International trade

Another way to measure the performance of the pharmaceutical industry is by its success in international trade. In several countries the industry is amongst the top five net exporters. However, as Table 4.8 shows, not all industrialized nations run surpluses on their balance of trade in pharmaceuticals (nor do all the less industrialized nations run deficits).

Of the countries listed in Table 4.8, Japan ran the largest deficit in 1989 followed by Italy, Luxembourg, Spain, Greece, the Netherlands and Portugal. Large imports by value do not necessarily imply a deficit: Germany was

Table 4.8   Pharmaceutical Exports, Imports and Net Balance of Pharmaceutical Trade,* 1989 (millions of ECU)

Country	Exports	Imports	Net trade
Belgium	1 101	989	112
Denmark	794	344	450
France	2 487	1 689	798
Germany	4 040	2 260	1 780
Greece	58	207	−149
Ireland	594	292	302
Italy	972	1 650	−678
Luxembourg	–	279	−279
Netherlands	1 018	1 142	−124
Portugal	57	144	−87
Spain	437	652	−215
United Kingdom	2 816	1 484	1 332
Switzerland	2 856	706	2 150
Japan	655	1 805	−1 150
US	3 121	1 805	1 316

Notes: * Exports and imports include raw materials, intermediates and finished-form products. Exports are f.o.b; imports are c.i.f. It is not possible to add up the EC member states' figures to obtain an overall figure because of the significant amount of intra-EC trade.

Sources: Industry sources (details available from the author).

the biggest importer in 1989 yet still managed to achieve a significant net surplus.

The importance of pharmaceuticals in world manufacturing output is not adequately shown by the industry's share of world trade. Many companies have operating establishments in overseas markets which are serviced from local sources rather than by exports. Companies can try to expand foreign sales in a variety of ways: direct export is only one such method and this happens usually at an early stage in trade, or where the market is relatively small or where the political climate in the recipient nation is somewhat unfavourable. More common approaches are the licensing of a local manufacturer or of a distributor to produce and sell in specific countries; other marketing agreements; or the establishment of a local subsidiary in overseas markets. These arrangements are not fully reflected in trade statistics.

Patterns of trade in pharmaceuticals can be explained in part by the location of the industry, but demographic factors and differences in public policy and in institutional and regulatory frameworks across countries are also likely to be important.

4.4.3 The leading firms

As Table 4.9 indicates, the importance of the national leader with respect to the world league differs significantly, with the ranking varying from first to 178th. The dependence of each leading firm on its sales from pharmaceutical business also varied from 12 per cent in Belgium to the maximum of 100 per cent in Ireland, Portugal and the UK. The third row shows the 1990 profits/sales ratio for the leading firm in each country.

4.4.4 Wider issues

Data on employment, R and D expenditure, innovative record, and contribution to the trade balance are useful indicators of behaviour and performance, but they do not provide information on broader issues.

For example, how should the contribution of pharmaceutical products to improvements in the quality of life and in life expectancy be calculated? How should the benefits of pharmaceuticals which reduce the length of stay of the patient in hospital, or which reduce the need for hospitalization in the first place, be assessed? Products that speed up the recuperation period also offer gains to society by enabling patients to get back to work earlier, or to be less of a burden on the rest of their family through quicker recovery. Furthermore, many pharmaceutical products (such as vaccines) exist to prevent disease; others (e.g. anti-depressants) alleviate the suffering of those burdened with ill-health. How should their benefit to society be calculated?

Table 4.9   Profile of Leading Company[1] in Each Country, 1990

Country	World rank[2]	Dependence on pharmaceutical sales[3] (%)	Ratio of profits to total sales[4]
Belgium	48	12.0	6.5
Denmark	50	67.0	10.2
France	20	19.7	10.5
Germany	4	18.4	4.9
Ireland	161	100.0	11.0
Italy	44	88.5	15.8
Netherlands	32	14.1	6.5
Portugal	178	100.0	–(0.8)
Spain	113	71.1	–
United Kingdom	2	100.0	28.1
Japan	11	64.3	5.3
US	1	82.5	–

Notes:
1. The leading company in each country is determined by its total sales in that country.
2. World rank is determined by total world sales.
3. The dependency ratio maximum is 100, i.e. all income to the company comes from its business in pharmaceuticals.
4. A minus sign implies negative profits of the leading company.

Sources: Industry sources (details available from the author).

4.5   Public policy and regulation

4.5.1   Approval systems

Public policy and the regulation of the pharmaceutical industry are of such complexity that this section can offer only a brief assessment of some key issues. The first concern for public policy is that pharmaceutical products seeking marketing approval must be of a minimum standard in quality, safety and efficacy. Probably the most conspicuous catalyst in the demand for regulation on these three aspects resulted from the thalidomide tragedy of the early 1960s. The product was discovered in Germany in the mid-1950s and used as a sedative from the late 1950s, first in Germany – where it was available without prescription – and then in eleven other European nations, Canada, Australia, Asian and some African states. That the product never received approval in the US was due to the vigilance and existence of that country's regulatory authority, the Food and Drug Administration.

Each EC member state has its own marketing approval system but there have been moves since the early 1970s to offer a more unified approach. One way to achieve this is to offer mutual recognition of marketing approvals: the EC 'multistate' option under Directive 75/319/EEC embodied the concept of allowing marketing authorization by an approved authority in one member state, on the basis of only one dossier, to be used as the basis for reciprocal marketing authorization in at least five other named member states. The directive set up the Committee for Proprietary Medicinal Products (CPMP) to act as a 'postal bureau' and to offer opinions (not legally binding) to national authorities on such marketing applications. This system was altered under Directive 83/570/EEC, which reduced the number of other named states and offered improved channels of communication between companies and the CPMP.

The multistate system is expected to evolve into a decentralized system of mutual recognition based on the spirit of the Treaty of Rome, in which each member state recognizes the validity of another member state's marketing authorization granted on the basis of accepted criteria. Member states would use a procedure of mutual cancellation to avoid multiple review, and unresolved difficulties would be dealt with by an agreed binding arbitrator.

An alternative avenue for marketing applications and authorities exists through the centralized route. The centralized procedure, which came into effect in July 1987, is mandatory for most biotechnology products and optional for high-tech products (e.g. NCEs). This procedure aims to give a marketing authorization which is valid in all member states, with the decision over approval being taken by the Commission. Currently, however, the ultimate decision on whether to grant approval or not still remains with individual member states. The system of mutual recognition and the centralized procedure are designed to be complementary and are aimed at opening up the options for marketing applications.

There is currently debate about whether a fourth hurdle – 'socioeconomic worth' – should be introduced, in addition to the present quality, safety and efficacy requirements, as a prerequisite for marketing approval. Moves to introduce this requirement for animal health products have surfaced but have so far been defeated. However, the spirit of the argument may yet be extended to pharmaceuticals for human consumption. It has already permeated the French and Norwegian health care systems.

4.5.2   Prices, consumption and reimbursement

There is no simple relation between consumption and prices in Europe. In the early 1990s the Netherlands and Denmark had relatively high prices but relatively low consumption rates; the UK, moderate prices and low consumption; Belgium, France and Greece, low prices but high consumption; Germany high prices and high consumption; and Italy, low prices and low consumption.

Only in Denmark, Germany (up until the late 1980s), the Netherlands and the UK has there in some sense been price freedom. In Belgium, France, Greece, Portugal and Spain a new product is only allowed as a charge on its social security when a price has been agreed between the government and the manufacturer. Such price regulation may impact at various stages in the supply path such as the dispensing, wholesale and/or manufacturing levels.

The regulated price may be based on the cost of manufacturing from a particular source or on the price of existing products in the therapeutic class in the market. For example in France the French Economic Commission sets the maximum reimbursable price, whereas the Transparency Commission decides whether a product is reimbursable at all and at what rate. Prices may be referenced with prices elsewhere: the Irish example has already been outlined.

Prices are also regulated by purchase taxes, reimbursement rates or indirectly through the regulation of the profit margins that wholesalers or dispensing physicians are permitted on the final price. The relevant EC directive on pricing and reimbursement is 89/105/EEC; this deals with the transparency of measures regulating the pricing of pharmaceutical products and their inclusion within the scope of national health insurance systems. Article 1 of the directive makes it clear that if national authorities decide to have their own price or profits regulation policy or to have limit lists, they must operate within the terms of the directive. However there is no provision in this 'transparency' directive which *requires* national authorities to operate such a system, and derogation is always a possibility.

4.5.3   Profits

One nation in the EC, the UK, has explicitly set controls on the profits that are made by companies selling to the nation's health insurance system. The misnamed Pharmaceutical Price [*sic*] Regulation Scheme aims to influence the pharmaceuticals bill of the UK health insurance system by allowing (but not guaranteeing) a specified rate of return on capital employed in supplying pharmaceutical products to the UK National Health Service. The allowable 'profits' were a function of the economic contribution the company made to the UK economy, e.g. in terms of employment, R and D and exports. This non-statutory scheme had its roots back in the late 1950s and came up for renewal in October 1992.

4.5.4 Cost controls

A variety of tools used in cost control efforts affect both the supply of and the demand for pharmaceuticals. Direct price control is one route. Another is the use of positive lists of products sent to prescribers and others, listing a set of products, e.g. by non-proprietary name, which can be reimbursed by the health insurance system. Such lists exist in Belgium, Denmark, France, Greece, Italy, Portugal, Spain and the UK. A product's presence on the positive list does not, however, guarantee full reimbursement. The health care systems in Belgium, Denmark, France, Italy and Spain operate lists where only a *portion* of cost of a product qualifies for reimbursement, with the patient having to pay the residual. (In France part of the patient's co-payment may be recouped through the Mutuelles insurance system.) Another attempt at cost control is seen in the provisions of the German Health Reform Act, which came into effect on 1 January 1989. This includes a reference pricing scheme under which the sick funds (*Krankenkassen*) would reimburse only a single fixed price (the reference price) for certain groups of products. This price is based on average daily treatment costs, and the patient is expected to pay the excess.

Yet another route for cost control is the use of negative lists containing products that are explicitly excluded from health insurance reimbursement. Such lists are in place in Belgium, Germany (from late 1991), Ireland, the Netherlands and the UK. The lists can affect prices and consumption rates in a variety of ways. For example, admission to the lists is a form of price control. Differing reimbursement rates, delays in the appearance of a product in the official list, the transfer of a product from the reimbursable to the non-reimbursable list, the linking of the reimbursement lists with the prices and the marketing approval process, and changes in the status of the product (e.g. from PoM to OTC) are all likely to affect prices and consumption.

Other cost containment measures used by national governments include positive encouragement of the prescribing and dispensing of generics, out-of-patent products and 'parallel' imports. Such policies may, however, create difficulties. For example, generic substitution by dispensing pharmacists creates serious and as yet unresolved problems in relation to: liability implications; tracking for the prescriber; diluting the professional judgement of the physician; and undermining the physician's control of the patient's regimen.

Two further avenues for cost control are physician audit or increases in the amount that the patient pays for the product. Health insurance systems do of course have considerable purchasing power, which may be used to extract price discounts for items dispensed against social security prescriptions or to impose price cuts or price freezes (as occurred in the Netherlands in the early 1990s).

4.5.5 Advertising

Across Europe there are disparate rules and conditions attached to the advertising of human-use pharmaceuticals. For instance in the early 1990s all medicines in Greece were officially classified as PoMs and no consumer advertising was permitted. No TV- or radio-broadcast advertisements were permitted in Belgium or Denmark in the early 1990s.

The primary purpose of the EC 'Directive on Advertising of Medicinal Products for Human Use' was not to harmonize member states' systems but to dilute trade barriers caused by the different national rules. In February 1991 the European Parliament's Economic and Monetary Committee considered the draft directive and amended it to require the following minimum information on any pharmaceutical advertisement: the name of the product, information necessary for correct use, any restrictions in use, possible interactions with other substances and any other special recommendations. In addition the committee recommended that the adverts should convey the message that the patient should ask the doctor or pharmacist about risks and side-effects. On a first reading of the draft directive by the European Parliament on 12 June 1991 MEPs rejected the 'minimum information' amendment and instead accepted much less demanding amendments which simply required advertisements to carry the statement 'Any medicine can be dangerous if used incorrectly – Consult your doctor', and another statement telling the reader of the advertisement: 'Read the Label'. The amended directive was given final assent early in 1992. However, the debate about advertising will grow not least in relation to the target audience. If there is to be a greater financial contribution from the patient for pharmaceuticals then the argument for more advertising direct to the potential consumer is strengthened.

4.5.6 Intellectual property

Two important aspects of such property are considered here: the dossiers submitted to marketing authorities for marketing approval; and patents.

Some nations allow a successful dossier to be referred to by other companies ('second' applicants) who want to market a similar product, hence reducing duplication but bringing in serious liability problems and an infringement of intellectual property. Allowing such referrals also dilutes the incentive to be first to apply for marketing approval.

Under Directive 87/21/EEC there is only limited protection from second applicants. This directive permits second applicants to seek and receive 'permission to refer' to the first company's dossier within ten years of the granting of the first marketing licence in the EC. If an application for a generic product is made beyond the ten-year period then an abridged application (showing only the quality of the copy product and bioavailability/bioequivalence with the first product) may be made. The directive does not stop second applicants submitting at any time a full dossier collating their own clinical trials data provided this does not infringe the intellectual property rights of the first applicant.

The period required for the administrative and regulatory reviews prior to application for marketing approval may mean that the effective patent life (the length of time that a product on the market is covered by a patent) is shorter than the nominal patent period, perhaps by as much as 50 per cent. Indeed data on Belgium, France, Italy and Sweden have shown that an average development time of between 8 and 10.7 years existed in the late 1980s. The effective patent life has been falling. This is a phenomenon which is not unique to the EC: Japan and the US have also experienced such problems. However, in the early 1980s these two countries changed their laws. For example the 1984 US Drug Price Competition and Patent Term Restoration Act increased basic patent protection to 17 years and provided for up to five years' restoration for time lost due to pre-marketing regulatory requirements.

In the early 1990s the European Commission's proposal for a 16-year effective patent life protection period was aired and in late 1991 the EC Council of Ministers agreed on a 15-year period for pharmaceutical patents. The amended proposal is now going through the EC legislative system and at the time of writing it was expected that the new system could be in place by the end of 1992. The new system may, however, still discriminate against treatments that at present take longer to test and evaluate such as those relating to Alzheimer's disease, multiple sclerosis, motor neurone disease and some cancers. So R and D efforts may become biased towards products that take a shorter period of time to test, for example in clinical trials. The cost to health care of the discrimination against longer-term developments could be high: for example in 1990, 280 000 new cancer cases were admitted to hospitals in Germany alone.

4.6 Conclusion

This chapter has demonstrated the importance of the pharmaceutical industry in the EC, and has suggested that many of the effects of the industry are diverse and difficult to quantify. The chapter should also serve to undermine some of the more sensationalist misconceptions of the industry.

The science-based, innovation-orientated nature of the industry suggests that if the framework of analysis is to be realistic it must be couched in dynamic rather than static terms.

The extensive regulation of the pharmaceutical industry raises important issues of public policy. There is a pressing need for much more research on the regulation of an industry whose effects are felt by the industry, purchasers, consumers and not least health care markets. This research would not only benefit the industry, the regulators and the parties directly involved, but might also serve to refine if not redesign some of the academic community's 'tools of the trade'.

Further reading

Andersson, F. (1990), *The International Diffusion of New Chemical Entities* (Sweden Linköping Studies in Arts and Science 51), Linköping University.

Ballance, R., Forstner, H. and Pogany, J. (1992), *The World's Pharmaceutical Industries: An International Perspective on Innovation, Competition and Policy*, Aldershot: Edward Elgar.

Burstall, M.L. and Senior, I. (1985), *The Community's Pharmaceutical Industry*, Luxembourg: Commission of the European Communities.

Comanor, W.S. (1986), 'The Political Economy of the Pharmaceutical Industry', *Journal of Economic Literature*, **24**, (3), September, 1178–217.

Grabowski, H. and Vernon, J. (1990), 'A new look at the returns and risks to pharmaceutical R & D', *Management Science*, **36**, (7) July, 804–21.

Macarthur, D. (1987), *The EEC Environment for Medicines: Progress towards Harmonisation*, Richmond, Surrey: PJB Publications.

OECD (1990), *Health Care Systems in Transition*, Paris: Organisation for Economic Cooperation and Development.

Schmalensee, R. and Willig, R.D. (1989), *Handbook of Industrial Organisation*, Amsterdam: North-Holland.

Sermeus, G. and Adriaenssens, G. (1989), *Drug Prices and Drug Legislation in Europe – An Analysis of the Twelve Member States of the European Communities*, Brussels: Bureau Européen des Unions de Consommateurs (BEUC/112/89).

Statistical Office of the European Communities (latest edition), *Structure and Activity of Industry*, Luxembourg: Eurostat.

Taggart, J. (1993), *The World Pharmaceutical Industry*, London: Routledge.

Teeling-Smith, G. (ed.) (1992), *Innovative Competition in Medicine*, Whitehall, London: Office of Health Economics.

Walker, S.R. and Griffin, J.P. (eds) (1989), *International Medicines Regulations: A Forward Look to 1992*, London: Kluwer.

5 Biotechnology

Leonie Marks

5.1 Introduction

5.1.1 What is biotechnology?

The term 'biotechnology' came into widespread usage during the mid-1970s with the advent of a number of scientific breakthroughs, particularly in the area of genetic engineering (Oakey *et al.*, 1990, p. 5). Biotechnology can be narrowly defined as the 'application of scientific and engineering principles to the processing of materials by biological agents to provide goods and services' (OECD, 1989, p. 4). It involves the use of genetic engineering techniques[1] to transfer genes which exhibit a desirable trait between different living species or organisms – plants, animals and micro-organisms (National Research Council (NRC), 1987, pp. 16–17).[2]

A broad definition of biotechnology would include, in addition to the use of genetic engineering techniques, the use of tissue culture techniques[3] to reproduce organisms in controlled settings and the use of micro-organisms to produce chemicals of commercial interest. This broader definition is more appropriate when considering industrial applications of biotechnology.

5.1.2 Biotechnology as a process

The 'output' of the biotechnology industry, until recently, has largely been the development of more efficient 'procedures' for conducting research into potentially useful products and processes rather than the production of marketable products. The industry is at the take-off stage. In the long run, however, it is anticipated that biotechnology will yield new and novel products while at the same time allowing existing products to be produced more efficiently. With the use of genetic engineering techniques, biotechnology firms will eventually be able to produce (for example) an improved variety of wheat, tolerant to drought, or a new species of cattle which produces more milk. These are process innovations. Alternatively, biotechnology firms may produce new final products (product innovations) – novel pharmaceutical products and novel forms of animals and plants which have not been previously produced.

Biotechnology firms, apart from providing 'final' products, may also provide 'intermediate' goods for other industries. Cuphea is a wild plant grown in Mexico which produces lauric acid. Lauric acid is a feedstock for the soap and detergent industries. The development of cuphea, through the use of genetic engineering, could eventually provide a cheaper input for those firms which currently use chemicals as feedstock.

Biotechnology firms also provide services, such as research and development (R and D), to other firms. These firms may be either new biotechnology firms (NBFs) or large established firms (LEFs).

It can be argued, on one level, that biotechnology firms do not constitute a distinct industry because they do not produce the same or similar products. The biotechnology industry does not fall into the usual Standard Industrial Classification (SIC) of industries,[4] or into Nomenclature Générale des Activités Economiques des Communautés (NACE) which is the general industrial classification of economic activities used in EC statistics. Instead, biotechnology firms are linked by the use of a common technique or 'process' technology. They operate in numerous industries including the health, agriculture, chemical, food, energy and service sectors (waste disposal/management, effluent treatment, oil recovery). Table 5.1 provides some idea of the scope of those industries potentially linked through the use of biotechnology.

Firms operating within the industry fall into two distinct (although not mutually exclusive) groups: companies that have pioneered R and D in new biotechnologies, to so-called NBFs, which provide services (technical R and D) to other firms within the industry or have marketed their own products; and the larger, established companies which may be conducting their own research into biotechnology or contracting research services from the NBFs and public research institutes.

5.1.3   Historical development of the European biotechnology industry

Biotechnology may be characterized as having three periods of historical development (Advisory Council for Applied Research and Development, 1980). First-generation biotechnology has its roots in fermentation techniques used to produce drinks (wines and beers), food (cheese and bread) and fuel (Oakey *et al.*, 1990, p. 8). By the nineteenth century the industrialization of biotechnological production had gone some way in the European brewing industry as local firms began to increase their sales in European cities. Problems of process reliability meant that only small-scale production was possible. In Britain, for example, brewing was limited to cooler times of the year. In other European cities major investments were made in cellars and ice stores (Yoxen, 1989, p. 20).

Large-scale fermentation techniques used to manufacture solvents, such as acetone and butyl alcohol from starch, were first used during the First World War. Such solvents were used in the manufacture of munitions (Yoxen, 1989, p. 21). These manufacturing processes used a bacterial culture for the

Table 5.1   Biotechnology according to Industrial Sector

Chemicals
>   Organic (bulk)
>   Ethanol, acetone, butanol, organic acids
>   Organic (fine)
>   Enzymes
>   Perfumes
>   Polymers (mainly polysaccharides)
>   Inorganic
>   Metal beneficiation, bioaccumulation and
>   leaching

Pharmaceuticals
>   Antibiotics
>   Diagnostic agents (enzymes, antibodies)
>   Enzyme inhibitors
>   Steroids
>   Vaccines

Energy
>   Ethanol (gasohol)
>   Methanol (biogas)
>   Biomass

Food
>   Dairy, fish and meat products
>   Beverages (alcoholic, tea and coffee)
>   Baker's yeast
>   Food additives (antioxidants, colours, flavours, stabilizers)
>   Novel foods
>   Amino acids, vitamins
>   Starch products
>   Glucose and high-fructose syrup
>   Functional modifications of proteins, pectins
>   Toxin removal

Agriculture
>   Animal feedstuffs, hormones, regulators and chronobiology
>   Veterinary vaccines
>   Ensilage and composting processes
>   Microbial pesticides
>   Rhizobium and other N-fixing bacterial inoculants
>   Mycoorhizal inoculants
>   Environmental stress resistance
>   Herbicide resistance
>   Plant growth regulators
>   Plant cell and tissue culture (vegetative propagation, embryo production, genetic
>   improvement)

Service industries
>   Water purification
>   Effluent treatment
>   Waste management
>   Oil recovery

Source: Bull *et al.* (1982), with additions from author.

first time and are known today as bioprocesses (NRC, 1987, p. 41). Oakey *et al.* (1990, p. 9) argue that this development paved the way for sustained involvement by the bulk chemical producers in fermentation-process technology and in the use of biotechnology in the production of smaller-volume chemicals, for example, citric acid and vitamins. Fermentation processes were largely superseded in the inter-war years by the development of chemical alternatives. However, by the 1940s microbiology, biochemistry and chemical engineering were becoming distinct disciplines. The integration of these disciplines in different applications provided the core of second-generation biotechnology.

Second-generation technology emerged after the Second World War and covers the period from the 1940s to the 1970s. It involved larger-scale fermentation in the brewing and, later on, sewage treatment and chemical industries. There were enormous improvements in efficiency, in yields from fermenting cells, in fermenter design and in extraction and purification of the final product (Oakey *et al.*, 1990, p. 9). As a result, there was a prodigious increase in the range of products manufactured using biotechnology including many novel, fine and speciality chemicals, food products and additives, as well as pharmaceuticals (*ibid.*). Today, advances in biotechnology have renewed interest in uses of bioprocessing in agricultural and forestry commodities. For example, many scientists hope that bioprocessing could have a significant effect on fuel production through the manufacture of biomass energy from alcohol produced from seeds, grains and sugar. At the moment (other than in countries such as Brazil) there are competitive alternatives such as petroleum, gas and coal (NRC, 1987, p. 41), but oilseed fuel derived from rape is starting to be used in non-oil-producing EC countries.

Third-generation biotechnology is characterized by the use of genetic engineering techniques. This stage of industrial development grew out of advances in genetic engineering outside of the industrial R and D centres – largely through medical research conducted in university laboratories sponsored by the government (Oakey *et al.*, 1990, p. 11). The initial development of the technology within the public sector has had a significant impact on the subsequent development of the industry.

5.2   Importance of the biotechnology industry within Europe

5.2.1   *An overview*
As already suggested, the biotechnology industry links a number of industrial sectors across Europe via a common process technology, so it is extremely difficult to identify the full impact and importance of the European biotechnology industry. Data are not available on the degree of activity relating to biotechnology in any given sector. Nevertheless, a general over-

view can be given of the industries affected by biotechnology and their overall contribution to production, employment and net exports from Europe to the rest of the world. While this level of analysis may overstate the current importance of the biotechnology industry within Europe, it is not unreasonable to suggest that biotechnology will play a significant role in future productivity gains and structural change within the sectors identified. Such an analysis gives an insight into the qualitative nature of the industry. Any quantitative analysis should be treated with caution.

While the potential of biotechnology is recognized to be substantial, many developments currently being explored are decades from reaching full application, so the reliability of any predictions about future progress is limited. As technical progress will also depend on the institutional, social, political and legislative environment that unfolds over the next decades, predictions at this stage of the industry's development are further weakened.

Tables 5.2a, 5.2b and 5.2c incorporate those sectors which are linked through the use of biotechnology and whose future development will be strongly influenced by developments in biotechnology. The tables contain data on agriculture and pharmaceuticals, which are dealt with separately in

Table 5.2a   European[1] Biotechnology Industry Production, 1985–90 (millions of ECUs)[2]

Sector	Agriculture[3]	Chemicals	Pharmaceuticals (health care)	Food, drink & tobacco	Total all sectors
1985[4]	157 829	240 473	32 397	269 795	700 494
1986	184 596	229 331	37 775	304 268	755 970
1987	181 078	236 857	40 407	307 957	766 299
1988	185 718	265 704	45 814	326 187	823 423
1989	200 938	289 045	48 100	350 451	888 534
1990[5]	N/A	293 790	50 500	356 759	N/A

Notes:
1. European 12 including: Belgium, Denmark, Germany, Greece, Spain, France, Ireland, Italy, Luxembourg, Netherlands, Portugal and UK. Sectors are classified according to NACE unless otherwise specified.
2. Production is gross turnover excluding VAT. Figures are in current prices and exchange rates.
3. Final agricultural production includes contract work at agricultural producer level (Germany, France, UK and Spain) and other taxes linked to production (Italy).
4. Figures for the year 1985 are for EC 10 for the food, drink and tobacco industry and agriculture.
5. 1990 figures across sectors are estimated. 1989 figure for pharmaceuticals is estimated.

Sources: Eurostat, *Basic Statistics of the Community*, Luxembourg: Eurostat 1990, 1991; CEC (1991b).

Table 5.2b   European¹ Biotechnology Industry Employment, 1985–90
(000s)

Sector	Agriculture[5]	Chemicals	Pharmaceuticals (health care)	Food, drink[4] & tobacco	Total all sectors
1985	10 373	1 905	400	1 866	14 544
1986	10 090	1 910	400	2 261	14 661
1987	9 884	1 910	443	2 277	14 514
1988[2]	8 529	1 922	445	2 274	13 170
1989	9 027	1 941	445	2 260	13 673
1990[3]	N/A	1 945	447	N/A	N/A

Notes:
1. European 12 including: Belgium, Denmark, Germany, Greece, Spain, France, Ireland, Italy, Luxembourg, Netherlands, Portugal and UK. Sectors are classified according to NACE unless otherwise specified.
2. Figures for agriculture 1988 exclude Greece.
3. 1990 figures are estimated. 1989 figure for pharmaceuticals is estimated.
4. Figures for the year 1985 are for EC 10, figures for 1986–90 are for EC 12.
5. Agricultural employment is for EC 10 only for 1985.

Sources: Eurostat, *Basic Statistics of the Community*, Luxembourg: Eurostat 1990, 1991; CEC (1991b).

Chapters 2 and 4 of the present book. These data are included here for the sake of completeness, although they may not be fully consistent with some of the statistics given in the two chapters because of the different sources used.

The four sectors included in the tables account for 10.5 per cent of total employment within the EC or 13 673 million in 1989. Two-thirds of this employment is within the agricultural sector, where the potential impacts of biotechnology are likely to be the greatest. Total output of these sectors was 888.5 billion ECUs in 1989 or 20 per cent of total community output. Overall these sectors are net exporters, generating 23 billion ECUs of net exports to the rest of the world, or 41 per cent of total net exports in 1989.

The Senior Advisory Group on Biotechnology (SAGB) has projected that 2 million more jobs may be created by the year 2000 through the introduction of competitive biotechnology in the sectors identified[5] (SAGB, 1990, p. 8; CEC, 1991a, p. 1). One and a half million jobs may be created in agriculture, 280 000 in chemicals and pharmaceuticals, 250 000 in health and 113 000 in food. However, little of this employment is likely to occur through European NBFs. If the experience of the UK is typical then employment growth in NBFs will be moderate, in contrast to that experienced by some of the better known US NBFs (Oakey *et al.*, 1990, p. 68).

Table 5.2c   *European[1] Biotechnology Industry Net Exports, 1985–90*
           (millions of ECUs)[2]

Sector	Agriculture[4]	Chemicals	Pharmaceuticals (health care)	Food, drink[5] & tobacco	Total all sectors
1985	(12 235)	26 325	3 129	2 540	19 759
1986	(13 659)	22 214	3 697	2 551	14 803
1987	(12 148)	22 315	3 835	3 992	17 994
1988	(12 667)	24 161	3 969	2 115	17 578
1989	(9 336)	23 790	4 153	4 527	23 134
1990[3]	N/A	24 016	3 819	N/A	N/A

Notes:
1. European 12 including: Belgium, Denmark, Germany, Greece, Spain, France, Ireland, Italy, Luxembourg, Netherlands, Portugal and UK. Sectors are classified according to NACE unless otherwise specified.
2. Net exports are defined as the trade balance of the community with the rest of the world and are in current figures.
3. 1990 figures are estimated. 1989 figures for pharmaceuticals are also estimated.
4. Agriculture is defined as including food and live animals chiefly for food.
5. Figures for the food, drink and tobacco industry for 1985 are for EC 10; figures for 1986–90 are for EC 12.

Sources: Eurostat, *Basic Statistics of the Community*, Luxembourg: Eurostat 1990, 1991; CEC (1991b); Eurostat, *Agriculture Statistical Yearbook 1990*, Luxembourg: Eurostat, 1990.

SAGB also gives some indication of the potential growth in sales of biotechnology-derived products up to the year 2000. The present world market for biotechnology products in the health and pharmaceutical sectors is 1.2 billion ECUs. By the year 2000 this is projected to have grown to 23.9 billion ECUs. Similarly, for chemicals the world market for biotechnology products is currently estimated to be 0.1 billion and is projected to be 14.6 billion ECUs by 2000. Agriculture and food product sales are currently worth 2.4 billion ECUs and are projected to be 40 billion by 2000. Even environmental biotechnology products,[6] which constitute some 0.4 billion ECUs in sales, are projected to reach sales of 2 billion ECUs by 2000 (SAGB, 1990, p. 7).[7]

5.2.2   Chemicals

In the chemical sector, biotechnology is likely to affect downstream branches of the industry such as pharmaceutical and medical products, agrochemicals and to a lesser extent detergents. Upstream branches of the industry include basic chemical products – basic inorganic chemicals and basic organic and petrochemicals. The main outlets for these products are almost exclusively downstream sectors (CEC, 1991b, p. 8–4). The agrochemicals and fertilizer industries each constitute 2 per cent of chemical industry production, whereas the pharmaceutical industry constitutes 17 per cent.

Agrochemicals include insecticides, fungicides, herbicides, plant growth regulators and all other chemicals designated for crop protection and development (CEC, 1991b, p. 8–33). Europe is currently the world leader in the agrochemical market, with the EC's plant protection market estimated to be worth 5.3 billion ECUs in 1988. Forecasts for 1995 put its value at approximately 5.6 billion ECUs. In comparison, the US market (the second largest) was estimated to be 4.7 billion in 1988 and by 1995 will have stabilized at 5.1 billion ECUs (CEC, 1991b, p. 8–33).

Biotechnological products are likely to be developed as alternatives or 'substitutes' for existing products within the agrochemicals sector. For example, the bioinsecticide *Bacillus thuringiensis* (Bt) uses natural pathogenic bacteria rather than chemicals to kill pests. Bt is likely to displace or reduce the use of chemical pesticides in agricultural production. It is already produced and marketed in developed countries and some developing countries are in the process of setting up production facilities. However, product displacement is not quite as clear-cut as the foregoing analysis would imply. Farmers are likely to use an integrated approach to pest management, that is, a range of control techniques. In the future, chemicals are likely to be used in pest management programmes along with biological control and bioinsecticides such as Bt.

In the case of other agrochemical products, such as herbicides, the possibilities for substitution are likewise unclear. Chemical and seed companies are developing herbicide-resistant plants which may increase, rather than reduce, the use of a specific herbicide (although the use of chemical herbicides in general is likely to be reduced). Clearly, it is in the interests of the chemical and seed companies to be at the forefront of developments in biotechnology in order to ensure market share in future products.

The fertilizer industry produces and markets single fertilizers such as nitrogen (N) or phosphates (P) as well as a range of complex fertilizers containing compounds of N, P and K (potassium). Intermediate products such as ammonia are also used in other parts of the chemical industry. In 1989 the EC produced 50 million tonnes of fertilizer with an estimated value of 6.6 billion ECUs. The Community accounts for some 12 per cent of world production and is the fourth largest producer after the Soviet Union, the US and China.

An enhanced understanding of plant species and their needs is liable to bring about a gradual decline in fertilizer consumption, that is, substitution towards alternative biotechnology-derived products. For example, inoculants such as Rhizobia, a symbiotic bacteria, increase the ability of certain plants to take up nitrogen from the soil. Such plants will use nitrogen products more efficiently and, therefore, require less of them.

5.2.3 Pharmaceuticals

Production of pharmaceutical products increased by almost two-thirds between 1985 and 1990 (see Table 5.2a). The EC is currently the leading world location for pharmaceutical production and exports of pharmaceutical products, with an external trade surplus of 3.8 billion ECUs in 1990. Genetic engineering and monoclonal antibody technology have already had a significant impact on the industry.[8] The latter technique allows firms to produce large quantities of very specific antibodies. Antibodies are important scientific tools which can be used as diagnostics. Recombinant DNA (rDNA) or genetic engineering techniques have been used to produce products such as human insulin, human growth hormone and alpha interferon, and novel products such as tissue plasminogen activator (tPA) and interleukin-2 (IL-2) (Daly, 1989, p. 37). Human insulin, growth hormone and alpha interferon are natural products which have already been marketed. Future new products such as the tPA and IL-2 have a large market potential (*ibid.*); for example, tPA is used for dissolving blood clots.

5.2.4 Agriculture

In agriculture, applications of biotechnology will affect livestock production and also crop production. Developments in livestock production include the improvement of animals through genetic selection; enhanced food nutrition; increased reproductive efficiency; greater control of diseases and pests; and the development of growth hormones, bioregulators and diagnostic kits. Plant biotechnologies are being developed to improve resistance to environmental stresses; create new species; regulate plant growth; control diseases; improve plant nutrition; create microbial insecticides; create herbicide-resistant plants; improve digestibility of forages and enhance metabolic efficiency (Marks, 1990, p. 7). The technology is likely to affect all sectors of agribusiness, the companies supplying inputs (chemicals, seeds), livestock breeders, and the end-users, i.e. the farmers themselves.

5.2.5 Food and drink

Biotechnology will also affect the processing and retailing, packaging and distribution, of food. The food industry may be affected by the use of biotechnology to preserve products such as fruits and vegetables. It is also likely to lead to further improvements in fermentation technology. The use of genetically modified micro-organisms in food production or for the production of food ingredients (flavours, sugar substitutes and so on) will allow for further diversification and improvement of food quality (CEC, 1991b,

p. 15–5). Biotechnology should allow firms to develop better methods of diagnosis, analysis and control of contaminants and to achieve higher standards of quality of food products (Mainguy, 1986, p. 80). Progress in the form of biotechnology is unlikely to lead to spectacular technological leaps but rather to 'continuing and systematic changes ... [with] a greater mastery of traditional processes' *ibid.*, pp. 80–1).

5.3 Demand and supply

5.3.1 Demand characteristics
Biotechnological products can be characterized according to their elasticity of demand. Because biotechnology links a number of industries producing a range of products, elasticities will vary both across and within industrial sectors. In general, bulk products derived using biotechnology show a high own-price elasticity of demand because they are challenged by other products or processes (Hacking, 1986, p. 21). For example, single-cell protein (SCP) has a very high own-price elasticity of demand because it competes with direct substitutes such as soy or fish meal. Demand for food and animal feed is also price sensitive. Intermediate groups of products, such as organic acids and amino acids, approximate unit elasticity as they do not have direct substitutes (*ibid.*). Most pharmaceuticals are examples of products with highly inelastic demand, particularly when a drug is new and there are no effective substitutes. In health care, a patient's welfare is of the utmost important to the doctor, who is less concerned with price characteristics (Hacking, 1986, p. 21). Elasticity of demand is likely, therefore, to be low. Low elasticity of demand also characterizes genetically engineered agricultural products, although individual farmers face highly elastic demand curves. One incentive for farmers to introduce new crops is to improve their product quality, thereby differentiating their product from that of their competitors (for example genetically engineered tomatoes which are able to mature longer before harvesting have superior taste and storage characteristics).

Hacking (1986, p. 22) argues that for many biotechnologically derived products the situation is not as clear-cut as the above categorization would indicate. For many products the demand curve may have own-price elasticity which differs depending upon the market where it is sold. For example, the demand for antibiotics may be highly inelastic in the human medicines market but very elastic in the animal feed market.

5.3.2 Supply characteristics
Supply characteristics also vary across sectors. Supply is likely to be fairly inelastic at capacity for the production of ethanol (fuels) from corn, for example, because of the nature of the huge investment in plant. Up to

capacity, however, supply is fairly elastic. Pharmaceutical products are likely to have fairly inelastic short-run supply curves, due to the considerable time taken for product development. However, as products often have a short product life cycle, plants are often built to be flexible (even at the expense of cost efficiency) (Hacking, 1986, p. 27), which may increase the elasticity of supply.

For farmers, the supply is very inelastic in the short run for crops and livestock but fairly elastic in the long run. This is unlikely to change with the advent of biotechnology products, although innovations such as frost tolerance and drought resistance may increase the elasticity of supply of certain crops.

5.4 Market structure and market behaviour

Any overview of the market structure and market behaviour of the European biotechnology industry needs to be undertaken at the sectoral level. An attempt is made to assess the degree of competition between existing firms within each sector and to examine the influence of the NBFs which straddle the different market sectors.

5.4.1 Chemicals

The European chemical industry is a highly concentrated industry where five companies share more than 40 per cent of EC production. Amongst the top ten world chemical companies seven are European. Chemical firms are mainly located in Germany and the UK; with France, the Netherlands, Belgium and Italy each having one of the top ten European firms (in terms of sales). Among the 30 top world chemical companies 17 are European (13 based within Europe) 10 are American and 3 are Japanese. Other producers have appeared on the world stage more recently, for example Brazil and South-East Asia, but the major share of production remains within the European and American groups (CEC, 1991b, p. 8–5).

Today the chemical industry can be regarded as a mature industry at the end of a period of rapid growth and technical development which has been dominated by petrochemicals and polymers (Hacking, 1986, p. 31). Future competition is likely to be between biotechnology and a particular chemical 'process' rather than between companies. There is an increasing tendency within the European industry for vertical integration from production of raw materials to distribution which should create further barriers to entry. Unlike in Europe, in Japan (a latecomer to the field of biotechnology) large chemical companies have been one of the main developers of biotechnology.

5.4.2   Pharmaceuticals

Chapter 4 provides an assessment of the extent and nature of competition in this industry, and demonstrates the complex nature of the issues involved, especially in relation to barriers to entry. These issues are not examined again here. However, it is worth pointing out that NBFs are unlikely to be able to compete with existing pharmaceutical companies in the long run due to the high costs of R and D and marketing (see section 5.4.5). It is also interesting to note that pharmaceutical companies are pursuing different strategies with regard to the NBFs. For example, Bristol-Myers and Eli Lilly have recently acquired NBFs (*The Economist*, 1988, p. 4). Eastman Kodak, on the other hand, has acquired Sterling Drug while at the same time helping to establish a biotechnology institute at Cornell University. This has enabled Eastman Kodak to forge closer links with biotechnology firms and the university sector (*ibid.*).

5.4.3   Agriculture

The reader is referred to Chapter 2 for a discussion of the structure of agricultural production. In the context of this chapter it is worth noting that agriculture is already very advanced in crop and animal breeding, in its use of fertilizers and pesticides, and in mechanization. The main effects of biotechnology will be in the 'supplying' industries, through development of better varieties of crops, pesticides and so on. These developments should ensure that the agricultural sector remains competitive and is further rationalized, with smaller, less efficient farmers leaving the industry. Agriculture remains a politically sensitive area within Europe. A recent decision by the European Commission not to allow the use of bovine somatatrophin (bST) within the European dairy industry, where there is already overproduction of milk, illustrates the point.[9]

5.4.4   Food and drink

The food and drink industry is diverse in structure, with both small firms and large multinational enterprises (MNEs) operating within the sector. In Europe, northern markets are more highly concentrated than those in the South. European markets are less highly concentrated than those in the US, which suggests that concentration will increase within Europe as the single market comes into force (CEC, 1991b, p. 15–5). Product and process innovations resulting from developments in biotechnology will give the larger companies a substantial advantage over their smaller competitors, especially as firms tend to compete more on quality and product diversification (brand proliferation) than price. Biotechnology will afford food manufacturers the opportunity to develop food products which are more 'natural'. MNEs likely to be affected by such developments are already involved in multiple consumer markets such as confectionery, snacks, dry pasta, biscuits, industrial baking and frozen foods. This should increase concentration across these markets.

Biotechnology will also have a significant impact on food processors (Hacking, 1986, p. 28); for example, it has already reduced costs of starch production through the use of enzyme technology. Food processors, such as the Italian food company Ferruzzi, are vertically integrated and heavily involved in transforming basic products such as sugar, starch, maize and soya into food products. Such firms stand to gain from further process innovations and are in a market position to eliminate weaker competitors as a result.

The European food and drink industry is already becoming increasingly concentrated both through direct investment and acquisitions (CEC, 1991b, p. 15–5). Mergers and acquisitions have been motivated by a desire to achieve economies of scale in advertising and to consolidate the power of the food manufacturers against retailers. There is also an increasing tendency towards larger-scale plants. Advertising costs and integration are significant barriers to entry.

In contrast to the pharmaceutical producers, most food firms are high-volume, low-margin operations and their profits (based on gross sales) are low. R and D expenditure has also tended to be lower in the food industry, the European food companies being more interested in minor changes in food quality than in conducting basic research in biotechnology which would lead to new products and improved processes. This has provided a market niche for NBFs, which provide expertise in the basic technology. Their role is unlikely to be competitive in the long run (see section 5.4.5). In contrast, in Japan, the large food and drink companies originally involved in fermentation technology have been some of the main investors in biotechnology (Fransman and Tanaka, 1991).

5.4.5 *Relationship between the LEFs and the NBFs*
As stated in the introduction, the NBFs have emerged as suppliers both of products and of R and D services. Given the high costs of R and D, marketing and patenting, one would expect the LEFs to have a considerable advantage in developing biotechnology. Large companies are in a relatively better position to commit the resources for the time that is necessary to achieve a return on investment. However, smaller start-up firms have tended to have greater flexibility and faster response times in developing biotechnology (CEC, 1991c, p. 4). So far, NBFs have exploited product niches and/or research niches where they have a competitive advantage. They have overcome initial financial constraints, either through access to venture capital, or through equity stakes. It remains to be seen whether they can overcome

other more persistent barriers to entry such as marketing barriers and econo-mies of scale.

The pattern of emergence of NBFs differs across countries. In the US, NBFs played a significant private sector role in developing the biotechnology industry. Backed by venture capitalists, many professors, who perceived the commercial potential of their work, left the university sector to set up their own companies (*The Economist*, 1988, p. 1). Genentech, a California-based company, was the largest and most well known of these companies, becom-ing a significant supplier of biotechnological products and services. It has since been taken over by Hoffman La Roche, a European pharmaceutical company (CEC, 1991c, p. 29).

In Europe, and in particular the UK, NBFs have also had a crucial role in the development of the biotechnology industry. They have provided a simi-lar link between public research institutes and the market-place.

If the UK experience is typical of the rest of Europe (the UK, Germany and France have the strongest biotechnology industries, which are at a simi-lar stage of development) then new firm formations peaked in 1982, one year after the United States. In the period 1970 to 1988, according to *The Economist*, (1988, p. 1), some 600 biotechnology companies were founded, nearly all of them in the US. In Britain, for example, in the period 1976–86 43 NBFs were established (Oakey *et al.*, 1990, p. 67). However, more re-cently the European Commission has estimated that some 800 firms (includ-ing LEFs as well as NBFs) are active in the field of biotechnology within Europe. By comparison there are 1 000 firms active in the US and 300 in Japan (CEC, 1991a, p. 1). In the initial stages it is likely that these firms were product based, as university professors exploited the immediate market potential of their research. However, as the industry has developed, NBFs have become more service based, or research 'boutiques' (Oakey *et al.*, 1990, p. 46).

While the majority of the NBF start-ups have remained in the industry since the early 1970s (out of the 600 biotechnology firms mentioned earlier, by 1988 fewer than 10 had gone bankrupt or been taken over despite incur-ring considerable losses since being founded: *Economist*, 1988, p. 1), their future position is somewhat tenuous (as the recent acquisition of Genentech would indicate).

Some NBFs compete directly with the LEFs in terms of products already marketed. For example, a US firm has developed 'probiotics' which are potentially safer and more effective for use in animal feed than antibiotics. These products are direct substitutes for the antibiotics developed by the pharmaceutical companies in this market. On the whole, however, the NBFs lack the necessary marketing and managerial skills, scale and 'push' needed for full product development across several markets. Other NBFs have progressed from R and D contracting to licensing and on to joint ventures. Increasingly, large firms are either undertaking R and D in house or with an equity stake in the NBF. It is unclear at this time, given the increasing equity involvement of large companies, how far the smaller NBFs will be able to expand on their own or survive without being taken over.

5.4.6 Research and innovation

As should be clear from the discussion so far, the biotechnology industry has developed around a core of new research techniques. In this sense the industry is still very young and has been extremely innovative (see section 5.5). In order to examine the industry's research record it is necessary to identify the role of public institutions (national governments and the EC Commission) as well as the role of firms.

The role of national governments and the Commission Since 1982 the Commission has initiated a series of research and technological development programmes (often complementing national R and D programmes) in the field of biotechnology. The Commission views its initiatives as being interactive with those of EC member states and the biotechnology industry itself. The initial emphasis of these programmes was on research and training, although the focus has now widened significantly.

The third and latest research initiative by the Commission runs from 1990 to 1994 and is called BRIDGE – Biotechnology Research for Innovation, Development and Growth in Europe – with a budget of approximately 100 million ECUs. In February 1992 the Council adopted an R and D programme in the field of biotechnology which extends the BRIDGE programme and provides additional funding of 162 million ECUs (CEC, 1992, pp. 6, 18). At least 10 per cent of funds are allocated to basic research, with between 5 and 7 per cent allocated to the training of researchers. The mandate of this programme is wider than earlier initiatives in that the Commission is interested in examining the ethical, social and environmental implications of biotechnology (3 per cent of the budget is allocated to this task).

In addition to such centralized expenditure, national governments have publicly financed R and D expenditure. In 1987 (latest figures available) Germany and the UK each spent 185 million ECUs from public funds on biotechnology R and D. France spent 170 million ECUs and Italy 50 million. The total public expenditure for that year (depending on source) ranges from 800 million ECUs (CEC, 1991a, p. 4) to twice that level: 1 600 million ECUs (CEC, 1991c, p. 4). By comparison, the US spent 2.5 billion ECUs (CEC, 1991a, 1991c, p. 4). European Community expenditure has been far more fragmented than in the US or Japan. Only the UK, Germany, France and the Netherlands have attempted to coordinate R and D policies and programmes in biotechnology (Eurostat, 1991, p. 52).

Three conclusions may be drawn from the above. First, currently the aggregate of national expenditures far exceeds that at the Community level (although national expenditure is concentrated among only a few countries). Second, despite higher levels of expenditure at the national level, overall levels of public expenditure fall considerably behind that of the US (Europe's main competitor). Third, the EC is faced with the difficult task of coordinating policy at the national and Community level, with some countries lacking policy initiatives in biotechnology research. As future developments in biotechnology will crucially depend on the level and quality of R and D expenditure undertaken, within both the public and private sectors, the future competitive position of the EC may be undermined. Evidence would seem to indicate that this is already the case (see section 5.5).

The role of private firms   Data and evidence on the degree of expenditure by the private sector on biotechnology R and D remains scattered and largely incomplete. In many cases it is difficult to separate biotechnology work from other R and D activities in the major companies, so only an approximate analysis can be given. The large European chemical companies such as ICI, Sandoz and Ciba-Geigy were spending up to one-third of their R and D budgets on developing expertise in biotechnology in 1988 (*The Economist*, 1988, p. 4). In 1987 the percentage of total turnover devoted to R and D (of all kinds) was 4.5 per cent for the chemical industry, or 10.5 billion ECUs (CEC, 1991b, p. 8–6), therefore approximately 3.5 billion ECUs were spent on biotechnology R and D. In particular sectors of the chemical industry, such as agrochemicals and pharmaceuticals, the percentage of total turnover devoted to R and D rises to 10–15 per cent (CEC, 1991b, pp. 8–6, 8–55). For example, the pharmaceutical industry devoted 5 billion ECU to R and D in 1988 (15 per cent of turnover), one-third being devoted to development of biotechnological products.

These figures probably under-represent the level of R and D expenditure (as a percentage of turnover) by the industry as a whole. For example, the UK biotechnology industry was spending 29 per cent of sales in 1988 on R and D (equivalent to 73 billion ECUs), and 28 per cent in 1989 (projected to fall to 25 per cent in 1991). Such high expenditure is characteristic of an industry in its start-up phase, when future sales are often dependent on existing R and D expenditure and the phasing of such expenditure affects the figures. What does seem clear from the above figures is that, despite the late start by the private sector in initiating research into biotechnology, R and D by the private sector clearly outstrips public expenditure at both the national and Community level. The level of expenditure within the UK is probably not out of line with that of other leading countries within Europe, such as Germany and France.

Whilst it can be argued that R and D expenditure does not guarantee profitability *per se*, nevertheless such expenditure is likely to be a significant determinant of the future competitiveness of the European biotechnology industry, and of that of the other industries linked to it.

5.5 Performance

There are a number of possible measures of industry performance such as share of international trade, productivity, profitability and innovative record. As the biotechnology industry is still very much in its infancy, some of these measures, such as profitability, are inappropriate. For example, only the very top biotechnology firms in the world (such as Genentech) were making profits as late as 1987 (*The Economist*, 1988, p. 4). Indeed, most of the biotechnology companies (NBFs) launched since 1970 have made losses.

One way of mapping the performance of biotechnology firms (and of government and university research institutes) is through the number of patents applied for over a given period. Patent statistics contain a number of pitfalls for the unwary, but they do provide one indicator of research effort and innovative record.

Table 5.3 provides cross-section data on the performance (based on the number of applications filed at the European Patent Office(EPO)) of the EC versus Japan and the US for the period 1986–89. The European countries with the most innovative record are (as one would expect) Britain, Germany and France. Europe and the US have both shown strong performances over this period, although in the majority of categories identified the US is ahead of Europe. Japan is also strong in certain areas.

Table 5.3 does not trace the progress of the industry in different countries over time. Table 5.4, however, provides an insight into the progress of Europe versus the US and Japan over the 1980s in the field of agrobiotechnologies. From Table 5.4 it is clear that the EC had an innovative advantage in the early 1980s versus the US and Japan but by 1987 the US had matched the performance of Europe in terms of patent applications. If the trend continues, the US will overtake Europe in quantitative terms in the 1990s (CEC, 1991d, p. 47). In other areas of research, such as AIDS research and cancer research, the pattern of performance is somewhat different. The EC, from the early 1980s, has lagged behind the US in both, while Japan has tended to compete at the same level as the EC in cancer research but has lagged behind in AIDS research (CEC, 1991d, Annex 2, p. 9).

Within the EC, Germany dominates in the field of agrobiotechnology with about 40 per cent of all applications filed with the EPO over two periods, 1983–85 and 1986–88. France and other EC countries lag behind, with less

Table 5.3   Patent Applications in Biotechnology, 1986–89 (%)

Classes	Japan	US	EC total approx.	United Kingdom	West Germany	France	Belgium	Netherlands	Denmark	Italy	Spain	Others	Total number demanded
												Country of origin	
A	8	15	56	10	15	13	1	7	2	8	1	21	318
B	17	50	11	0	0	11	0	0	0	0	0	22	18
C	9	40	34	6	8	10	2	4	1	1	0	17	268
D	20	40	30	6	11	6	2	2	2	2	0	10	1 517
E	19	42	29	6	9	6	2	3	2	1	1	10	996
F	31	31	30	5	12	6	1	4	2	2	0	8	616
G	14	54	24	7.5	10	4	0.5	1	0.5	0.5	0	7	390

Classes:
A = manufacture of dairy products.
B = novelty products and procedures for obtaining them.
C = medicines.
D = general biotechnology.
E = genetic engineering techniques.
F = fermentation processes.
G = use of micro-organisms to facilitate research processes and in evaluation of research products.

Source: CEC (1991c).

Table 5.4 Number of Patent Applications at the European Patent Office: Agrobiotechnologies, 1980–88

Priority year	EC 12	United States	Japan	Other	Total
1980	45	11	6	9	71
1981	36	17	7	11	71
1982	42	22	15	13	92
1983	61	40	18	23	142
1984	51	40	17	18	126
1985	58	69	31	26	184
1986	85	65	25	19	194
1987	81	67	27	20	195
1988	74	87	40	21	222

Source: CEC (1991d).

than 20 per cent of all applications over the two periods. The UK accounted for approximately 20 per cent of all applications in 1983–85. These increased to about 25 per cent in the period 1986–88 – a strong growth performance. The number of patents filed with the EC also reveals a high share of international cooperation within the EC and, more importantly, between the EC and other countries (such as Switzerland, the former East Germany, Austria and Canada). International cooperation appears to be more important for the countries that have smaller resources devoted to R and D. However, there have been few cases of international cooperation between MNEs. Most of the examples of research cooperation result from internationally mixed inventor teams and some cross-sector cooperations between companies and public institutions (CEC, 1991d, p. 51). This would indicate that government coordination and public research play a significant role in ensuring cooperative research, which would otherwise not be undertaken by the private sector.

5.6 Public policy

There are a number of key policy areas where national governments and the Commission may exert an influence over the future competitiveness and development of the biotechnology industry. Such areas include taxation and financial incentives for firms; government funding of basic and applied research; training; regulation and legislation (intellectual property law); anti-trust law; university/industry/international cooperation; and, finally, public perception and consumer choice (CEC, 1991c, p. 5).

The main problem facing the European biotechnology industry versus its competitors is that of fragmentation; that is, each national government pursues its own strategy with regard to R and D, training, regulation and legislation. Such fragmentation can create non-tariff barriers to trade and, perhaps more importantly, a climate of uncertainty which may prohibit investment in R and D and capital formation by firms both within and outside Europe. Bearing this in mind, the Commission has been concerned to coordinate legislation and regulate the industry at the Community level to avoid duplication and, hence, uncertainty and unnecessary costs to industry.

The objective of the Commission is to create a single European market in biotechnology. However, given the rather lengthy legislative procedure within Europe, the right legislative framework may take longer to develop than in competitor countries, such as the US, for example, where the Food and Drug Administration can act fairly autonomously. In this final section only a few key policy issues are addressed.

5.6.1   Patent legislation

An issue of immediate importance is that of intellectual property rights, or the right to patent life forms. With recent developments in the field of biotechnology, current legislation does not provide firms with adequate protection of the results of their research. The economic case for providing biotechnology firms with patent protection is that as biotechnology requires high-cost R and D, which is particularly risky, firms need to be able to capture the rewards of their efforts. Patents grant the firm a temporary monopoly over a production process or a particular product. Differences in exclusivity in the granting of patents may have adversely affected the European industry (especially in pharmaceuticals) as the US and other competitors have a longer period of protection. Costs of obtaining a patent may also be higher in Europe as European Patent Office costs are equivalent to three times the cost of applying to a national government (EPO, 1981).

In addition to the potential benefits to be gained through the granting of patents, patents incur costs to society. While they may encourage the development of high-cost and high-risk technologies, they decrease the benefits that society would have enjoyed from the existence of an invention if that knowledge had been available to all producers. From a welfare point of view, information, once produced, should be freely available to all firms. The granting of a patent on a life form and, in particular, a patent on a process innovation, may give considerable rights to the private company, which might charge a high price for such technology. It may also encourage the firm to consolidate its monopoly position in the future. The question for European policy-makers (which does not appear to have been addressed by the Commission) is: would such research be better undertaken in the public domain (where information is freely available) or should patent or intellectual property right legislation be enacted to encourage private enterprise (national or international) to develop the technology? (Marks and Papps, 1992, p. 24).

5.6.2 Regulation

Regulation of the biotechnology industry falls into two main areas: environmental protection and antitrust legislation. With regard to environmental protection, the potential for both beneficial and harmful effects of biotechnologies poses a challenge to policy-makers. They need to find the right degree of regulation of the industry in order to protect consumers and the environment from potential hazards. The community currently has two sets of directives in place: 'horizontal' directives which relate specifically to the environment and to the protection of workers in the workplace, and 'vertical' directives which relate to specific sectors and products affected by biotechnology. Horizontal legislation tends to safeguard positions not covered by sectoral and product legislation. The Commission's view is that existing and proposed legislation are enough to ensure adequate protection of health and the environment.

Uncertainty about potential changes in regulations or new regulations may deter investment within the biotechnology industry. Unnecessary regulatory burdens increase costs to industry and may hinder product development. The cost of regulatory failure is also likely to be high. Two recent decisions by the US government have laid a regulatory framework for US firms which may give them a competitive advantage over European firms. In February 1992 the Bush administration issued a set of guidelines for genetically engineered food products within the biotechnology industry. These stressed that in order to block the development of biotechnology products strong evidence would have to be presented to suggest that they were a potential hazard. This puts the burden of proof on consumer and environmental groups rather than on the biotechnology firms, and supports the idea of genetically altered food. Then in May 1992 the US government announced that producing new food types by genetic engineering is not inherently more dangerous than producing it by any other method and such food does not need extensive pre-market testing. In addition, the FDA will not require identifying labels on genetically altered products under the new policy (*Financial Times*, 1992, p. 6). Such a step has yet to be taken within Europe. This is a significant breakthrough for the agricultural and food industries in the US, gives US firms a considerable advantage over European firms, and reduces uncertainty over future product development. It is likely to lead to further increases in investment in biotechnology within the US.

5.6.3   Public perception

For the biotechnology industry to achieve its development potential it requires public support, both for research undertaken and the products developed. However, the current view within the EC is that there is poor perception of biotechnology both by the public and by policy-makers.

In 1991 a survey of public opinion was carried out by the Directorate-General Science, Research and Development (DGSRD) of the Commission of European Communities and Consultation Unit for Biotechnology in Europe (CUBE) (DGSRD/CUBE, 1991). A number of interesting results emerge from this survey. First, the term 'genetic engineering' is less well known and has a more negative connotation than 'biotechnology'. This would indicate that the industry has to give careful consideration to its use of such terminology when promoting its activities. Secondly, and not surprisingly, the two principal sources of information used by Europeans are the television and newspapers. The most reliable sources of information, however, are considered to be consumer and environmental organizations and schools or universities (industry sources are less trusted). This would indicate a perception problem from an industry standpoint which will need to be overcome. Thirdly, 50 per cent of Europeans believe that biotechnology will improve their way of life over the next 20 years and only 10 per cent believe it will make them worse off. Those who are more optimistic are men, young people, people with a higher level of education or those in higher income groups. These groups are also the best informed regarding the technology. Fourthly, most Europeans tend to agree that research into biotechnology is worth while and should be encouraged. Exceptions are in the areas of research on farm animals (58 per cent of Europeans think it a bad idea) and, to a lesser extent, on food (42 per cent think this a bad idea). Support for biotechnology also depends directly upon the risk associated with the application. The greater the perceived risk, the lower the support. Finally, regardless of nationality, most Europeans consider that all types of research into biotechnology need to be regulated and controlled by the government. So in order to maintain public confidence regulation must be seen to be effective, especially where applications are perceived as high-risk. In general, contrary to the view of the Commission, there is good public support of the biotechnology industry across Europe, although there is room for improvement of public perception in certain areas. This support needs to be carefully managed by both industry and government.

5.6.4   Information

One final area for public policy is the weakness of the Community versus its competitors in the area of bio-informatics. Information and data bases in the Community concerning the biotechnology industry are often fragmented and incomplete. Researchers within the Community rely on the comprehensive data bases in the US. The US, because it possesses the world's major biotechnology information infrastructure involving both data bases and specialist software, has the potential of controlling the sources and flow of information in biotechnology. US firms therefore have a considerable advantage over EC firms, as up-to-date knowledge in a science that is developing so rapidly is crucial for competitiveness (CEC, 1991c, p. 6).

5.7 Conclusion

The introduction of new biotechnology techniques across Europe will allow for the development of new products and production processes which, if managed carefully, will provide considerable benefits to Europe in the coming decades. At the moment European producers are in a strong position *vis-à-vis* their competitors. They have shown a strong performance in terms of R and D expenditure and innovation as measured by patent applications within Europe over the 1980s, but it is questionable whether this performance will be as strong over the next decade. While the position of European firms should be strengthened by the arrival of the single European market, the US is providing increasing competition in biotechnology products. It has already caught up with the European firms, which enjoyed a competitive lead in key applications of the technology during the early 1980s. The US is also taking a greater share of the investment which is flowing into the biotechnology industry, and recent regulatory decisions are likely to ensure that the US maintains these investment flows.

The key policy issue for the remainder of the 1990s will be to ensure that a single European market in biotechnology is in place. This should help to secure future investment within Europe and maintain its long-term competitive position.

Notes

1. Genetic engineering involves the alteration of the structure of the chromosomes of a cell to change the genetic characteristics of the species.
2. Micro-organisms are any tiny, usually microscopic, entities capable of carrying on living processes. They may be pathogenic (toxic). Kinds of micro-organisms include bacteria, fungi, protozoa and viruses. Fungi are usually included with micro-organisms, even though they also fall into a group of plants which includes moulds, mushrooms, mildews and rusts. These plants have no leaves or flowers, and reproduce by means of spores.
3. For example, micropropagation techniques are used in plant research. Micropropagation is a complementary technique to genetic engineering as it allows researchers quickly to multiply plants which have been selected for their desirable traits.
4. This makes the task of evaluating industrial activity at the national and European level extremely difficult, as data are inadequate.
5. These new jobs will either replace current jobs based on present technologies or constitute net new employment from enhanced European competitiveness in these sectors.
6. Environmental applications of biotechnology have not been examined in detail and are not included in Tables 5.2a, 5.2b and 5.2c.

7. Estimates of the current size of the market for biotechnology products and market projections vary considerably depending on source. For example, CEC (1991a) estimates of world sales of biotechnology-derived products (excluding fermented foods and drinks) totalled 7.5 billion ECUs in 1985 (larger than the SAGB calculations). Latest estimates for the year 2000 predict sales rising to between 26 billion and 41 billion ECUs (lower than the SAGB estimate).
8. Monoclonal antibody technology involves the use of experimental animals which are immunized against a particular antigen followed by fusion of cultured tumour cells with spleen cells from the immunized animal. The hybrid cells are then cultured, tested for specificity and the level of antibody activity. The successful hybrid cells (hybridomas) can be frozen for future use or injected into a laboratory animal to produce a tumour which becomes, in effect, the manufacturer of the specific antibody.
9. bST can increase milk yields by up to one-third.

References

Advisory Council for Applied Research and Development (1980), with the Advisory Board for the Research Councils and the Royal Society, *Biotechnology: Report of a Joint Working Party (the Spinks Report)*, London: cited in Oakey *et al.*, 1990.

Bull, A.T., Holt, C. and Lilly, M.D. (1982), *International Trends and Perspectives in Biotechnology: A State of the Art Report*, Paris: Organization for Economic Cooperation and Development.

Commission of the European Communities (CEC) (1991a), *Biotechnology: Ending the Fragmentation of the European Market to Produce an Even More Competitive Industry*, Spokeman's Service – Information Memo 18 April, 4 pp.

CEC (1991b), *Panorama of European Community Industries 1991–1992*, Luxembourg: Office for Official Publications of the European Communities (Eurostat).

CEC (1991c), *Commission Communication to Parliament and the Council Promoting the Competitive Environment for the Industrial Activities Based on Biotechnology within the Community*, SEC(91) 629 final, Brussels: CEC, 19 April.

CEC (1991d), *Patents as Indicators of the Utility of European Community R&D Programmes*, Luxembourg: CEC, June.

CEC (1992), *Re-examined Proposal for a Council Decision Adopting a Specific Research and Technological Development Programme in the Field of Biotechnology (1990–1994)* (COM(92) 60 final – SYN 265), Brussels: CEC, 28 February.

Daly, P. (1989), 'Future Pharmaceutical Markets and Human Care', in E. Yoxen and V. Di Martino (eds), *Biotechnology in Future Society. Scenarios and Options For Europe*, Luxembourg: European Foundation for the Improvement of Living and Working Conditions.

Directorate-General Science, Research and Development of the Commission of the European Communities (DGSRD) and Concertation Unit for Biotechnology in Europe (CUBE) (1991), *Opinions of Europeans on Biotechnology*, Brussels: European Coordination Office.

The Economist (1988), 'Biotechnology: Inherited Wealth' (Biotechnology Survey), *The Economist*, **307**, (7548), 30 April.

European Patents Office (EPO) (1981), *Protecting Inventions in Europe* (EPO Information Leaflet), Munich; EPO Press and Public Relations Department.

Eurostat (Office for Official Publications of the European Communities) (1991), 'Promoting the Competitive Environment for the Industrial Activities Based on Biotechnology within the Community', in 'European Industrial Policy for the 1990s, *Bulletin of the European Communities*, Supplement 3/91, Luxembourg: Eurostat.

Financial Times (1992) 'Approval for Gene-altered Food', *Financial Times*, **31,768** (Week 22), 22 May.

Fransman, M. and Tanaka, S. (1991), 'The Strengths and Weaknesses of the Japanese Innovation System in Biotechnology', Edinburgh Institute for Japanese–European Technology Studies (JETS), JETS Paper 3, University of Edinburgh.

Hacking, A.J. (1986), *Economic Aspects of Biotechnology*, Cambridge: Cambridge University Press.

Mainguy, P. (1986), 'The Impact of the Development of Biotechnology in the Agro-food Area', in Duncan Davies (ed.), *Industrial Biotechnology in Europe: Issues for Public Policy*, London: Frances Pinter.

Marks, L.A. (1990), 'An Analytical Framework for Assessing the Potential Impacts of Biotechnologies on Third World Agricultural Sectors', MA thesis, Department of Economics, University of Calgary.

Marks, L.A. and Papps, I. (1992), 'Identifying the Costs and Benefits of Projects: an Example from Biotechnology', *Project Appraisal*, **7**, (1) March, 21–30.

National Research Council (NRC) (1987), *Agricultural Biotechnology: Strategies for National Competitiveness*, Washington, DC: National Academy Press.

Oakey, R., Faulkner, W., Cooper, S. and Walsh, V. (1990), *New Firms in the Biotechnology Industry: Their Contribution to Innovation and Growth*, London: Frances Pinter.

Organization for Economic Cooperation and Development (OECD) (1989), *Bio Technology Economic and Wider Impacts*, Paris: OECD Publications.

Senior Advisory Group on Biotechnology (SAGB) (1990), *Community Policy for Biotechnology: Economic Benefits and European Competitiveness*, Brussels: SAGB.

Yoxen E. (1989), 'Historical Perspectives on Biotechnology', in E. Yoxen and V. Di Martino (eds), *Biotechnology in Future Society. Scenarios and Options for Europe*, Luxembourg: European Foundation for the Improvement of Living and Working Conditions.

Further reading

Molnar, J.J. and Kinnucan, H. (eds) (1989), *Biotechnology and the New Agricultural Revolution*, Boulder, Colorado: Westview Press.

Russell, A.M. (1988), *The Biotechnology Revolution: An International Perspective*, Sussex: Wheatsheaf Books.

Tombs, M.P. (1990), *Biotechnology in the Food Industry*, Milton Keynes: Open University Press.

Yoxen, E. and Green, K. (eds) (1990), *Scenarios for Biotechnology in Europe: A Research Agenda*, Shankill, Co. Dublin: European Foundation for the Improvement of Living and Working Conditions.

Yoxen, E. (1987), *The Impact of Biotechnology on Living and Working Conditions*, Shankill, Co. Dublin: European Foundation for the Improvement of Living and Working Conditions.

6 Motor vehicles

Garel Rhys

6.1 Introduction

In the early 1990s the motor industry represented just under 10 per cent of the EC's manufacturing output. Directly and indirectly it employed almost 9 million people, with 2.5 million in vehicle and component making. In dynamic terms through its R and D, and investment in production and information systems, the industry is central to technological developments in the EC, and contributes greatly to the Community's trade with a surplus of well over 20 billion ECUs a year, in contrast to a total EC trade deficit covering all sectors of almost 30 billion ECUs in 1991. R and D in such a large sector of EC industry is important in maintaining and developing the EC's total technical base, as well as increasing the sophistication of vehicles.

In many ways the EC motor industry's external trade position shows its strength and its weakness. In 1991 the industry's surplus of 22 billion ECUs was mainly due to the component sector (14 billion ECUs). If the contribution of commercial vehicles (CVs) is then removed, the balance for the car sector is only about 2 billion ECUs. A key factor limiting the car surplus is the challenge posed by the Japanese motor industry, which dominates world trade in cars.

The single internal market did not appear overnight at the end of 1992, but was established regulation by regulation. However, the motor industry was already one of the most 'European' of industries and had done much to anticipate 1992. It has long regarded Europe as one market and already operates on this basis. It is not fanciful to say that a transnational company like Ford had achieved its own 1992 when it created 'Ford of Europe' in 1967.

The design, development, production and marketing of vehicles on a West European rather than a narrow national basis had started to emerge in the 1960s and subsequently gathered momentum. This chapter examines the emergence of a 'European' motor industry and the impact the EC has had on this process. Its main focus is on car production, although reference is also made to CVs and components.

6.2 Costs

Despite new technology, new flexible equipment and new operating systems, which can reduce the fixed costs of R and D or can put a variety of vehicles along a production line thereby reducing the car-specific optimum, large scale is still needed for optimality in many of the car making processes (Table 6.1). Thus while the *shape* of the long-run average cost curve may change, the minimum efficient scale is hardly altered.

Table 6.1   *Optimum Scale in Various Processes*

	Annual volume
Casting of engine blocks	1 000 000
Casting of various other parts	100 000–750 000
Power train machining and assembly	600 000
Axle machining and assembly	500 000
Pressing of various body panels	1–2 000 000
Final assembly	250 000
Paint shop	250 000

Source: Author's estimates.

Table 6.2   *Volume to Average Unit Cost Relationship*

Output per year	Index of costs
100 000	100
250 000	83
500 000	74
1 000 000	70
2 000 000	66
3 000 000	65

Source: Pratten (1971); author's estimates.

The relationship between volume and costs (Table 6.2) shows that minimum efficient scale is around 2 million units a year (Pratten, 1971). Hence the production figures for the leading full line producers (i.e. those making a full range of volume-produced cars from minis to large executive cars) indicate that the Europe-wide production totals for Ford and General Motors (GM) has put them on a par with the other four firms (Table 6.3). However, even by 1986 when the total production of Ford and GM had become comparable with all the leading firms, apart from Volkswagen (VW), Ford (UK) only made 320 000 cars and Ford (Germany), including Belgium, 725 000, with GM (by Opel) making 903 000 cars in its German operation,

Table 6.3   European Production of Six Leading Firms (000s)[1]

	Ford[2]	PSA[3]	GM[4]	VW[5]	Fiat[6]	Renault
1970	857	525[7]	990	1 835	1 891	1 143
1975	743	1 205[8]	753	1 255	1 454	1 235
1980	1 023	1 722[9]	942	1 517	1 479	1 817
1985	1 297	1 545	1 333	1 735	1 203	157
1986	1 406	1 591	1 363	1 870	1 628	1 428
1990	1 604	1 978	1 718	2 397[10]	1 873	1 514
1991	1 590	1 836	1 685	2 441	1 632	1 547

Notes:
1. Figures corrected for possible double counting in the official statistics. The following data on production outside Europe may be helpful for comparative purposes. In 1991 Toyota made 3.2 million cars in Japan and 350 000 in the USA. The figures for Nissan were 1.9 million and 120 000 respectively. General Motors and Ford made 3.2 million and 1.2 million cars (GM) respectively in the USA.
2. From 1990 including Jaguar.
3. PSA refers to Peugeot Société Anonyme.
4. From 1990 including Saab.
5. From 1970 to 1980 SEAT is excluded from VW total. SEAT is included from 1986.
6. From 1986 includes Alfa Romeo.
7. Figure for Peugeot only.
8. Figure for Peugeot and Citroën.
9. Figure includes Peugeot, Citroën and Talbot.
10. From 1990 includes Skoda.

Source: Society of Motor Manufacturers and Traders (SMMT); company information.

280 000 in Spain and 150 000 (by Vauxhall) in the UK. Thus on their own and without integration none of the US firms' European national companies approached optimum size. It may have been that without integration of their respective operations neither Ford nor GM would have survived in the EC to reach the strong market positions they had in 1990.

The need for a viable scale to match the US transnationals and the other European firms also led Peugeot to embark on a takeover programme in the 1970s. The company purchased Citroën in 1975 and Chrysler's European interests in 1979. The purchase of Citroën doubled Peugeot's size to 1.5 million units and the purchase of Chrysler produced an operation with a theoretical capacity of 2.6 million units. However, the Chrysler (quickly renamed Talbot) models declined in appeal, whilst Peugeot was faced with an immense task of rationalization to realize the potential economies of scale. In 1980–84 the combine lost £755 million, and its share of the West European market fell from 18 per cent in 1978–79 to 11.5 per cent in 1984 (see Table 6.5). From that point, armed with a reinvigorated product range, the group's finances improved significantly.

Unit costs are reduced not only by operating at optimum scale but also by reducing input prices, such as wage costs (Table 6.4). Consequently GM concentrates the manufacture of its small supermini in low-wage Spain, and VW may do the same. As the labour content does not increase proportionately with the size of the car, superminis are relatively labour intensive to make. As long as productivity is good it makes economic sense to produce them in low-wage economies, even though the car plants in these countries have the same capital to labour ratio as other EC factories. The strength of this argument will diminish as further automation, especially in final assembly, reduces the overall labour content involved in car production, and labour costs in countries like Spain (*and* the UK) increase to more closely match those elsewhere in the EC (Table 6.4). Already Fiat has chosen its FSM subsidiary in Poland, bought in 1992 to make its new mini car, largely for unit labour cost reasons.

Table 6.4   World Auto Industry Wage Costs (DM per Hour)

Country	Gross hourly earnings		Total wage costs		
	1990	1991	(1980)	1990	1991
Sweden	24.56	25.60	28.6	43.72	45.41
Germany	24.30	25.87	26.9	41.87	44.47
USA	23.76	25.58	24.8	32.07	35.05
Belgium	16.93	17.83	28.1	31.83	33.65
Italy	14.59	14.62	17.1	31.67	31.57
Netherlands	16.86	17.39	23.3	31.20	31.86
Japan	22.03	26.05	14.5	28.64	33.87
Spain	17.13	17.81	12.6	28.43	29.56
France	13.76	14.50	19.7	26.01	26.43
United Kingdom	18.27	19.46	15.0	25.58	26.64

Note: 'Wage costs' includes social costs such as pensions and payroll taxes. In 1991 social charges in the UK were only 36.9% of hourly earnings. This was low in European terms but comparable to US and Japanese levels.

Source: Verband der Automobilindustrie e. V. (VDA), Frankfurt.

6.3   Demand

Cars and CVs provide a flow of transport services. In the case of cars the product is also desired because it confers on its owner various attributes, not the least of which are prestige and status. The relevant dependent variable in the demand equation is not so much the demand for new cars as the demand for car ownership. The latter may include the purchase of cars of different vintages ranging from the new to, say, those over ten years old. Indeed, in any one year in the EC three times as many used cars may be sold as new ones.

The main independent variables are price and per capita disposable income. Estimates of long-run price elasticity of demand for cars as a whole vary from –0.6 to –1.7 while income elasticities range from 1.1 to 4.2. However, price elasticity estimates for the products of *individual* firms vary between –2.0 and –7.0. Advertising and demographic, locational and credit factors also influence car demand. Population density is also a significant independent variable, being a proxy for a number of factors (e.g. the nature of public transport) which are inversely related to the demand for car ownership. Hence the densely populated EC will never reach US per capita car ownership levels, everything else (such as per capita real income, real prices of cars) being equal. Again severe short-run changes in car demand are generated by changes in credit terms. For instance, it has been suggested that a change in the minimum hire-purchase deposit, say from 33 per cent to 20 per cent of the price of a car, increases car demand by the same extent as a 2 per cent growth in national income (Silberston, 1963). Often analysis is carried out in terms of quality-adjusted (e.g. hedonic) pricing. The myriad specifications and opportunities for changes in vehicle 'quality' make car demand a particularly appropriate area for such an approach. Often when quality-adjusted pricing is introduced, price competition becomes even more apparent in the EC motor industry. Own-price elasticities as high as –8 can be generated here.

In the long term, environmental factors such as exhaust emissions, energy use, noise, congestion and recycling demands could affect the demand for car ownership and hence the demand for new cars. In short, many aspects of government policy have affected (and will affect) vehicle demand, be it legislation that affects road and rail passenger and goods transport, vehicle sales and user taxes, road building or traffic constraint policies (see also p. 150). So far nothing has fundamentally undermined the human desire to obtain access to personal mobility via car ownership. Whether future environmental concerns will do so remains to be seen.

6.4 The industry's structure: some key features

6.4.1 Cars

Market share Motor vehicle production in the European Community and Western Europe generally has been dominated by six mass producers of cars, but with a significant position being held by car-makers who concentrate on more specialized parts of the market. Car *sales* are also dominated by these European-based firms, but over 10 per cent of West European car sales are now made by Japanese firms, many of whom have established vehicle production facilities in Western Europe. A small share is held by East European and other Asian producers. The recent distribution of the market between the leading firms is shown in Table 6.5.

Table 6.5 Share of West European Car Market (%)

	1973	1978	1982	1984	1985	1986	1990	1991
Volkswagen Group[1]	11.3	11.5	11.8	12.1	12.9	14.7	15.5	16.5
Fiat[2]	14.9	11.8	12.5	12.7	12.2	14.0	14.6	12.8
Peugeot Group[3]	5.6	18.0	12.4	11.5	11.6	11.4	13.2	12.0
Ford[4]	10.6	13.2	12.4	12.8	11.9	11.7	11.7	11.9
General Motors[5]	10.1	10.7	8.7	11.1	11.4	10.9	12.1	12.1
Renault	10.3	11.8	14.7	11.0	10.7	10.6	9.9	10.0
Rover	9.0	4.9	3.7	3.9	3.9	3.5	2.8	2.6
Others[6]	28.2	18.1	25.8	24.9	25.4	23.2	20.2	22.1
for example								
Daimler-Benz	2.0	2.5	3.2	3.2	3.3	3.4	2.8	3.3
BMW	1.4	2.1	2.8	2.7	2.5	2.8	2.7	3.1
Volvo[7]	2.1	1.7	2.0	2.1	2.2	2.5	1.8	1.5

Notes:
1. From 1986 VW's figures included SEAT (1.6%).
   From 1990 they included Skoda's share of about 0.2%).
2. From 1986 Fiat's figures included Alfa Romeo (1.5%).
3. From 1978 the Peugeot Group's figures include both Citroën and Chrysler, although the latter was bought on 1 January 1979.
4. From 1990 Ford included Jaguar (0.1%).
5. From 1990 General Motors included Saab Automobile (0.4%), in which it had a 50% equity holding and managerial control.
6. In 1973 'Others' included Citroën with 5.3% of the market, and Chrysler with 7.8%. By 1984 'Others' included a Japanese share of almost 10%, which had grown to 11.8% in 1986 and 12.3% in 1991.
7. Volvo figures include Swedish and Dutch-sourced sales.

Source: Derived from SMMT data.

Of the six leading 'full line' producers (Table 6.6) Ford and General Motors are the European operations of American transnational companies. The four remaining firms are European owned. Of the two French companies the Peugeot Group is a private sector company and Renault is state owned. (Since 1990 Renault and Volvo have been linked through cross-shareholdings.) Fiat of Italy is privately owned and like Peugeot the founding family has a major shareholding. Volkswagen-Audi is 18 per cent owned by the State of Lower Saxony, the Federal Government having sold its 20 per cent shareholding in 1988.

Table 6.6   Share of West European Production (%)*

	1985	1986	1990	1991
Volkswagen Group	16.0	16.1	18.3	19.3
SEAT	1.9	1.8	–	–
Fiat	11.1	12.7	14.3	12.9
Alfa Romeo	1.9	1.8	–	–
Peugeot Group	12.9	13.7	15.1	14.5
Ford	12.1	12.1	12.2	12.6
GM	12.3	11.8	13.1	13.3
Renault	13.1	12.3	11.5	12.2
Rover	4.3	3.5	3.5	3.1
Others	14.4	14.2	12.0	12.1
for example				
Daimler-Benz	5.0	5.1	4.4	4.5
BMW	4.0	3.7	3.8	4.2
Volvo	3.7	3.6	2.8	2.2

Note: *Only West European production is included here. Hence VW does not include Skoda of the Czech Republic.

Source: Derived from SMMT data.

The Rover Group (formerly BL) became a subsidiary of British Aerospace in 1988, and Honda took a 20 per cent equity holding in 1990. Rover is the smallest of the full-line producers. Indeed, by 1987 it had a smaller share of the West European car market than Daimler-Benz, the largest of the specialist makers. As a result, Rover's strategy has been to try to cultivate its own specialist image in recognition of its lack of scale, and to move upmarket but still with a wide range including superminis.

The 'Others' category is a fluid group. Up to 1986 both Alfa Romeo and the Spanish SEAT company were included, but both were then bought by larger companies (Fiat and Volkswagen respectively). This category currently includes companies such as BMW, Daimler-Benz and Volvo, Japanese firms such as Nissan, Honda and Toyota, and ultra-specialists such as Rolls-Royce and Porsche. Jaguar was included in this category, after 1984, when it hived off from the then BL Company, but in 1989 it became a Ford subsidiary. The difficulty of being small in the motor industry is shown by the fact that even ultra-specialists like Ferrari and Aston Martin are now owned by large groups (Fiat and Ford respectively), and by the events of 1989–90 when many medium-sized firms linked with big companies to survive.

The transnational nature of the industry   The development of a 'European' motor industry – with a firm's production, and in some instances R and D facilities, located in more than one European country, and vehicle designs being determined increasingly by European, rather than national, tastes and requirements – is characteristic of a transnational enterprise, or in this context, a 'European' one. Hence the establishment of a 'European' motor industry has in some instances been part of the process by which vehicle firms develop what is in effect a transnational mode of operation.

The most highly developed transnational firms owning or controlling facilities engaged in R and D and production outside their country of origin are Ford and GM. However, all the European-owned large full-line producers have transnational facilities, as does the specialist maker Volvo, which has an assembly plant in Belgium and an associate company in Holland. The other European specialist producers and Rover in essence serve their markets from their home base alone, the former being very successful in capturing the top end of the market throughout the world. However due to a combination of a high cost base and new Japanese competition, the German specialists are contemplating investing elsewhere, especially in their largest market, the USA. VW has the largest major manufacturing presence *outside* Europe, mainly in Latin America and China.

The strength of the integrated European operations of Ford and GM should ensure that they play a significant and central role in an integrated world motor industry. The US transnationals are the most 'European' of firms, as they regard Europe not just as one market but also as being suitable for an integrated production operation. This allows the companies to think of optimum-size plants, optimum-size model runs, European-wide model programmes and integrated distribution.

Intra-EC trade   So the six leading full-line producers of cars in the EC are all in some ways transnational or 'European'. They sell their cars on a West

European basis and design them with the wider European customer in view. Although Fiat make cars in Poland and (what was) Yugoslavia, in Western Europe they only produce cars in Italy (but make CVs in Italy, the UK, France and Germany). However, the other large producers all operate in a major way in up to four European countries (Table 6.7). Amongst the specialists only Volvo has car production facilities in the EC outside its home market.

Table 6.7   Production in EC Countries, 1990[1] (000s)

	UK	Germany	Belgium	France	Italy	Spain
Ford	330	594	312	–	–	326
GM	256	1 030	–	–	–	377
PSA	117	–	–	1 958	–	255
Renault	–	–	–	1 317	–	254
VW Group[2]	–	1 930	–	–	–	467
Fiat	–	–	–	–	1 869	–

	Sweden	Netherlands
Volvo	248	121

Notes:
1. Due to the local content GM's Belgium assembly figures are included in its German figures. Similarly VW's, Volvo's and Renault's Belgian figures are included in home totals. In 1992 Sweden was still of course an EFTA country.
2. Skoda's Czech production in 1990 was 187 181 cars.

Source: SMMT.

Until the end of the 1950s, when the moves to free trade began to be effective, high intra-European tariff barriers (Table 6.8) meant that cars were made for distinctive home markets and sold abroad wherever possible. Cars represented national characteristics, be they wealth, the fiscal system, terrain or geography and climate. In the late 1950s and the 1960s tariffs began to fall and the car-makers in the original six members of the EC began to sell on a Community basis. As the essentially national designs were sold more widely, the successful companies obtained economies of scale whilst maintaining their distinctiveness.

In the 1970s and throughout the 1980s the EC expanded and established free trade arrangements with EFTA countries. This effectively created a West European car market. Encouraged by this development the car-makers established integrated production and selling organizations. The car companies not only spread vehicle production into different countries (see Table

Table 6.8   Tariffs on Cars, 1950–90 (% of Customs Value)[1]

	US	Japan	France	Germany	Italy	UK[2]
1950	10	40	35	35	35	33.3
1960	8.5	35–40	30	13–16	31.5–40.5	30.0
1968	5.5	30	0/17.6	0/17.6	0/17.6	17.6
1973	3.0	6.4	0/10.9	0/10.9	0/10.9	10.9
1983	2.8	0	0/10.9	0/10.5	0/10.5	0/10.5
1986	2.6	0	0/10.0	0/10	0/10	0/10
1990	2.5	0	0/10.0	0/10	0/10	0/10

Notes:
1. The Community countries had zero tariffs on intra-EC trade but a common external tariff against others. Since the early 1980s there have been no tariffs between the EC and EFTA on car imports.
2. UK had zero tariff on EFTA imports (e.g. from Sweden).

Source: Deptartment of Trade and Industry; Toyota Motor Company.

6.7) but established component plants in yet more locations, for example Ford in France. To obtain the maximum share of the West European market the car-makers had to cater for a wider European customer. So although national characteristics are still evident in the products of the European-owned producers (Fiat's bias to small cheaper cars; VW's focus on light medium, relatively expensive, family cars), and although these firms are strongest in the *segment* of the European market which reflects their position in the home market, there is nonetheless a great convergence of vehicle attributes. Cars are now mainly designed for a European market. In this way the EC market has forced the mass producers to make a full line of vehicle types; otherwise they would have been excluded from whole segments of their new 'home' market, which would have lowered their market share and made it impossible for them to compete in sales volume and price.

As a result of the break-out from domestic markets in the 1950s and 1960s, and the integrated activities of the 1970s and 1980s, the former due to lower trading barriers (Table 6.8) and the latter to firms availing themselves of structural changes made possible by the creation of a tariff-free enlarged market, trade in cars grew rapidly within the EC as presently constituted from under 1 million cars in 1960 to almost 6 million in 1990 (output increased by 2.7 times). This trend will be reinforced further by the post-1992 emergence of more attributes of a single market.

In 1985 no less than 60 per cent of EC car exports were to other Community countries, and in 1991 it was 65 per cent. Hence, the export perform-

ance of the European-based car firms was largely dependent on regional
sales, with Renault, VW and Fiat, as well as the US transnationals, supplying third-country markets from local plants or other non-European facilities.
Many of the sales to the 'rest of the world' are of specialist cars such as
Mercedes, BMW and Jaguar: here Europe has a comparative advantage,
especially where 'image' is concerned. However, new Japanese products
such as Toyota's Lexus marque and Nissan's Infinniti range indicate that in
the 1990s the EC producers will meet sharper competition in these specialist
sectors.

Intra-company activities   The essential feature of transnational operations
is intra-company trade. This occurs where one subsidiary of a company sells
components or complete cars to another. In the case of cars they are sold
through the 'home' firm's distribution network. This gives rise to 'tied
importing'.

In the mid-1980s some 40 per cent of UK imports, 25 per cent of French
and 30 per cent of German consisted of intra-company trade due to the
location policy and integrated approach to manufacture and sales of the US
and European vehicle companies. French tied imports stem from the activities
of PSA and Renault, whereas the UK and German figures mainly stem from
the US firms. In addition VW contributes to this activity via its SEAT and
Skoda subsidiaries. In the UK the Ford (Table 6.9), and GM balance of
payments figures in the 1980s reflected increased tied importing and reduced
vehicle exports, a trend that is being reversed in the 1990s.

Table 6.9   UK Motor Industry's Balance of Payments (£ million)

	1978	1979	1980	1981	1982	1988	1989	1990	1991
Ford	+£601	+£761	+£57	–£164	–£263	–£1 110 (est.)	–£1 400 (est.)	–£1 297	–£214
All motor industry	+£773	–£287	+£593	+£469	–£973	–£6 100	–£6 600	–£4 600	–£1 000

Source: SMMT; Ford Motor Company.

Table 6.9 shows that in the 1980s Ford's negative balance accounted for
over one-fifth of the UK's total adverse balance in motor products. If to this
is added the impact of Vauxhall, which had a deficit of £850 million in 1986,
and Peugeot, then intra-trade in the 1980s often accounted for about half the
total deficit on UK motor products trade. As well as 'tied imports' the higher
'foreign' content of each car affects the balance of payments. So whilst a

Rover mini is 98 per cent UK by value most Rovers are now 60–80 per cent, Vauxhalls are about 63 per cent, and UK-made Fords 75 per cent. On the other hand, GM's German Opel cars have 85 per cent German content.

In traditional vehicle-making centres where car firms have usually made a full range of vehicles, and where each car was almost 100 per cent locally made, the emergence of tied imports and the reduced local content of home production, produced controversy. Industrial and political opposition have been encountered as tied imports and imported components were seen as alternatives to increased domestic output, and a cause of reduced employment. If one country amongst a number receives a disproportionate number of tied imports, and much of its vehicle output is made by assembling components imported from elsewhere, such views may not seem unreasonable. However, to obtain US or Japanese-type efficiency requires specialization and integration as well as internal improvements. In Europe this means intra-European trade, and a reduction in the national content of cars as items are bought abroad.

6.4.2 *Commercial vehicles*

The EC is the third largest market for CVs in the world, but the biggest for heavy vehicles. The sector is divided between car-derived vans and micro vans up to 1.8 tonnes gross weight, medium vans of 1.8 to 3.5 tonnes, and trucks above 3.5 tonnes. The last category is subdivided into light, medium and heavy trucks ranging up to 40 tonnes (38 tonnes in the UK and Ireland) for international haulage in the EC. In some EC countries even heavier trucks can be used on internal duties. In addition there is a large bus and coach sector with its allied specialized bodybuilders, supplying a considerable market in the EC for road public transport. To a degree the heavy truck and bus sectors have a dedicated component sector, including complete diesel engines, axles, brakes and transmissions.

In 1956 there were 72 major truck makers in the EC but by 1992 only six major groups remained, accounting for 95 per cent of the market. Thus the CV sector is now more concentrated than the car sector. The market leaders are Daimler-Benz with 34 per cent of the market for trucks over 3.5 tonnes, Volvo-Renault (20 per cent) and Iveco (Fiat) (18 per cent). These are followed by three medium-sized firms, MAN, Scania and Daf-Leyland, each with 6–11 per cent of the EC–EFTA market. A few small firms such as ERF, Dennis and Ginaf remain. The truck customers want access to products that deliver 'tonne kilometres' efficiently. From the 1970s the larger producers demonstrated their capability to meet this need at minimum cost, thereby putting pressure on smaller firms, and even the medium-sized firms found it difficult to compete. The main rivals to the European producers are the four large Japanese producers: Toyota-Hino, Isuzu, Mitsubishi and Nissan Diesel.

Toyota-Hino has small and simple assembly operations in Ireland and Portugal, but the efficiency and strength of local producers together with the highly competitive conditions and marginal profits in the 1980s forced the Japanese to pause in determining whether or not to fully enter the EC market with heavy products. If the EC motor industry has a comparative advantage, it is in the heavy truck and bus sector, an area where the Japanese do not have a large home market.

The minimum scale for cab and powertrain production, as well as R and D, is still beyond the scale of operations of even the largest EC firms, so the industry in Europe is not in long-run equilibrium. The need to meet stricter environmental regulations aimed at CVs in the 1990s will put further pressure on firms' resources, which could result in further alliances and mergers.

6.4.3   Components

Almost 50 per cent of the value of a vehicle consists of bought-in components, materials and services. Of this about 80 per cent is identifiable components such as brakes, electronic equipment, metal forgings and castings. So about 40 per cent of the value of a vehicle is accounted for by the products of the material and component sector. Of course, many components are made by the vehicle firms themselves, often by free-standing subsidiaries such as Fiat's foundry or electronic companies. The component firms supply both the original equipment (OE) market and the large replacement market, with the former directed at the 15 million new vehicles made each year in Western Europe and the latter at the 165 million cars, trucks and buses in use.

In 1991 EC component production was 88 billion ECUs, of which 25 per cent was accounted for by the replacement market. Employment in the sector was one million, or 2.4 per cent of total EC industrial employment. Germany, France, Italy, Spain and the UK account for over 90 per cent of total employment and production. In fact, as befits its dominance of vehicle production, Germany accounts for 43 per cent of EC production by gross value. The percentages for France, Italy, Spain and the UK are 22, 14, 10 and 9 respectively. The figure for the UK reflects the relative decline of its motor industry during the last 30 years, the high foreign content of many UK vehicles, and the particular inefficiencies of the UK component industry in the 1970s and 1980s. In terms of delivery times, product price, quality, service back-up and new product development the UK fell behind its main rivals. Only in the 1990s are these trends being reversed significantly.

An individual car has about 20 000 separate items of 2 000 separate types. This, plus the tendency of vehicle firms to buy from national suppliers, has led to a fragmented industry: there are about 4 000 major independent component and material suppliers in the EC. Of these 1 200 are in Italy, 700 in Germany, 500 each in Spain and France, and 400 in the UK. The remaining 700 are in the other EC countries. There are only 150 suppliers employing more than 1 000 people but they account for 50 per cent of total EC employment in the sector.

The sector is relatively concentrated in Germany, France and the UK but very fragmented in Spain and Italy. As a result, of the top 20 component suppliers, excluding firms producing materials such as sheet steel, seven are German, six are British and three are French. Of the remainder, one is Italian and three are American owned. The largest firms are Bosch (Germany), which dominates the world markets in many areas of electronics componentry, Valeo of France and Fiat's Magnetti Marelli of Italy. However, the UK firms, GKN, Lucas, BBA, T and N, Pilkington and BTR are genuine 'EC-wide' firms and indeed have a global presence.

Vehicle component purchasing in the EC is still nationally focused. Whereas over 50 per cent by value of vehicles are exported, if often only to elsewhere in the EC, the value for components is less than 10 per cent. Mercedes buys 92 per cent of its components locally, VW 81 per cent and Fiat 87 per cent (Boston Consulting Group, 1991). The 'open frontier' of the single market post-1992 and the competitive shake-out in a components industry which is too fragmented will serve to reduce this. On the other hand pressures for 'Just-In-Time' (JIT) delivery may be a counterbalance, although excellent logistics and communications in the EC should allow JIT to coexist with cross-border supplies.

European vehicle firms tend to be more vertically integrated than the Japanese. The EC car firms account for 56 per cent of value-added (10 per cent from component firms they control) compared with 30–40 per cent in Japan. The US car companies account for 55–65 per cent of value-added. This means that the new Japanese car plants could add significant business to the EC component sector. Together, in the mid-1990s, Toyota, Honda, Nissan and IBC in the UK will buy around £3 billion of EC components, material and services a year, of which two-thirds will be from the UK.

Japanese motor vehicle firms tend to have far fewer suppliers than their EC counterparts. Whereas the latter have between 800 and 2 000 direct suppliers, the Japanese have about 200 each. This is achieved by a system of 'tiers' in which the first-tier supplier deals with the second and third tier as a major contractor. This may be the trend in the EC. Already between 1980 and 1990 the average number of suppliers per vehicle firm has fallen from 1 800 to 800 and this will go further; it will cause a shake-out in the sector.

Of the top 1 200 suppliers in EC countries some 35 per cent were foreign owned in 1990. The USA accounts for 30 per cent of foreign ownership, and Germany and the UK account for about 20 per cent each. The high proportion of German-owned components firms in Spain, for instance, followed the investment there by VW, Opel (GM), and Ford. The Japanese are establishing some component production in the UK but it is likely that this will be limited: Japanese vehicle firms have indicated that they will seek to buy from local suppliers and joint ventures, and only if they are unable to obtain products locally will they encourage Japanese firms into the EC market. This is different to the US, where almost 1 000 Japanese component firms have established themselves, but the greater relative efficiency of the EC component sector could preclude this being repeated in Europe.

Of Japanese component investment in the EC, over 40 per cent is in the UK. This is because of the concentration of Japanese vehicle firms, low labour cost, English language, good industrial relations and positive official attitudes. Indeed partly because of inward investment from the USA, EC and Japan, Wales has become a major centre for automotive suppliers, with over 150 establishments.

6.5   Behaviour

6.5.1   Pricing

In the 1950s and 1960s car firms still tended to regard export sales in the EC and Western Europe as precisely that, and not as sales to a unified regional market. As a result firms often used their strength in the home market to charge lower ex-works prices abroad. However, because of tariffs and a policy of not provoking the national champion into cut-throat retaliation, retail prices were normally higher than for domestic products. Furthermore, imports tended to be aimed at sectors where the national champion was absent, or already weak, and not central to such a firm's prosperity. The strategy was based upon a slow build-up of sales, in order to avoid domestic retaliation, and maintaining and enlarging the sales network. A strong network was essential if competitive pricing policies were to be introduced with any hope that they would have an impact on sales volume.

In the 1970s the construction of such sales networks, especially by the US transnationals, the integration of markets, the production of a full range of vehicles made by the major producers and the necessity to maintain volumes to keep facilities occupied and unit costs controlled, changed competitive strategies. Prices became more closely aligned in more aggressive competition with those of the national champion. So whilst specialists like Daimler-Benz and BMW charged higher prices abroad than at home because of skilful overseas marketing aimed at creating a differentiated image which bore a price premium, the volume makers used their extra marketing strength and full and modern product ranges to add price competition to various non-price measures, to compete head on with the national champion. As the European market in the 1970s became more integrated, European pricing became more homogeneous. This tended to reduce the opportunities for discriminatory pricing between home and foreign markets since the national champion found it prudent to lower its internal price as imports became more aggressive and competitive.

Differential pricing has, however, not disappeared from the Community car market. Various factors such as different levels of sales tax in the Community (for example 15 per cent in West Germany, but up to 197 per cent in Denmark), price controls in some markets (e.g. Belgium), differences in specifications and variations in consumer preferences, and different price discounts, produce the conditions for price discrimination by car-makers provided they can separate their markets. This they are able to do partly through consumer ignorance of price comparisons for similar cars across countries, but mainly through the selective distribution systems. In this way the car-makers determine who can sell their cars, thereby restricting entry to the new car retail sector. This prevents independent retailers buying cars in a cheap market and selling them in a dear one, undercutting the price in the official network. As consumer ignorance of price differentials was reduced in the post-1979 period due to media publicity, the non-homogeneity of car prices in the EC became a contentious issue. The ability to charge differential prices is shown in Table 6.10.

Table 6. 10   Comparative Car Pre-tax Prices in the EC

	UK	GER	F	I	NL	B	L	IRL	DK	SP
1975	100	97.8	101.3	103.4	93.4	90.2	91.3	93.1	86.4	–
1980	100	80.7	80.3	87.0	74.1	76.7	73.7	82.0	64.7	–
1981	100	72.0	71.7	–	65.6	65.2	64.5	83.3	53.3	–
1982	100	75.1	72.4	77.2	71.9	61.4	62.8	93.3	55.0	–
1983	100	83.0	81.0	87.0	–	72.0	–	–	–	–
1984	100	85.0	88.0	93.0	–	77.0	–	–	–	–
1986	100	85.5	85.5	95.2	82.0	80.0	82.0	100	66.0	–
1989	100	85.0	82.0	92.0	81.0	76.0	79.0	106	62.0	93
1990	100	86.0	79.0	–	–	75.0	–	–	60.0	–

Source: Bureau Européen des Unions de Consommateurs.

The position in 1975 shows the 'normal' position, where car companies charge lower prices in markets in which there is no indigenous motor industry. In these markets there is no particular 'goodwill' shown towards any particular maker, as there would be in its home market. So all car-makers charge lower ex-works prices in Belgium and Denmark than at home. By 1980 the UK fell out of line, for whereas the relationship between prices in West Germany, France and Italy on the one hand and Belgium on the other did not greatly change compared with 1975, car prices in the UK rose in relative terms. This was due to a disproportionately high inflation rate, compounded by an appreciation of sterling. The strength of Ford in the UK market and the wish by the Europeans to make profits in the UK meant that importers did not reduce UK prices to a level which threatened the existence of all UK car-makers. By the mid-1980s the differentials had fallen, to widen again in the strong markets of 1989–90.

6.5.2 Investment

Changing patterns   During the 1960s and 1970s the move to free trade was accompanied by a preference to invest at home by the European-owned car firms. As a general rule no firm was interested in building new manufacturing capacity outside the home country except to overcome trade barriers. The exception to this was investment in Belgium, where major transnational investments amounted to over £2.5 billion (1990 prices) in products and plant. The country was attractive because of its strategic location, good communications, easy availability of labour and low wages. The Belgian government's policy was to exploit these advantages and to provide employment in depressed areas. Tax and other incentives were offered in competitive bidding against other countries to attract the motor industry to Belgium, especially US investment.

Without intra-EC free trade, Belgium could not have attracted foreign investment on anything like this scale. Ford exported 96 per cent of output and VW 85 per cent as the national market was small, yet highly competitive. So Belgium became a centre of the 'European' motor industry. The country attracted a volume of investment that would not have been possible if Belgian government policy had been to erect trade barriers and require firms to cater for the local, but small, market. The development of car-making in Belgium was very different to that in say Denmark or Ireland, where small assembly facilities had been geared to meeting small local needs.

In the 1980s investment by European car-makers moved away from being made on a nation-state basis, to being part of an integrated, rationalized European organization. This process has now developed to the stage where investment in Europe as a whole has to be justified on a global basis. This reflects the gathering pace of the US, and now Japanese, transnationals' strategy of worldwide rationalization and integration of production in optimum-size plants, servicing a world network of output and sales. Even so, the 'worldwide' sourcing of components means just that, and is not a euphemism for the wholesale shifting of production to low-wage countries.

Of the European-owned car firms VW, Renault and Fiat have invested overseas, but only VW is really a world producer. VW uses Brazil and

Mexico to make specific types of vehicle, Mexico to supply engines and transmissions to Europe, and Nissan in Japan to build cars for the Far East. So far none of the overseas investments by the European transnationals have been very profitable, and in general the efforts of various national producers to become multinationals on US lines have been a cash drain rather than a source of strength. The withdrawal of VW and Renault from US car-making confirms this. The low profitability is not unconnected with the fact that the overseas plants of European car-makers are now located in underdeveloped countries. In contrast the US transnationals have a major presence in the developed countries of the world. It is the latter that provide the largest and most prosperous car markets.

Japanese investment in Europe   Historically, the Japanese car-makers have not been truly transnational, although new investment in North America and Europe in the 1980s and 1990s is changing this pattern. The Japanese motor industry developed during the period of a general freeing of world trade under GATT, so they have been able to grow via direct exports to the world in a way that was not open to the US and European firms during their formative and growth years. In order to reduce their exposure should free trade be threatened, the Japanese first responded to requests by countries who were experiencing pressure on their balance of payments and their indigenous car industries by voluntary export restraints (VER). Then in the 1980s they turned to direct investment overseas. This is a new departure for the Japanese. So far, compared with their American developments, Japanese investment in Western Europe has been limited. However, there are clear indications that this state of affairs is altering. By the year 2000, Japanese companies could be producing around 1.7 million cars and 250 000, mainly light, commercial vehicles in Western Europe. This trend is being spearheaded by Nissan. In 1980 it bought 35.8 per cent of the equity in Motor Iberica, the Spanish commercial vehicle and tractor maker, and Nissan's first venture into European car-making was a joint venture with Alfa Romeo in Italy. This was announced in 1980, but the vehicle was not a success and by 1987 production had ceased. It was Nissan's developments in the UK which were the forerunner of things to come.

In 1981 Nissan reached an agreement with the British government to embark on a feasibility study for the manufacture of 200 000 cars a year plus an engine plant. In 1988 this was expanded to include the production of a second car with planned output in 1992–93 growing to *at least* 200 000 units a year. In 1992 the target was raised to 300 000 by 1994. The local EC content of these vehicles accounted for 80 per cent of the ex-works price, having reached 70 per cent in 1988. In 1988 Nissan announced that a design and development centre would be established in the UK to develop vehicles for European tastes. Hence, Nissan was in a rudimentary way beginning to duplicate what Ford and GM had established in Europe. By the late 1990s Nissan could be making 500 000 vehicles in the UK, reflecting an investment of over £1 billion.

In addition, in 1992 Honda opened a car assembly plant alongside its engine plant in Swindon. This followed a series of links established with the Rover Group. Although the stated annual capacity of the Honda car plant is 100 000, an economic level of production for an assembly plant would be 200 000 vehicles a year. It is likely that Honda will achieve this some time in the 1990s.

As well as these developments the smaller Japanese vehicle firm Suzuki also operates in Europe. In Spain it has a 17 per cent shareholding in Land Rover Santana, a Rover Group associate. Santana's main activity has been the assembly and part-manufacture of Land Rovers, but an increasing part of its business is the assembly of Suzuki's light four-wheel-drive vehicles. General Motors owns 4.9 per cent of Suzuki's equity and 40 per cent of Isuzu, which makes a full range of commercial vehicles. In turn Isuzu owns 3.5 per cent of Suzuki. All three of these firms are involved with IBC Vehicles, the joint venture established in 1987 by GM (60 per cent) and Isuzu (40 per cent) to take over GM's Bedford van operations in the UK. Although IBC seems to represent in effect a family of GM-related firms, it is under Japanese managerial control. In the early 1990s, Suzuki established a plant in Hungary, and a joint venture with VW in Spain.

The most powerful of the Japanese vehicle firms, Toyota, is joining Nissan and Honda in the UK. In 1989 its only European facilities were a small assembly plant in Portugal making 5 000 vehicles a year, and a tiny operation in Ireland where Toyota's Hino associate made trucks in a joint venture with local capital. However, to become a global company with over 10 per cent of world car sales and to put itself in a position to challenge the US giants, Toyota had to establish an integrated manufacturing facility in Europe making powertrain as well as assembling vehicles, hence its decision to invest in the UK. The initial capacity of the plant, which opened in 1992, is 250 000 vehicles a year to be achieved by 1997, but this should increase to over 400 000 by the turn of the century.

Mitsubishi is building a 200 000 units a year car plant with Volvo in Holland, and Mazda is likely to establish car and commercial vehicle assembly and manufacturing plants. This will add to the number of European-based producers and will intensify competition. If the Japanese firms increase their European market share from the 10 per cent they had in the early 1990s to the 30 per cent plus they now have in the US, then Japanese investment will be accompanied by serious, if not terminal, pressure on some of the existing producers. The result would be a massive restructuring of the present European motor industry. This would include mergers, as well as more joint ventures through cooperation and collaboration. To give Europe a breathing space an 'Accord' negotiated between the EC and Japan in 1991, and lasting until 1999, will constrain Japanese car and light CV imports to their 1989 level of 1.23 million. All sales increases will come from transplant production. After 1999 the Europeans may have to face a truly free market where Japanese competition is concerned. This assumes that the political and industrial vested interests in the EC do not obtain further protection. The Japanese industry has been strong enough to make the huge expenditures required to establish facilities in Europe, and to produce a steady flow of new models, perhaps with five-year life cycles, although this may not be so in the future. The Europeans with the seven-year-plus product cycles needed to amortize investment would face intense pressure from such 'fresh' model introductions. The US companies via their financial links with Isuzu, Suzuki, Mazda and Mitsubishi, and joint ventures with Toyota and Nissan, could derive benefits which at least partly offset the threats to their existing European facilities. The European-owned firms would be much more vulnerable given that they have much less developed global organizations to call upon, and given their dependence on the West European market for most of their financial well-being. Initially the full line producers would be most affected, but as the Japanese move further and further upmarket even the specialists could feel the pressure.

In total, Japanese investment in Europe exceeds £3 billion in 1992. This compares with VW's £10 billion five-year investment programme (1992–96), an amount equalled by Mercedes Benz and exceeded by Fiat (£13 billion).

6.5.3   R and D

The European-owned transnationals conduct the bulk of their R and D in Europe. The large market allows the vehicle-makers to fund research, development, design and engineering, although the vehicle-makers often find it prudent to share such costs in joint ventures. The European operations of the US transnationals are of such a scale that they too undertake most of their own R and D, design and engineering, but there is now a world dimension to such activities. However, such is the expertise of Ford and GM's European operations, especially in the quality of their human resources, that not only are their European subsidiaries self-sufficient in R and D, design and engineering, they are also a major source of programmes that have worldwide applications. In future car firms may divide their investment between 'centres of excellence'. This might mean Europe concentrating on certain sizes of car and types of components, with other areas of the world, say the USA and Japan, being given responsibility for others.

6.6   Employment

In the EC the fall in employment in the industry after 1979 was dramatic, particularly in the UK, whose experience was paralleled only in the US. Employment in the UK motor industry fell to under 250 000 in 1992, compared with 520 000 in 1970 and 425 000 in 1979. One-third of the fall in UK employment was caused by plant closures and the matching of capacity and output to demand. The remainder was due to the elimination of over-manning and the switch by Vauxhall and Talbot to largely assembly-only operations. Hence many factors other than transnational integration were instrumental in reducing motor industry employment in the UK. On the continent, Fiat reduced its workforce by 25 per cent between 1979 and 1983, whilst Renault embarked, in 1985, on reducing its workforce by 24 per cent (25 000 people) over a two-year period, with further jobs lost subsequently. In 1983–85 Peugeot reduced its French workforce by 30 000 (20 per cent). In total, between 1979 and 1990 Italy lost 150 000 jobs and France 140 000, and more than 400 000 EC jobs in car making alone disappeared in the period 1980–90, reducing the workforce to 1.2 million. About 200 000 were shaken out in the component sector, reducing employment to one million, and 70 000 in CVs.

By 1992 even Germany was not immune to these pressures. Between 1979 and 1990 total motor industry employment in Germany *rose* by 79 000 to reach almost one million, but to remain competitive the German industry may have to shed 30 per cent of this in the 1990s. Already GM is seeking to reduce its German workforce by 5 per cent a year over the period 1992–96 with the other car-makers announcing employment reductions in 1992 total-ling 50 000. These moves are designed to catch up on productivity increases elsewhere in the EC and to combat Japanese competition.

The main reasons for job reductions in the 1980s was the need to rational-ize the West European motor industry to make it fully competitive with the Japanese. At the same time over-capacity and the resulting price competition made it necessary to reduce the workforce, both by bringing capacity into closer proximity with demand and by eradicating overmanning and other X-inefficiencies. (X-inefficiencies refer to the problems that stem from factors such as poor management, quality, organization, industrial relations and so on, rather than those experienced by firms trying to survive when they are really too small (or big) to compete. That is, they are inefficiencies that stem from sources other than sub-optimum scale.) In addition, the introduction of new production equipment reduced the labour to capital ratio. Any resultant increase in demand for skilled labour was more than offset by the disappear-ance of unskilled jobs.

6.7 Performance

Productive efficiency varies between the countries of the EC, but the greatest differential is between the EC and Japanese motor firms. Within the EC the German motor industry (including Ford and GM) is the most efficient in terms of output per employee, although the other EC motor industries closed the gap in the 1980s. In 1990, with German productivity set at 100, that in the French car industry was 92, Italy was 76 and the UK was 68, improving from 34 in 1980. However the Japanese figure in 1990 was 150.

The 1990s have seen an erosion of the German motor industry's productivity advantage. Indeed UK productivity, following Japanese investment and improved performance by the traditional firms, could match Germany's in the late 1990s. This loss of Germany's productivity advantage, together with a rapid increase in the cost of its inputs (Table 6.11), has led to a fall in German competitiveness.

Table 6.11   Productivity and Unit Labour Costs: Average Annual Percentage Change, 1980–90

	Productivity	Unit labour costs
UK	8.1	0.5
France	5.8	0.4
Spain	5.5	1.5
Japan	5.0	1.3
Italy	3.6	1.4
US	3.3	0.7
Germany	1.9	2.4

Source: Verband der Automobilindustrie e. V. (VDA), Frankfurt.

German unit costs have grown not only because of increased payments, especially social provisions such as insurance, but also because of reduced working hours. The average annual number of hours per worker in Germany is 1 500 compared with 2 200 in Japan, 1 700 in Spain and 1 800 in the UK. The German cost base increased more than productivity and the competitiveness of the market ensured that profitability fell (Table 6.12). By 1991 VW had the highest costs of the EC mass producers and in 1992 BMW announced its intention to build a plant in the USA with cost considerations being a main influence. So whilst the German car industry is still the most productive in the EC, the lower cost base in Spain or the UK can offset this. For instance in 1991 GM cars cost £260 less per unit to make in the UK

Table 6.12   Profits before Interest and Tax (% of Sales)

	1984	1990
UK	1.8	9.0
France	2.1	13.0
Germany	6.0	5.8
Japan	4.0	4.0

Source: Derived from company data.

compared with Germany. Japanese-style productivity and UK input costs will make the UK motor industry highly competitive in the 1990s.

Productivity comparisons within and between companies mainly reflect national factors. A transnational like Ford in 1991 took 28 hours in Germany, 34 hours in Spain and 39 hours in the UK to make a Fiesta car. However, although intra-European differences exist the main differential is with Japan.

By 1990 the average Japanese mass production plants assembling car bodies, painting, and finally assembling cars were twice as efficient as the EC average in terms of labour hours required. Taking account of *all* the manufacturing functions, such as machining engines and transmissions, the productivity difference was around 25 per cent. In 1980 it took 24 hours to assemble a car in Japan, 34 hours in the USA and 41 hours in the EC. In 1990 the figures were 17, 26 and 34 respectively. In 1992 a fully operational Japanese-owned car plant in the UK equalled the performance in Japan. Comparisons of the Japanese profit and productivity performance suggests that the competitive gains were being used to develop an increasing flow of new models, to price competitively and to embark on overseas investment rather than increase unit profits. However, Japanese margins will have to increase.

Other performance indicators show the challenge the Japanese pose for the traditional EC producers. In 1990 stock turnover in Japan was four times better than in EC car plants. This reflected a more extensive use of JIT systems, and greater efficiency in the use of manufacturing processes and systems. The Japanese plants in the EC will duplicate much of this efficiency.

The 'dynamic' competition provided by the Japanese is equally challenging. The EC motor industry takes up to five years to develop a new car compared with three years in Japan, and the EC needs 2.9 million engineering hours for development compared with 1.7 million in Japan. So not only do the Japanese use less resources in developing cars which often have more design novelty than new EC models, but they can in principle either replace cars more quickly or cover more market sub-segments. This can result in major non-price competition. Furthermore, although the EC car industry has increased the flow of patents from around 800 a year in 1970 to 1 300 in 1990, the Japanese increase was from 200 to 1 500 a year over this period (Womack *et al.*, 1990). This reflected another dynamic strength: that since the mid-1980s the Japanese have spent more on vehicle R and D that the EC vehicle industry. However, both spend over £4 billion a year, with the German-based industry, including Ford and GM, accounting for over 50 per cent of this figure.

In future EC best practice may be found as much in the UK with its Japanese and US-owned plants as in the German motor industry. To survive in a free market the other EC producers must match this level of perform-ance. Early indications show that this has been recognized, with the French motor industry's productivity improving to close the gap to 10 per cent behind the Japanese car plants in the UK

6.8 EC policy

The motor industry's activities are of interest to many of the EC's director-ates. Social and trade matters are clearly important, as are technological affairs. However it is competition (DG4) and industrial strategy (DG3) where most of the central debate occurs..

The Competition Directorate has been keen to ensure that the Commu-nity's vehicle consumers are not exploited by the industry and seeks to eliminate anti-competitive partitioning of the market unless such behaviour can be shown to be in the public interest. This was the case in 1985 when the industry's selective distribution system was given a block exemption from Article 85 of the Treaty of Rome. As the whole ethos of '1992' has been to create a truly single market and to promote competition, DG4 has been very active in the 1990s in putting the interest of the consumer first. For example it introduced regulations designed to moderate price differentials, given that the car-makers were allowed to maintain their selective distribution system. As long as there are no special reasons for low ex-works prices in certain markets, such as high sales taxes (Denmark) or price control (Belgium) the Commission may intervene where ex-works prices diverge by at least 12 per cent for a year, or 18 per cent at any time. It may even abolish a firm's 'selective' sales network to remove price distortions. The Commission has shown a willingness to interfere in business arrangements which in turn might affect prices and it is maintaining vigilance in monitoring pricing behaviour.

DG4's concern with consumer interests has caused some friction with DG3, which has wanted to see the development of a strong EC motor industry able to compete with the world's best, which in recent years has meant the Japanese. So undermining selective distribution could open up more sales outlets to Japanese firms in the free-for-all that would occur, which would threaten the market shares and viability of the EC producers. The trend is to greater competition, industrial restructuring and free trade but whereas DG3 wants the motor industry to be given time to improve efficiency, and therefore to be restructured to meet competition – hence its support of the EC–Japanese 'Accord' in 1991 – DG4 is prepared to see competition increasing first and market forces dictating any restructuring.

Environmental and transport policy, inasmuch as it affects such areas as vehicle emissions, energy use, noise pollution, vehicle weights and road transport liberalization in the EC, will have profound effects on the R and D costs facing the industry, the investment needed in plant, and competition in the 'user' industries. Factors involved here affect costs of production on the one hand, and demand conditions on the other. The harmonization of safety-related vehicle regulations, as exemplified in the creation of EC-wide Type Approval in 1992 to replace national regimes, reduced costs facing vehicle firms in that they only had to meet one authority's regulations rather than twelve. However it also helped non-EC car firms to penetrate the market.

Some countries – for instance Italy and France – have been more ready than others, such as the UK, to countenance protectionism. In the UK there is no longer a nationally owned motor industry of any size so the vested interest is less. Furthermore, UK domestic policy has sought to maximize Japanese inward investment in order to generate wealth, jobs, and favourable effects on the balance of payments. The EC motor industry has been one of those areas where *dirigiste* and free market ideas have clashed.

6.9   EC's effects on the motor industry

The creation and development of the EC has had important effects on the broad structure of the industry: for example the EC was directly responsible for the emergence of Belgium as a major car producer. In addition the preferential trading arrangements with Spain, before it entered the EC, led to Ford and GM establishing facilities there. Hence, the *de facto* broadening of the Community to include Spain was instrumental in attracting US transnational investment, which integrated Spain's motor industry with that in the rest of Europe. These moves by the US firms then forced the French firms to respond. VW purchased the ailing SEAT from the Spanish government, and started using Spain to make superminis for Europe. In the 1990s Portugal has attracted major investment by Ford and VW in a joint venture.

The EC has also had other effects on the structure of the European motor industry. Initially firms endeavoured to strengthen their operations so as to be able to compete in an increasingly freer 'home' or regional market. This resulted in a tidying-up process whereby domestic mergers occurred. In Germany VW bought NSU and then Daimler-Benz's share in Audi. In the UK, to meet the challenge of large competitors, the British Leyland Corporation was formed out of British Motor Holdings and Leyland Motors Corporation. In France Peugeot grew from being a medium-sized French firm into one of the largest concerns in Europe by buying Citroën and Chrysler's European operations. At the same time small-scale high-cost operations – such as Fiat's German subsidiary, Ford's Dutch car plant and virtually all of Ireland's vehicle assembly industry – were closed. European integration and rationalization had no place for suboptimal facilities. This process meant that the three major EC car-producing countries (France, Germany, Italy) had one (or in the case of France, two) major domestic champions.

Although the emergence of European free trade has increased the integration of the European motor industry the country that has benefited most is Germany. The free trade environment in Europe allowed the dynamic and efficient German motor industry to expand and to take the lead in the West European industry. The two US transnationals used their efficient German operations to spearhead European integration, the German specialists used free trade to dominate the top of the market sectors in Europe, and the German national champion, Volkswagen, more than held its own (see Table 6.1) against the other full line producers. In commercial vehicles VW did well in light and medium vans and Daimler-Benz dominated the heavy truck market not only in Europe but in much of the rest of the world. The German component industry used the growth of its customers to expand, to dominate EC component production, and to provide over 60 of the top 100 firms in Europe.

6.10 Conclusion

The EC is a vital centre of worldwide car production and will remain so for the foreseeable future (Table 6.13). In addition, the Community will be an important part of the transnational worldwide operation. The European 'home' market is vital for the transnational growth of the European-owned companies. A solid home base conducting the bulk of R and D and providing the managerial 'know-how' to conduct diverse operations on an integrated basis is a necessity. An integrated operation spreading costs and overcoming 'absolute cost' barriers allowed a facility like VW's in the USA to survive on a volume of 100 000 units for as long as it did. No domestic newcomer could have survived for so long on such low output figures. Initially, the US transnationals used their US base to support the development of European subsidiaries. Now those operations have become integrated and are largely self-supporting. However, as cars developed for world sale now cost over £1 billion to develop and build, this can best be financed and amortized on the

Table 6.13 Car Production (000s)

	EC	US	Japan
1984	10 349	7 773	7 073
1985	10 804	8 185	7 647
1986	11 398	7 829	7 810
1987	12 086	7 099	7 891
1988	12 624	7 111	8 198
1989	13 321	6 824	9 052
1990	13 238	6 077	9 948
1991	12 796	5 439	9 753
Forecast			
1995	14 700	6 200	10 100
2000	15 500	7 500	10 500

Source: SMMT (1984–91); Centre for Automotive Industry Research, Cardiff Business School (1995, 2000).

basis of world production and sales, so the European owned transnationals and the US transnationals in Europe are looking to a global strategy.

In the 1990s the motor industry in the EC will face the opportunities presented by the single market, but also challenges. The threat of Japanese competition including the transplants, extra competition within the EC itself, the possibility of over-capacity and its consequence, and the challenge of meeting environmental issues, will threaten the existence of all but the most efficient vehicle-makers. As a result those who believe that competition is the only way to establish an EC motor industry capable of meeting the world's best will have to contend with those who believe that an industry as important as the motor industry must be protected against the full blast of world competition until it has increased its efficiency significantly. In many ways the future of the EC motor industry will measure the EC's commitment to genuine free trade.

Even so, the development of a single market in the EC, and the stronger free trade links with the EFTA countries, means that more than ever the motor industry's operating environment will be a 'European' one. The removal of non-tariff barriers, the harmonization of standards, and longer production runs, should produce cost savings in Europe for each car made. However, as the long established policy of cooperation and collaboration designed to reduce unit costs is likely to continue in any event, it might be stretching matters to claim that '1992' is the motivating force. These cost savings are needed just to remain profitable in a highly competitive market. The creation of a single internal market will merely be the latest but not the last episode in the process of changing the operating environment of vehicle firms from the national to the 'European' level, a process in which the motor industry of the EC has long been in the vanguard.

References

Boston Consulting Group (1991), *The Competitive Challenge Facing the European Automotive Components Industry*, London: BCG–PRS.

Pratten, C.F. (1971), *Economies of Scale in Manufacturing Industry*, London: Cambridge University Press.

Silberston, A. (1963), 'Hire Purchase Controls and the Demand for Cars', *Economic Journal*, **73**, 32–53 and 556–8.

Womack, J.P., Jones, D.T. and Roos, D. (1990), *The Machine That Changed the World*, New York: Rowson Associates.

Further reading

Abernathy, W. (1978), *The Productivity Dilemma*, Baltimore: Johns Hopkins University Press.

Banville, E de., Chanaron, J-J. (1990), *Vers un système automobile européen*, Paris: CPE-Economica.

Dunnett, P.J.S. (1980), *The Decline of the British Motor Industry*, London: Croom Helm.

Hawkesworth, R.I. (1981), 'The Rise of Spain's Automobile Industry', *National Westminster Bank Quarterly Review*, February, 37–48.

Jenkins, R.O. (1977), *Dependent Industrialisation in Latin America: the Automobile Industry in Argentina, Chile and Mexico*, London: Praeger.

Maxcy, G. (1981), *The Multinational Motor Industry*, London: Croom Helm.

OECD, (1983), *Long-term Outlook for the World Automobile Industry*, Paris: OECD.

Rhys D.G. (1989), *The Motor Industry in the European Community*, Hertford: IMI.

Roos, D., Altschuler, A., Anderson, M., Jones, D., Roos, D. and Womack, J. (1984), *The Future of the Automobile*, London: Allen & Unwin.

Seidler, E. (1976), *Let's Call It Fiesta*, Cambridge: Patrick Stevens.

Sleigh, P.A.C. (1989), *The European Automotive Components Industry: A Review of Eighty Leading Manufacturers*, London: Economist Intelligence Unit.

Vernon, R. (1979), 'The Product Cycle Hypothesis in a New International Environment', *Oxford Bulletin of Economics and Statistics*, **41**, 255–68.

7 The defence industries*

Nick Hooper and Digby Waller

7.1 Introduction

7.1.1 The importance of the defence industries

The defence industries form an important sector in the European economy by virtue of their size. Other characteristics reinforce this position: they play a significant role in ensuring that the armed services can maintain the security of European nations, and defence industries are often at the forefront of technology. Above all, defence is a political market-place; it involves large expenditures of public money by politicians; and many people hold strong views about the need for defence and the form it should take, not least over nuclear weapons. As a result, economists must adopt an approach which can allow for and build upon the political nature of defence, such as through public choice economics.

The importance of the defence industries does not make them immune to the significant structural changes which have characterized other European industries over the past 20 years, as discussed in other chapters of this book. Indeed, with the ending of the Cold War and expectations of a peace dividend the defence sector faces a period of major restructuring. Fundamental questions are being asked about the nature and source of any threat to the security of Europe which may arise in future, and the role of European nations in the security of other parts of the world (Kirby and Hooper, 1991). This military and strategic assessment will then influence the size and structure of the armed services. The equipment needs of such future military forces will have implications for the future of European defence industries.

Alongside the debate over the meaning of security after the Cold War, there is a growing movement for defence to be taken into the framework of the European Community. Since the inception of the Community, defence has been one area left to national governments. While a common foreign and security policy may be some way off, there are moves towards military collaboration. The growing involvement of the Commission in the European defence industry lags somewhat behind the Europeanization of production brought about by commercial pressures.

*This chapter is based on work funded by the Leverhulme Trust, whose help is gratefully acknowledged. Responsibility for the contents and any errors remains with the authors.

This chapter considers the structure of the European defence industry against the background of the changing security situation. The next section considers the definition of defence industries. This is followed by an analysis of the size of defence production in Europe, and the present structure of defence industries is discussed. The role of international collaboration in defence production is considered through a case study of the EH 101 helicopter and the trend toward the internationalization of production is discussed in the context of the EC and the Single European Market. Finally, the major trends which will influence the future of the European defence industry are considered.

7.1.2 Defining the defence industries

A simple definition of defence industries would comprise suppliers to the armed forces. However, like all communities the services (or their agents, the Ministries of Defence) buy a wide range of items, from cutlery to nuclear submarines. The simple definition would thus encompass almost all of European industry as potential if not actual suppliers.

The scope of defence industries can be narrowed by introducing the concept of *strategic goods*, those items which have a specific military function. Article 223 of the Treaty of Rome essentially embodies this approach when it allows national governments to protect security interests connected with the production of, or trade in, arms, munitions and war materials (Brzoska and Lock, 1992). Table 7.1 lists the products covered by Article 223. This provision does not apply to products not intended primarily for specific military purposes. Although items such as armaments and nuclear submarines are clearly intended primarily for military purposes, the distinction is less clear for other goods, and there is now a third category of *dual use* goods recognized as falling between strategic and non-strategic items. Such dual use goods and technologies may consist of, incorporate or be derived from civilian capabilities which may be used for lethal purposes or to improve overall military capability.

It is more constructive to consider military and civil goods as being on a continuum. The boundary between defence and civil production may be close to the lethal weapons end of the spectrum during peacetime, but may move in time of war to encompass a wider range of goods, perhaps including fuel and food. As well as maintaining defence-specific capabilities, a country can provide industrial support for its armed forces by converting civilian factories to military production as tension increases and conflict threatens.

The categorization of industries as defence will be influenced by the structure of the industry. For example, if nuclear submarines are built by specialist builders there will be a nuclear submarine industry as part of the defence sector. However, if submarines form a small part of the output of

Table 7.1 List of Products under Article 223

Portable and automatic firearms
Artillery and smoke, gas and flamethrowing weapons
Ammunition for the above
Bombs, torpedoes, rockets and guided missiles
Military fire-control equipment
Tanks and specialist fighting vehicles
Toxic or radioactive agents
Powders, explosives and liquid or solid propellants
Warships and other specialist equipment
Aircraft and equipment for military use
Military electronic equipment
Camera equipment specially designed for military use
Other equipment and material – parachutes and parachute fabric; water
    purification plant specially designed for military use; military command
    relay electrical equipment
Specialized parts and items of material of a military nature
Machines, equipment and items exclusively designed for the study, manu-
    facture, testing and control of arms, munitions and apparatus of an exclu-
    sively military nature included in the list.

Source: Brzoska and Lock (1992).

diversified shipbuilding companies such companies may not be included in
some definitions of the defence sector. The issue then arises whether parts of
the industries (or companies) should be included in the defence industry,
with the remaining parts excluded.

Economic theory would suggest that industries may be divided between
strategic and non-strategic using the concept of opportunity cost. Those
industrial capabilities which would be of strategic value are those which the
military are prepared to support by forgoing other expenditure. In other
words, the military may consider some industrial capabilities to be of such
value that they are prepared to give up extra equipment, facilities or manpower to keep that industrial capability in existence (Hooper, 1990).

Here again, difficulties arise in putting this conceptual approach into
practice. Unless faced with the loss of suppliers the military may not have
considered the value to them of industrial capacity. The assessment may
depend on the size of the defence budget – if forces and equipment are
already under pressure from budget constraints then the opportunity cost of
supporting industrial capacity will be high. In times of less stringent financial constraints the opportunity cost at the margin will be lower. There is

also likely to be disagreement if those who want the industrial capacity are not the forces which would bear the cost, for example if the army are asked to give up manpower to keep an aircraft industry.

There is now an issue over the extent to which EC member states need their own national defence industries. In other words, is there now a European defence industrial capability, rather than 12 national capabilities? This issue again raises the question whether member states require the capability to take independent national military action supported by their own national defence industries, or whether future military action will only take place as part of an EC or other multinational force (e.g. the UN) supported by an EC defence industrial base.

Politicians refer to the essential industrial capability necessary to support the military as the *defence industrial base*, usually without specifying exactly what constitutes that capability. Defence economists also recognize the concept of a *military industrial complex*, which applies the idea of pressure groups to the analysis of the interrelationships between the defence industry, the military and the government (MoD). Supporters of this approach suggest that the parties have a common interest in ensuring that defence budgets are maintained and that new high-technology equipment is developed and produced, thus continuing the arms race.

The characteristic which all these definitions have in common is that they refer to both the type of product and the customer. Goods of one type may be defence when supplied to MoD and not when supplied to other customers. In the context of this uncertainty over exactly what comprises defence, this chapter adopts a pragmatic approach to the interpretation of the defence industries of Europe, focusing on the larger companies and those most dependent on defence, while recognizing that from some perspectives other firms might be considered more important to the defence effort.

7.2   The European defence industries

7.2.1   The defence capabilities of EC countries

Defence procurement by EC member states in 1990 totalled 72 400 million ECU, with 87 per cent being accounted for by the four largest spenders, France, the UK, Germany and Italy (Table 7.2). Within this total, some 65 billion, or 90 per cent, is formed by defence equipment, the remainder consisting of infrastructure and operational items.

Even though all member states have armed forces and buy a wide range of defence equipment, not all members of the EC have capabilities to produce all types of defence equipment. All countries rely to a greater or lesser extent on imports of military equipment, particularly from the US.

Table 7.2   EC Defence Procurement, 1990

	Expenditure[1] ECUmn	Share %
France	22 685	31.3
UK	17 660	24.4
Germany	15 960	22.0
Italy	7 065	9.8
Spain	2 710	3.7
Netherlands	2 695	3.7
Belgium	1 155	1.6
Greece	1 090	1.5
Denmark	870	1.2
Portugal	400	0.5
Ireland	95	0.1
Luxembourg	15	0.02
Total[2]	72 400	100.0

Notes:
1. These figures are based on non-personnel expenditure, using NATO definitions. They include equipment, infrastructure and operations. They may be considered an upper estimate.
2. Total of percentages does not equal 100 due to rounding.

Source: Centre for Defence Economics estimates.

The EC member states can be classified into four groups according to their defence industrial capabilities:

- France, Germany, the UK and Italy – prime contractors for all weapon systems and a wide range of subcontract and supplier networks;
- Belgium, Denmark and Netherlands – limited capability in some systems and components;
- Greece, Portugal and Spain – embryonic defence industries, developed to contribute to domestic needs and introduce modern technology;
- Ireland and Luxembourg – small defence production limited to subcontract and supply.

The capabilities of the major European defence companies are shown in Table 7.3. Ireland and Luxembourg have very little in the way of defence industries, and no companies with the capability to produce complete systems. At the same time, France, Germany, Italy and the UK account for over 40 per cent of the companies with a capability in complete systems. The degree of sophistication represented by these numbers varies, however. For example, one-third of the companies which can produce complete systems are in ordnance, where the demands are perhaps less than those in other areas such as aerospace, submarines or tanks.

Table 7.3   West European Defence Industries: Complete Systems

	Bel.	Den.	Fra.	FRG	Gre.	Ita.	Net.	Por.	Spa.	UK	Total
Land equipment											
Tanks	–	–	2	3	–	2	–	–	2	2	11
Other vehicles	2	–	10	10	2	4	2	2	3	11	46
Ordnance	4	1	27	18	3	19	4	5	17	29	127
C3	2	2	19	10	1	18	1	2	5	17	77
Sea											
Shipbuilding	1	–	3	6	2	2	3	–	1	4	22
Submarines	–	1	1	3	–	2	1	–	–	3	11
Torpedoes	–	–	3	1	–	1	–	–	–	2	7
Other warships	–	–	6	3	–	2	2	–	1	4	18
Air											
Aircraft	1	–	7	5	–	5	1	–	1	11	31
Helicopters	–	–	1	1	–	2	1	–	1	3	9
Weapons	–	–	7	4	–	4	–	–	–	4	19
Missiles	–	–	2	–	–	1	–	–	–	1	4
Totals	10	4	88	64	8	62	15	9	31	91	382

Notes: The table shows the number of firms with a capability in each type of defence equipment. Subsidiaries and affiliates of major companies are counted separately where appropriate.

A company which makes more than one type of equipment (e.g. tanks and other vehicles) will be included in each of the appropriate entries; a company which makes more than one product of the same type is only counted once (e.g. two models of helicopter from one company count as one entry).

There are no data for Ireland or Luxembourg.

Shipbuilding and submarines include repair.

Source: Derived from Noyes and De Renzo (1990).

Component and subsystem suppliers are again concentrated in the four major countries, which account for over 80 per cent of the total with the UK alone having one-third. Suppliers to the aircraft industry are the most important single group. There has been a trend for prime contractors to see them-

selves as systems integrators, relying on specialist suppliers of components
and subsystems to provide the equipment to be integrated with the platform
to produce a complete weapons system. The top ten companies are shown in
Table 7.4

Table 7.4   The Largest European Defence Producers, 1989

Rank	Company	Country	Industry[1]	Arms sales US$mn	Total sales US$mn	Defence share %
1.	British Aerospace	UK	Ac El Mi SA	6 300	14 898	42
2.	Thomson SA	France	El Mi	4 320	12 027	36
3.	Daimler-Benz	Germany	Ac Eng Mv El Sh	4 260	40 634	10
4.	Direction des Constructions Navales	France	Sh	3 630	3 630	100
5.	GEC	UK	El	2 880	14 408	20
6.	IRI	Italy	Ac Eng El Sh	2 230	41 285	5
7.	Dassault-Breguet	France	Ac	2 200	3 059	46
8.	Aérospatiale	France	Ac Mi	2 190	4 969	44
9.	CEA Industrie	France	Other	1 820	5 254	35
10.	Lucas Industries	UK	Ac	1 640	3 655	45

Note: 1.   The industry code is as follows. Ac: aircraft; El: electronics; Eng: engines; Mi:
missiles; Mv: military vehicles; SA: small arms; Sh: ships.

Source: Anthony *et al.* (1990).

European defence companies are amongst the largest in the world, as
shown by their ranking in the world top 100 (Table 7.5), but even the largest
does not equal the biggest US companies in size. For example BAe is the
largest European defence company, with 1989 arms sales of US$6 300
million, but ranks only fourth in the world after McDonnell Douglas (US;
1989 arms sales US$8 500 million), General Dynamics (US; 1989 arms
sales US$8 400 million) and Lockheed (US; 1989 arms sales US$7 350
million). The next largest European company ranks twelfth (Thomson SA of
France; 1989 arms sales US$4 320 million) (SIPRI, 1991). Such compari-
sons must be approached with caution as the situation changes with each
takeover or merger of a company and each closure of a plant.

Table 7.5   European Companies in the Top 100 World Arms-producing Companies

	Rank in world 100					Number of companies 1989
	1–20	21–40	41–60	61–80	81–100	
UK	2	1	2	5	4	14
France	2	3	2		2	9
Germany	1		1	3	2	7
Italy		3				3
Spain		1				1
Netherlands			1			1
Totals	5	8	6	8	8	35

Source: Wulf, H., 'Arms Production', *SIPRI Yearbook*, 1991.

The share of output accounted for by defence varies between countries, as indicated in Table 7.6. In 1989 average dependence was greatest in the UK at 10.2 per cent, just ahead of France at 9.7 per cent. German companies are much less dependent (4.5 per cent). These averages hide a wide range of dependencies at the level of individual businesses, from almost 100 per cent for companies such as Vickers Shipbuilding and Engineering in the UK to 10 per cent for Daimler-Benz in Germany. Table 7.4 includes estimates for the top ten defence companies. The figures also depend on the industrial unit under consideration, as individual firms will typically be more defence in-tensive than the group or conglomerate to which they belong.

Table 7.6   Defence Dependency, 1988–89

	Number of companies No.	Arms sales 1989 $bn	Arms share of total sales (%)	
			1988	1989
UK	14	17.2	10.6	10.2
France	9	16.3	9.3	9.7
Germany	7	7.6	5.1	4.5

Notes: Based on world's largest 100 arms producers. Seventy out of the 100 largest defence companies in Western Europe operate from three countries – the UK, Germany and France – accounting for almost 80% of (domestic plus export) arms sales of the European top 100.

Source: Wulf, H., 'Arms Production', *SIPRI Yearbook*, 1991.

7.2.2   Some industrial characteristics

Traditionally, the defence industries were characterized by large, uncompetitive state-owned enterprises working closely with their customers, the defence ministry and armed forces, in a military-industrial complex. In such an environment, each party would pursue its own objective: industry seeking new and more costly technology to maintain contracts and profits; the defence ministry pursuing bureaucratic objectives such as prestige, security and increased numbers of jobs through complex and growing procurement decisions; and the armed services enhancing their position by demanding the newest and most sophisticated equipment. By pursuing their own objectives each reinforces the pressure for new technology and ever higher budgets, reinforcing the spiralling arms race.

The presence of one dominant buyer for defence goods, coupled with the need (for security reasons) to specify equipment at the forefront of technology and better than that possessed by potential adversaries, poses a severe problem for ensuring efficient procurement. Only in the US has demand been on a level capable of supporting competing development projects, under which rival aircraft, for example, can be developed and prototypes produced for assessment in flight. Typically in other countries one system has been chosen and a competition held at the design stage, if at all. As a result, critics have described the relationship between procurement executives and supplying companies as cosy (Hartley, 1991), rather than the arm's-length buyer–seller relationship of a competitive market. This has been seen as a particular problem in the UK, while other nations seem less disturbed by the prospect of collusion between customer and supplier.

The trend towards monopoly in defence production is driven by rising costs and the importance of scale effects. The increase in costs of successive generations of equipment is indicated in Table 7.7, with, for example, a Type 22 frigate costing four times as much as a Leander Class, which it replaced. Allowance must be made, however, for improvement in the performance of modern equipment. The high proportion of R and D in total costs and typical scale effects of the order of 10 per cent (Hartley, 1991) imply significant cost savings from single long production runs of one model. Even where competition exists for a new piece of equipment, cost pressures dictate that only one supplier will be chosen. It is by no means certain that the losers will remain in the defence business to provide competition for the next generation, which might not reach production for 20 years.

Those countries with state-owned or controlled defence industries may not be any more successful at maintaining essential capabilities than those which rely on private companies. Large, inefficient state-owned industries with inadequate cost control may undermine both the military and industrial capability of a country by absorbing an increasing share of the defence

Table 7.7 Comparative Programme Costs

Trident programme	4 times	Polaris
Type 22 Frigate	4 times	Leander frigate
Harrier GR1	3.75 times	Hunter
Sea Wolf missile	3.25 times	Sea Cat missile
Challenger 1 tank	2.25 times	Chieftain tank

Note: Comparisons are based on approximate programme costs.

Source: Cmnd 1559 (1991); HCP 369 (1991).

budget for state of the art projects characterized by delays and cost overruns. In such cases not only would the industrial capability fail to keep up with leading-edge technology, but the military would suffer directly in terms of the quantity and quality of equipment it received.

While the defence market is regulated in all member states of the EC, the form and extent of regulation varies considerably. Large, state-owned and controlled producers remain important in countries such as France while denationaliztion and contestability have perhaps progressed furthest in the UK. It is, however, the influence of procurement policy and practice and the attitude toward defence firms rather than ownership itself which has the biggest regulatory impact on defence industries. Thus Thomson, Aérospatiale and Matra have been declared 'national champions' by the French Ministry of Defence (Serfati, 1992), and receive financial and technological support from the state as part of a policy to ensure that a French (or French-led European) capability is maintained in selected industries, including aerospace and electronics. In Germany, obstacles to the creation of Deutsche Aerospace (DASA) were removed by the Minister of Economics (Brzoska and Lock, 1992). In both these cases the intent was to create national organizations on a scale which ensured their participation in European and global markets, at least as cooperative partners.

7.2.3 The defence industries in individual countries
Since the 1960s the French defence market has been dominated by the government's wish to develop national arms production, both for security reasons and as part of national industrial policy (Serfati, 1992). This effort was led by the Délégation Générale pour l'Armement (DGA), the government agency with responsibility for military R and D and production. The promotion of defence industries relied on both domestic and export sales, particularly associated with French colonial interests. As a result, the down-

turn in the defence market following the end of the Cold War required a change of direction for which the industry was ill prepared.

Despite this, the French arms producers, again led by the government, have reacted swiftly. There has been a rapid restructuring, including the privatization of parts of the DGA empire, with a view to establishing a strong position in the embryonic European market. At the same time, French companies have been active in taking over or forming alliances with companies in other EC states, and have acquired a dominant position in the Belgian arms industry through a series of takeovers. Discussions have even extended to collaboration with the UK on the nuclear programme, previously the heart of French independence.

The postwar development of arms production in Germany followed a different pattern, set by political and public sentiment in the aftermath of the war. With little public discussion of the issue, companies were left to develop arms production, most choosing to play down the importance of arms and to diversify their activities to include a large proportion of civil production. The exception was Bavaria, where arms production was used to turn an agrarian region into a high-tech manufacturing area (Brzoska and Lock, 1992). Arms production became a political issue with the dominance of Daimler-Benz towards the end of the 1980s. The federal government effectively accepted the arguments that survival of the defence industry required the creation of a European-scale operation when it removed the obstacles to the creation of DASA with the takeover of Messerschmitt-Bölkow-Blohm (MBB) by Daimler-Benz.

Thus in France the state acted over a long period to create a defence industry, and in Germany a passive federal state and an active *Land* (Bavaria) allowed the development of the industry. As a result, both countries have strong producers in a position to compete for a share of the new post Cold War arms market.

In the other major defence producer, the UK, the attitude of the government has been somewhat more ambiguous (Taylor, 1992). From the end of the Second World War through the 1970s the overriding thrust of policy was to control costs. Faced with global commitments, the demands of reconstruction and the budgetary demands of welfare policies in the face of poor economic performance, the period was characterized by cancelled projects and aborted efforts to stimulate a successful domestic defence industry. During the 1980s the emphasis was on the introduction of competition into the defence market, as the latest in the long line of efforts to control costs and bring expenditure into line with budget allocations. The state-owned industries were privatized, and foreign competition used to exert leverage on domestic companies. This policy had a dramatic effect on the industry, forcing rationalization and a move to establish a foothold in export markets through joint ventures and working agreements. As a result, many of the leading UK defence companies such as Rolls-Royce, GEC, BAe, and Lucas undertake little new work on their own.

The policy of competition was not without its problems. Many companies sought to reduce costs and risks by buying in components from around the world and concentrating on the integration of the platform, armaments, sensors and other elements to produce a complete weapons system. As a result, critics say, little money went into developing new fundamental technologies in the UK, leaving the industry and the MoD reliant on overseas suppliers. In addition, awarding a contract to one company inevitably meant that the competitors received nothing, and as a result might not be in the market for the next competition. Competition thus contained the seeds of its own destruction, giving a domestic monopoly to the winner and ultimately facing the government with the difficult choice of awarding work to the only UK supplier, or buying from overseas and closing the remaining UK capability. Examples such as the Westland affair gave no clear sign that the government had an underlying policy on whether competition and reliance on the market, or support for national defence industries, should have over-riding priority.

One result of the competitive policy has been a transformation of British defence companies. At the start of the 1980s they showed all the effects of a close and cosy relationship with their main customer. By the end of the decade the remaining British defence suppliers had been forced to learn how to survive in a highly competitive environment. The rationalization which occurred during this period put British companies in a strong position, ahead of many of their EC competitors, to face the cuts in demand that are expected to characterize the 1990s.

In contrast to the UK, Italian defence companies enter the 1990s somewhat behind in the adjustment process. Rationalization began late in Italy, and while the rest of the world is adjusting to the international market-place, Italian restructuring is still largely aimed at creating a viable industry for the domestic market (Parazzini, forthcoming). The Italian defence industry consists of a few large firms and a larger number of medium-sized companies. The industry is dominated by three major industrial groups which control 13 of the top 20 companies – IRI and EFIM, which are state owned, and the privately owned Fiat. For 16 out of the top 20, defence accounts for 50 per cent or more of their sales, but taken as a whole IRI has only 5 per cent of sales in defence and Fiat 3 per cent. Only in the case of EFIM are defence sales significant for the group as a whole, at 42 per cent. Despite the importance of the holding groups, until the creation of Alenia by the merger in 1990 of Aeritalia and Selenia none of the Italian defence companies approached the size of the largest European firms such as BAe, Thomson-CSF or DASA.

Even though the Italian defence industry underwent some rationalization and restructuring during the 1980s, it faces the downturn in market from a weaker position than France, Germany or the UK. While the major players have begun jostling for a place in the world market, Italian defence companies are still engaged in an attempt to find a structure to meet the Italian procurement needs. The reduction in defence spending may prove to be the catalyst which forces Italian defence firms to focus on European and world markets, rather than continue their slow progress toward efficient national production.

Belgium, Denmark and the Netherlands form a second group of defence producers with a limited scope of highly developed production in some systems and components. Belgium specialized in small arms and ammunition, having world-class companies in the field until the late 1980s. Restructuring has centred on the takeover of major producers by French arms manufacturers, with over half of Belgian defence production now in the hands of French companies.

The major capability in Denmark has traditionally centred on the production of warships, with associated expertise in systems and electronics. None of these companies operated on a European scale. Production in the Netherlands expanded to meet a domestic and export demand which peaked in the mid-1980s, leaving severe over-capacity even before the downturn in world demand. The naval shipyards have been badly affected, with little prospect of improvement in a market suffering from over-capacity. The electronics firm Philips, which was also struggling with mounting difficulties in civil markets, sold off its defence interests, including the largest Dutch defence producer, Hollandse Signaal-Apparaten. Much of the industry had been created around the licensed production of the F-16 aircraft, which is likely to provide maintenance and upgrading work for some time.

The third group of producers, with developing defence industries (Greece, Portugal and Spain), can be seen as market entrants during the 1980s. Defence production offered an opportunity to develop industrial facilities and to extend technological capabilities. The cost implications of supporting an embryonic industry will intensify as defence cuts reduce the scale of production. At the same time, continuing efforts to create new defence industries in less favoured regions conflict with a climate of reductions around the world.

7.2.4   The internationalization of the industry

An examination of the capabilities of individual countries provides only a partial description of the European defence industry. Over the last two decades there has been an increasing trend for the internationalization of defence production. There are two pressures behind this trend – increasing costs leading to pressures from government, and commercial moves to gain

Table 7.8 International Takeovers and Mergers in Arms Production, 1990

Takeovers

Buyer	Seller
SABCA (B)	Dassault Belgique Aviation (F/B)
Thomson-CSF (F)	NV Ohilips MBLE Defence (N)
Thomson-CSF (F)	Link-Miles (UK)
Thomson-CSF (F)	Ferranti Sonar Division (UK)
GIAT (F)	Fabrique Nationale (B)
GIAT (F)	parts of Beretta (I)
Finmeccanica (I)	Ferranti Italiana (UK)
Fiat (I)	Enasa (S)
Thorn EMI (UK)	MEL (UK military electronics part of Philips, N)
Astra Holdings (UK)	PRB (B)
Aérospatiale (F)/Alcatel (F)/Selenia (I)	parts of Space Systems Loral (USA)
MAN (WG)	Steyr Daimler Puch (Austria)
Sauer (WG)	Sundstrand-Sauer Co (USA)
Fincantieri (F)/Bremer Vulkan AG (WG)	Sulzer Diesel AG (Switzerland)
Finmeccanica (I)	FIAR (I, owned by Ericsson, Sweden)
Dowty Group (UK)	Resdel Engineering (USA)
BEI Electronics (USA)	part of Systron Donner (UK)

Mergers

Companies	Countries	New company
Matra	France	Eurodrone
MBB	W. Germany	
Aérospatiale	France	Eurocopter
MBB	W. Germany	
Selenia	Italy	CSEE Défense
CSEE	France	
MBB	W. Germany	DEFTEC
Santa Barbara (INI)	Spain	
BMW	W. Germany	BMW Rolls-Royce
Rolls-Royce	UK	
CESELSA	Spain	Aeronautical Systems Designers
SD-Scicon	UK	
Thomson-CSF	France	Eurodynamics } proposed merger
BAe Dynamics	UK	} abandoned
Aérospatiale	France	...
OFEMA	France	
AIROD	Malaysia	
Thomson-CSF	France	Defence Electronics of Singapore
Ferranti Technologies	UK	Ferranti Tech Asia
Allied Ordnance Co.	Singapore	

Source: H. Wulf, 'Arms Production', *SIPRI Yearbook* 1991.

access to markets where local participation is advantageous or essential (e.g. establishing a foothold in the embryonic single market: selling into the USA where a manufacturing presence is seen as essential (GAO, 1992); and selling to countries which require orders to be placed with local business to 'offset' the work lost overseas (Martin, 1991)). Recent examples of international mergers and takeovers are shown in Table 7.8

7.3   International collaboration

7.3.1   The costs and benefits of collaboration
The initial impetus for collaboration between European countries came from government efforts to save costs. New weapons are required to equal or better the perceived threat, which during the Cold War meant the Warsaw Pact. Both sides became embroiled in an arms race, in which weapon capabilities reflected perceptions about developments by the 'enemy' (Izard, 1988). The R and D programme required to develop new, state of the art weapons is expensive, and each generation typically costs more than the preceding one. By sharing the costs rather than duplicating R and D efforts, the partners in a collaborative programme were able to achieve substantial savings. Similar, though smaller savings were expected at the production stage from economies of scale and longer production runs. Collaboration also offers military benefits from the deployment of common equipment among allies, allowing for interoperability, common ammunition and spares and the ability to use maintenance facilities and so on in an emergency. The major European cooperative programmes are shown in Table 7.9.

As well as acknowledging real benefits, critics of collaboration point to the costs involved, arising from the acceptance of restrictions on specifications in order to reach agreement on a common design and from the inefficiencies of the cooperation process itself. Each nation wishes to have a share in the production, and work may be allocated to ensure that distribution matches the pattern of purchases rather than comparative advantage and most efficient production. Costs of collaboration will vary with the number of partners. According to the square root rule, costs increase with the square root of the number of partners: Martin (1991). Thus in a typical two-partner project the total cost may increase by about 40 per cent, although each partner would still save about one-third compared with a national project.

7.3.2   A case study of a collaborative project: the EH 101
The EH 101 helicopter is a collaborative programme between Italy and the UK. It illustrates the potential gains and the problems common to all collaborative programmes, while having some unique aspects. The programme grew out of the requirements of the UK and Italian navies for replacements

Table 7.9   Major European Cooperative Programmes

Programme	Countries
Inertial navigation system	Netherlands, Spain, UK, Canada
EH 101 helicopter	Italy, UK
Radar, Cobra air defence	France, Germany, UK
MLRS phase 3	France, Germany, Italy, UK, USA
Rescue tank	France, UK
European fighter aircraft	Germany, Italy, Spain, UK
A129 Tonal anti-tank helicopter	Italy, Netherlands, Spain, UK
RTM 322 helicopter engine	France, UK
Tiger helicopter	France, Germany
Trigat missile	France, Germany, UK
Air defence missiles (FAMS)	France, Italy, Spain, UK
Helios observation satellites	France, Italy, Spain
Midge	Germany, UK, Canada
NH90 helicopter	France, Germany, Italy, Netherlands
Long-range anti-ship missile	France, Germany
Aster surface-air missile	France, Italy
HOT 2 anti-tank missile	Euromissile – France, Germany
Milan anti-tank weapon	Euromissile – France, Germany
Roland surface-air missile	Euromissile – France, Germany

Source: CEC (1992).

for anti-submarine helicopters. However, while the basic performance specification remains dominated by the requirements of the Royal Navy (RN) and the Marina Militare Italiana (MMI), the EH 101 has become an integrated programme of a family of helicopters, comprising naval, military utility (army and airforce transport) and civil variants. As a result of the civil and military export elements of the programme the two industrial partners, Agusta (Italy) and Westland (UK) are sharing the financial risk of the civil and utility variants with the two governments.

The EH 101 programme dates from the mid-1970s. National replacement programmes for the Westland Sea King (UK) and Agusta SH3 (Italy) anti-submarine helicopters were pursued until 1978, when the governments of the UK, France, Italy and Germany signed a Declaration of Principles for Cooperation in Helicopter Programmes, followed in 1979 by a Memorandum of Understanding between the UK and Italian governments, agreeing in principle to collaborate on a Sea King and SH3 replacement. Contracts were placed with Westland and Agusta for initial feasibility studies, leading in

1980 to the formation of a jointly owned company, EHI, to manage the programme. A second Memorandum of Understanding was signed by the two governments in 1981, leading to joint project definition contracts. A third Memorandum of Understanding and contracts for the full development were signed in 1984, accompanied by an inter-governmental agreement for the civil variant.

At the same time, both companies needed a new helicopter programme if they were to develop their civil business. Neither could afford to develop a machine for the civil market which is led by the USA and France. By using the assured funding and orders from the military to develop a basic vehicle, the companies hoped to obtain a competitive position in a market comprising both replacement and new business.

In the event, the outcome has been mixed. By 1991 the basic helicopter had met the demanding design requirements and offered significant improvements in range, load capacity and productivity over competitors, particularly in the civil field. However, problems with the systems integration had delayed the naval variant, and the companies could not afford to complete development of the civil version in advance of the military. The whole integrated programme was thus delayed.

The problems with systems integration arose in part because EHI were prime contractors for the basic helicopter but were not responsible for ensuring that all the weapon systems and equipment were integrated into a working anti-submarine system. Eventually the UK MoD decided to appoint an overall prime contractor for the Royal Navy order. Two consortia submitted tenders, IBM and Westland being successful over BAe and GEC. While recognizing the improvement, the Defence Committee considered that there was still doubt over the successful outcome for the Royal Navy (HCP 243, 1991).

The EH 101 naval programme has progressively slipped over the course of development. For example, the commitment to full development by the two governments was delayed from 1983 to 1984. The first flight of the prototype (one of nine pre-production helicopters) was ten months overdue. Initial production orders were originally planned for 1989, with entry into service in 1991–92. In the event, the first production order for 44 anti-submarine warfare (ASW) EH 101s was placed in 1991 and entry into service is expected in 1994–95. So the overall programme slippage is in the order of three years for the naval programme, and up to five years for the utility and civil programmes.

The original 1978 estimates for the proposed UK national programme based on the Westland WG-34 indicated that development costs would be £650 million and total programme costs for the development and production of 74 anti-submarine warfare helicopters would amount to £1 500 million.

By 1980 estimated development costs had risen to £711 million. By comparison the cost estimate for the collaborative development of the helicopter was £427 million (all at 1980 prices). By reducing the initial offtake from 74 to 50, the MoD were able to restrict the total budgetary impact of the programme to the 1978 estimate of £1 500 million in current prices. In other words, the impact of inflation and cost escalation was offset by a reduction in the number of helicopters purchased. The agreement with Italy resulted in a cost share arrangement whereby the development cost of the common navalized helicopter was to be shared on a 50/50 basis and each partner government was to fund the cost of its own specific naval variant. Production workshare was to be proportioned according to national offtake.

By 1990 the cost of development had risen to £1 182 million (1990 prices), being a real increase of 28 per cent over the estimates prepared in 1983. The increase in development costs and the need to reduce numbers ordered to maintain budgetary targets imply that there has been a substantial increase in unit production costs.

Since the inception of the programme there have been significant changes in the international relations background which gave rise to the strategic need for an anti-submarine helicopter. This has led to questions about the number of systems likely to be required, if not as yet to suggestions for cancelling the programme. At the same time, the role for which the military utility variant was required has also been changing. The new security situation is likely to require greater mobility, giving rise to increased use of helicopters, but the size of the EH 101 may fall between two roles. While the RN have selected the EH 101 to replace both Lynx and Sea King, the Italian forces have chosen an alternative collaborative programme, the smaller NH 90 helicopter, for some of the roles originally envisaged for the EH 101; other tasks may need the greater heavy-lift capability of the Chinook. The civil variant is technically in advance of the competition, but may prove too costly to operate where greater range and load capacity are not such vital attributes.

The EH 101 programme illustrates the problems of collaborative projects: difficulties of agreeing requirements and combining them into a single product, leading in this case to three basic variants and individual national versions of each; time slippage; cost overruns; and the effect of changes in military requirements as a result of changes in international relations (the end of the Cold War).

Despite the shortcomings in the development programme, the EH 101 helicopter provides significant advances in operational capability and has enhanced the design and development capability of the collaborators. The dual objectives of military and cost benefits from collaboration have been reflected throughout the programme. In the long run, the collaboration seems likely to result in a high performance and competitive helicopter capable of meeting stringent naval, general military and civil requirements. The possibility of a substantial production run over 20–30 years offers the improvement in their competitive position sought by the two industrial partners. The industrial risk-sharing introduced into the EH 101 project may establish a precedent for future government–industry partnerships in dual use (civil-military) programmes. The success of the programme will not, however, resolve all the difficulties facing the two national industries in maintaining a competitive position in the helicopter market.

The EH 101 programme reflects both the costs and benefits of collaborative programmes. The costs arise primarily through delays and cost escalations; the benefits through spreading development costs over longer production runs, and through standardization of equipment between allied forces. There has been a learning experience which has increased the gains, but scope still exists for increasing the benefits and reducing the costs of collaboration.

Critics of collaborative projects also point to the difficulties of cancelling international programmes once they go wrong. However, the pressure of rising costs against relatively low and falling requirements will continue to make international collaboration an attractive option for government. There are also increasing commercial pressures which lead companies towards collaboration.

While the initial stimulus for collaboration on large defence projects came from governments seeking cost savings, many companies have adopted collaboration as central to their business philosophy. In some instances commercial pressures have led to the point where collaborative or joint production is the only European alternative to direct importing. Aircraft and aero-engines are examples, where even the previously independent French manufacturers are unlikely to pursue national projects in future. For European governments, collaboration may appear to offer irresistible savings, even after allowing for the costs of collaborating. But not all of the costs are financial, and in the same way as national industries were forced towards monopoly in an attempt to gain economies of scale so the EC can only support one US-scale supplier for each type of major equipment. While collaboration takes the form of project-based associations, scope for competition exists between consortia. Any tendency to establish more permanent joint ventures would, however, raise issues of monopoly.

International collaboration has been a major feature of European defence industries at the prime contractor level. However, focusing on the prime contractors does not provide a full picture of the defence industrial capabilities of a nation. Many technologies are developed and applied at the subcontractor level; indeed, many prime contractors are becoming systems integrators or assemblers, relying on subcontractors and suppliers for components. The ability to integrate systems into a total package is important, and without it a nation would not have a truly independent capability to develop and produce weapon systems. Equally, however, the technology in subsystems is crucial to the performance of the whole system.

The internationalization of defence production has perhaps proceeded further and faster at the subcontract and supply level than for prime contractors. Less attention has been paid to these supporting companies by governments, and capabilities may have been lost through decisions to import components and subsystems, taken without full assessment of the long-term consequences. The reliance of Europe and the USA on East Asia for microchips and other computer components is an illustration of this process of attrition. Indeed, the defence industrial capability of Europe may owe as much to the decisions of industry as to the desires of the governments concerned, and some capacities considered desirable by governments may have been lost through industrial choices.

7.4 The defence industry and the EC

The internationalization of defence production has occurred in parallel with that of civil industry. The initial impetus for defence was primarily cost-cutting for the major producers and technology transfer for the minor and emerging defence industries, followed by company-led restructuring in response to reduced demand. In contrast, the impetus on the civil side came from the Commission in the form of the creation of a Single European Market, from which defence was excluded.

Article 223 of the Treaty of Rome has generally been interpreted to imply that defence industries are outside the control of the Commission, not least by the governments of member states. This position is increasingly being challenged by the Commission, on the grounds that much defence procurement is now of dual-use military and civil technologies and as such should be subject to the competition, trade, investment and subsidy rules which apply to civil industry. The EC Competition Commissioner, Sir Leon Brittan, has initiated a review of the application of Article 223 (*Jane's Defence Weekly*, 1991).

The defence market has one characteristic which differentiates it from most civil markets – it is dominated by one purchaser, the national government. Virtually all defence equipment is developed for the requirements of the national military forces, with research and development paid for by the national government. Even collaborative projects are tailored to the individual needs of each partner, as for example with the development of specific British, German and Italian variants of the Tornado aircraft. Unlike the market for civil goods, the EC market for defence equipment will be controlled and organized by the customers, either as 12 individual states or those states acting together.

Extending the EC rules on competition to defence procurement will not obtain the full benefits from larger scale of production unless agreement is reached to standardize on common equipment. Such standardization has been notoriously difficult to establish in collaborative projects involving three or four partners, and has eluded the efforts of bodies such as the Independent European Programme Group (IEPG, comprising Belgium, Denmark, France, Germany, Greece, Italy, Luxembourg, Netherlands, Norway, Portugal, Spain, Turkey and the UK) which was formed in 1976 to promote European collaboration in defence equipment. Agreement on common weapon systems across all 12 EC member states seems unlikely without a common security and military policy, both currently outside the sphere of the Commission. Indeed, the full economic benefits of a single market in defence equipment may have to wait for a unified European military structure. The end of the Cold War and the dissolution of the Warsaw Pact has removed the main thread unifying European security – the common enemy. Until a new concept of security has evolved, achieving a common security and military policy seems even less likely (Kirby and Hooper, 1991). Sceptics might see the EC interest in the 'costs of non-Europe' as a lever by which the EC bureaucracy can exert pressure to extend their competence into the security arena.

Reductions in defence spending are creating new declining industries in Europe, in the same way as steel, shipbuilding and other traditional industries declined during the 1970s and 1980s. There have been calls for the creation of a Defence Diversification Agency to assist in the adjustment process (Oxford Research Group, 1992), along similar lines to the programmes for the steel and shipbuilding industries. Such an agency might fulfil a number of roles, from advice and assistance to funding investment in plant, equipment and training.

As with all large-scale manufacturing activity, much defence production is concentrated in particular locations, such as the Greater Munich area in Germany and Lancashire in the UK. Reductions in spending on defence equipment thus have a regional impact, and raise issues for the Community's regional policy. Many of the areas at risk are not covered by current regional policy, or they qualify for support for purposes other than industrial restructuring. Future regional policy needs to take into account the likely impact of defence cuts, as and when they occur.

Reductions in defence activity also have implications for the technological base of the Community, and hence for EC technology policy. Defence is seen as the leading edge of R and D, and as providing the technology base for much of civil production. While the balance has been shifting in recent years more towards civil leadership in R and D, the less-favoured nations have been relying on inward transfer of defence technology as part of their efforts to create an industrial base. A reduction in the need for defence production capacity and increasing interest in an EC-wide defence industrial base imply that an alternative technology transfer mechanism might be required, with implications for EC technology policy.

Some member states in less favoured regions such as Spain and Portugal were using defence procurement to develop high-technology manufacturing. Reduced defence requirements will not end the perceived need for a mechanism for technology transfer, and such states will want to continue to develop their defence industries unless an alternative mechanism for technology transfer can be found. EC technology policy may thus influence the future location and structure of defence production. If all member states are to share the burden of defence, each is likely to want a share of industrial activity and the benefits in the form of employment and income, as well as technology, which accompany it.

The EC interest in creating a European market for defence equipment is not the first effort in this direction. The IEPG has been promoting collaboration since 1976, focusing its efforts on three main themes: increasing visibility of opportunities; rationalizing research; and promoting collaboration (IEPG, 1990). Increasing visibility has involved member nations publishing bulletins of contract opportunities to facilitate cross-border tendering. The EUCLID programme coordinates and manages European defence research in an effort to reduce costs and strengthen the technology base. The IEPG encourages collaboration through harmonization of requirements, collaborative development, production or purchasing. Unlike the EC initiatives, which are described as fostering a single competitive market, the IEPG supports work-sharing (*juste retour*), at least for a transitional period. The importance attached to defence industries in view of their contributions to technology, employment and security suggests that rationalization on a European scale will become increasingly difficult without some form of offsetting compensation, whether in terms of work-sharing, industrial or regional aid or technology transfer.

7.5 Implications for the future

There has been concern about defence industries ever since the Second World War. Questions have been asked about the efficiency of industries, the procurement system and the effects on economic growth of the pre-emption of resources, particularly R and D, for military purposes. Two new developments suggest that in future the concerns will be different. First, the end of the Cold War has given rise to expectations of a peace dividend in the form of lower defence spending releasing resources which can be used to solve other social and economic problems. Secondly, the European Commission has turned its attention to defence, which, coupled with commercial pressures for internationalization of production, suggests that national interests will be less important in determining the future of defence industries.

The changed political situation in Europe and the world implies a need for a fundamental revision of the basis of security. The common element of European security which came from a common perception of the threat is not clear now the Warsaw Pact has been dissolved (Kirby and Hooper, 1991). While there is less likelihood of European nations undertaking military action on an independent basis rather than as part of an international force, the basis on which a common security and foreign policy might be built has been removed. Without a European security policy, the creation of an EC military force seems unlikely, leaving individual nations basing their equipment decisions, and hence their attitudes towards defence industries, on national criteria.

Whether the future lies in integrated European procurement, continuing national programmes, or some half-way house, the options for European defence procurement remain the same:

- support expensive national defence industrial bases;
- achieve some savings by collaborating on major projects;
- rationalize to form a Europe-wide industry;
- buy in from the US;
- Concentrate on R and D, building technology demonstrators but not putting them into production.

In the past, national ministries of defence had a dominant influence on the structure, conduct and performance of the defence industries through their procurement decisions. The future of the European defence industrial base will be determined by the nature and extent of the European Commission's role and by commercial decisions continuing the increasing internationalization of companies. The possibilities range between a European defence market controlled by reference to world competition, or a closed market shared out between member states. Whichever route is chosen – or evolves by default – the size and structure of European defence industries at the turn of the century will be very different from that at the start of the 1990s.

References

Anthony, I., Allebeck, A.C. and Wulf, H. (1990), *West European Arms Production*, Stockholm: SIPRI.
Brzoska, M. and Lock, P. (eds) (1992), *Restructuring of Arms Production in Western Europe*, Oxford: Oxford University Press for Stockholm Peace Research Institute.
CEC (1992), *Dual Use Industries in Europe*, Brussels: ERA Eurostrategies.

Cmnd 1559 (1991), *Statement on the Defence Estimates*, London: HMSO.
GAO (1992), *International Procurement: NATO Allies' Implementation of Reciprocal Defense Agreements*, GAO/NSAID, 92–126, Washington: GAO (March).
Hartley, K. (1991), *The Economics of Defence Policy*, London: Brassey's.
HCP 243 (1991), *Further Examination of the Procurement of the EH 101 and Attack Helicopters and the Trigat Missile Systems*, Defence Committee, London: HMSO.
HCP 369 (1991), *Royal Navy Submarines*, Sixth Report, Defence Committee, London: HMSO.
Hooper, N. (1990), *The UK Defence Industrial Base* (Working Paper 1), Centre for Defence Economics, University of York.
IEPG (1990), Copenhagen Communiqué, IEPG/Min/D–14, November, and attachment.
Izard, W. (1988), *Arms Races, Arms Control and Conflict Analysis*, Cambridge: Cambridge University Press.
Jane's Defence Weekly (1991), 'EC Awards to Meet Fair Trade Rules', 9 November, 49–54.
Kirby, S. and Hooper, N. (eds) (1991), *The Costs of Peace*, Chur, Switzerland: Harwood.
Martin, S. (1991), 'Economic Collaboration and European Security', in S. Kirby and N. Hooper (eds), *The Costs of Peace*, Chur, Switzerland: Harwood.
Noyes, R. and De Renzo, D. (eds) (1990), *Principal Foreign Defense Systems Producers 1990/91*, New Ridge, New Jersey: Noyes Data Corporation.
Oxford Research Group (1992), *Converting the Defence Industry* (Current Decisions Report 9), Oxford: Oxford Research Group.
Parazzini, S. (forthcoming), 'The Future of the Defence Firm in Italy', in A. Latham and N. Hooper (eds), *The Future of the Defence Firm in Europe, North America and East Asia*, Amsterdam: Kluwer.
Serfati, C. (1992), 'Reorientation of French Companies', in M. Brzoska and P. Lock (eds), *Restructuring of Arms Production in Western Europe*, Oxford: Oxford University Press for Stockholm Peace Research Institute.
SIPRI (1991), *World Armaments and Disarmament: The SIPRI Yearbook*, Oxford: Oxford University Press for Stockholm Peace Research Institute.
Taylor, T. (1992), 'The British Restructuring Experience', in M. Brzoska and P. Lock (eds), *Restructuring of Arms Production in Western Europe*, Oxford: Oxford University Press for Stockholm Peace Research Institute.

Further reading
Hartley, K. (1991), *The Economics of Defence Policy*, London: Brassey's.
A textbook on the economics of defence, with examples drawn from the UK.
Hartley, K. and Hooper, N. (1990), *The Economics of Defence, Disarmament and Peace: An Annotated Bibliography*, Aldershot: Edward Elgar.
A comprehensive bibliography of English-language literature on all aspects of the economics of defence, disarmament and peace.
World Armaments and Disarmament: The SIPRI Yearbook, Oxford: Oxford University Press for Stockholm Peace Research Institute (annual).
An annual review of issues affecting military security and disarmament, with comprehensive data on arms production and trade and arms limitation agreements.
Kirby, S. and Hooper, N. (eds) (1991), *The Costs of Peace*, Chur, Switzerland: Harwood.
An analysis of the political and military issues which will influence the future of European security, and their economic consequences.
Brzoska, M. and Lock, P. (eds) (1992), *Restructuring of Arms Production in Western Europe*, Oxford: Oxford University Press for Stockholm Peace Research Institute.
A survey of the reaction of defence industries to defence cuts.
Renner, M. (1992), *Economic Adjustments after the Cold War: Strategies for Conversion*, Aldershot: Dartmouth for UNIDIR.
A survey of how defence firms are reacting to defence cuts and the differing approaches to conversion to civilian production.

8 Construction

Michael Fleming

8.1 Introduction

The construction industry is responsible for all building and civil engineering work. It carries out a diverse range of activities covering the construction and repair (and also demolition) of buildings of all kinds, the installation of fixtures, fittings and services in them and completion work, such as glazing, painting and plastering, carried out by specialist contractors. It also covers the wide variety of civil engineering works such as roads, bridges, tunnels, dams, reservoirs, the laying of pipelines and related work such as the laying out of sports grounds, shaft drilling and mine sinking.

The nature of construction work is such as to make the industry distinct from all or most of manufacturing industry. Unlike manufacturing, in which production may be carried out at a fixed location and the products transported to customers in different markets, construction work has to be carried out on a site chosen by the customer. Although some parts of buildings may be prefabricated in a centralized yard or factory, ultimately the structures themselves have to be constructed at a specific location, fixed, as it were, to the site and, in the case of buildings, connected to mains services such as water, gas, electricity and sewerage. Unlike manufactured products, therefore, construction is not traded across national boundaries and as a consequence it is somewhat misleading to talk of a 'European' construction industry. There is instead a set of national industries. This is not to say, however, that the construction sector is devoid of international competition. This is transparently not the case. But the importance of international contracting, while extremely important for some firms, is a small part of the activities of the industry as a whole. It is estimated that currently only about 2 per cent of construction work in the EC is undertaken by non-national contractors (Male and Stocks, 1991).

In the rest of this section the relative importance of the industry in each country is examined. The rest of the chapter is concerned with the organization and structure of the industry, conditions of entry and competition, building economy, international contracting and the impact of the Single European Market.

8.1.1 Construction and the national economies

Construction is one of the largest industries in all countries. Table 8.1 gives relevant figures for most countries in Western Europe for 1989 (the latest year for which comparable data were available at the time of writing). It will be seen that in most countries the industry contributes around 5–7 per cent of gross domestic product and is responsible for around 7–9 per cent of total

Table 8.1   Construction in the National Economies, 1989[1]

Country	Shares of:			
	Gross domestic product	Employment		Gross fixed capital formation
		Persons	Employees	
Austria	6.8	n/a	7.6	47.8
Belgium	5.3	6.5	6.2	45.8
Denmark	5.8	6.9	6.5	55.0
Finland	8.5	8.8	8.8	57.6
France	5.3	7.2	6.7	53.4
West Germany	5.2	6.6	6.7	51.4
Greece	5.3[2]	6.8[3]	9.6[3]	53.5[2]
Iceland[2]	6.6	9.3	8.3	72.9
Ireland[4]	5.0	n/a	n/a	46.7
Italy	5.3	6.9	6.8	44.8
Luxembourg	6.5	9.7	10.1	49.6
Netherlands	5.8	7.4	7.4	52.4
Norway	5.4	7.4	6.9	73.3
Portugal[5]	5.6	9.0	11.6	54.9
Spain	8.3	9.0	9.5	61.1
Sweden	6.5	6.5	6.0	n/a
Switzerland[3]	7.6	n/a	n/a	n/a
United Kingdom	4.9	6.7	4.6	46.3

Notes:
1. Data relate to the year 1989 unless indicated otherwise.
2. 1988.
3. 1985.
4. 1987.
5. 1986.
n/a = not available

Source: OECD (1991), *National Accounts, Detailed Tables Vol II, 1977–1989*, Paris: OECD.

employment. In all countries, however, the economic significance of the industry is much greater than these figures would suggest, for it is by far the largest contributor to capital investment – generally contributing more than 50 per cent of total gross fixed capital formation each year.

In summary, the construction industry occupies a position of central importance in all economies and is responsible for a broadly similar relative contribution to total economic activity in each country.

8.2   Industrial organization

8.2.1   Structure of national industries

The organization and structure of the industry in each country is determined by factors relating to the nature of demand and supply. Construction demand is highly fragmented in terms of customers: it originates in every sector of the economy including individual consumers in the case of housing, all industrial and service sectors and the wide range of organizations responsible for infrastructure, public utilities and leisure facilities. The product – the construction facility itself – cannot be transported but, as noted above, has to be provided at a specific location. So, the demand for construction is highly dispersed geographically and the provision of construction services must also be similarly dispersed. This means that there is a natural advantage in a correspondingly dispersed organization of the industry. These factors are reinforced by factors on the supply side relating to the nature of construction activities themselves. These generally involve the use of heavy and bulky materials of low unit value such as cement, aggregates, bricks, concrete products and the like which are relatively costly to transport. This limits the economic scope for prefabrication, so more work is carried out on site than would otherwise be the case. Further, construction work cannot generally precede the receipt of orders (the only exceptions being speculative development by builders themselves – in the main, housing) but has to be carried out to meet the individual requirements of individual customers. These factors apply to all economies and play a predominant part in shaping the industry in each country. It is not surprising to find that the organization and structure of the industry in each country should display a number of significant resemblances.

The most notable feature with regard to the structure of the industry is the extent to which it is dominated by a large number of small firms in all countries. Taking the European Community as a whole, there are over one million firms in the construction industry with a total workforce of around 9 million – over 6.5 per cent of the working population (NEDC, 1990). Some 90 per cent of the firms employ fewer than 10 people and only just over 2 per cent employ more than 50 workers.

Table 8.2 *Size Distribution of Firms for Selected European Countries (%)*

Firm size	Belgium (1988)	France (1988)	Germany(a) (1989)	Luxembourg (1987)	Netherlands (1988)	Norway (1989)	Portugal (1987)	Spain (1980)	Sweden (1989)	Great Britain (1990)
Up to 5 employees	} 23.6	84.8	} 83.5	50.1	72.9(d)	70.8	84.5(d)	50.3(b)	73.1(d)	89.8
6–19 employees		11.7		33.1	13.5(e)	22.5	8.5(e)	36.4(c)	15.6(e)	7.5
20–49 employees	54.0	2.7	10.8	11.1	9.2	4.8	3.8	8.9	8.1	1.7
50–99 employees	12.8	0.5	3.5	3.6	2.8	1.2	} 3.1	2.5	1.9	0.6
100–199 employees	5.8	0.2	1.5	1.8	1.0	0.4		1.1	} 1.0	0.2
200–499 employees	3.2	0.1	0.6	} 0.5	0.5	0.3		0.5		0.1
500–999 employees	} 4.6	0.03	} 0.1		} 0.1	0.03		0.1	} 0.2	0.05
1 000 employees & over		0.02		–		–		0.2		0.03
Total %	100.0	100.0	100.0	100.0	100.0	100.0	100.0	100.0	100.0	100.0
Number	1 715	320 647	63 298	1 049	17 921	11 524	19 091	35 501	12 439	209 793

Notes:
Totals may not sum to 100 due to rounding errors.
(a) Federal Republic.
(b) Up to 4 employees.
(c) 5–19 employees.
(d) Up to 9 employees.
(e) 10–19 employees.

Source: *Annual Bulletin of Housing and Building Statistics for Europe*, **32** (1988) and **34** (1990) (UN, New York 1989 and 1991 respectively).

181

Table 8.3   Distribution of Employment (Employees) by Size of Firm for Selected European Countries (%)

Firm size (No. of employees)	Belgium (1988)	France (1988)	Germany(a) (1989)	Luxembourg (1987)	Netherlands (1988)	Norway (1989)	Portugal (1987)	Spain (1980)	Sweden (1989)	Great Britain (1990)
Up to 5 employees	} 6.8	20.8	} 34.0	5.9	24.0(d)	21.3	32.9(d)	6.9(b)	18.4(d)	16.7
6–19 employees		26.2		23.5	15.3(e)	29.2	10.1(e)	19.9(c)	13.0(e)	15.4
20–49 employees	34.1	18.7	20.4	23.5	21.4	19.1	10.1	15.5	14.0	13.0
50–99 employees	17.0	8.0	15.1	17.6	13.7	11.2		9.6	7.7	9.9
100–199 employees	15.9	6.1	13.1	17.6	9.2	7.9		7.6	} 11.6	9.4
200–499 employees	18.2	5.8	10.4	} 11.8	9.5	9.0	} 46.9	8.1		9.3
500–999 employees	} 8.0	4.1	} 7.0		} 6.9	2.2		4.5	} 35.3	7.6
1 000 employees & over		10.3		–		–		28.0		18.6
Total %	100.0	100.0	100.0	100.0	100.0	100.0	100.0	100.0	100.0	100.0
000s	87	1 383	1 009	16	262	89	206	554	207	773

Notes:
Totals may not sum to 100 due to rounding errors.
See notes (a)–(e) of Table 8.2.

Source: As for Table 8.2.

Table 8.4 Value of Output by Size of Firm for Selected European Countries (%)

Firm size (No. of employees)	Belgium (1988)	France (1988)	Germany(a) (1989)	Luxembourg (1987)	Netherlands (1988)	Norway (1989)	Portugal (1987)	Spain (1980)	Sweden (1989)	Great Britain (1990)
Up to 5 employees	} 5.5	25.2	} 27.7	7.6	20.7(d)	19.1	26.3(d)		18.5(d)	22.0
6–19 employees		18.7		22.7	12.3(e)	24.6	9.3(e)		7.7(e)	11.6
20–49 employees	31.6	15.0	19.8	23.6	19.3	17.7	10.3		10.9	10.5
50–99 employees	17.4	6.6	16.0	15.1	14.6	12.2			6.3	9.0
100–199 employees	16.8	6.2	15.2	21.1	11.4	8.5	} 54.1	n/a	} 10.9	9.3
200–499 employees	19.1	6.3	12.8	} 9.9	12.5	12.8				9.1
500–999 employees	} 9.6	6.6	} 8.5		} 9.2	5.1			} 45.7	8.2
1 000 employees and over		15.4		–		–				20.4
Total %	100.0	100.0	100.0	100.0	100.0	100.0	100.0		100.0	100.0
Value	279 800 million francs	600 601 million francs	126 590 million DM	27 409 million francs	52 108 million guilders	59 253 million kroner	456 117 million escudos		153 877 million kroner	£10 288 million

Notes:
Totals may not sum to 100 due to rounding errors.
n/a = not available. See notes (a)–(e) of Table 8.2.

Source: As for Table 8.2.

Data are not readily available for all European countries but broadly comparable data for ten selected countries are given in Table 8.2, which shows the distribution of the number of firms by size for various recent dates. It will be seen that in all countries for which data are available, well over half of the firms have no more than five employees, with the proportion rising to well over 80 per cent in some countries including France and Great Britain. At the other end of the scale some firms have 1 000 employees or more but the proportion of such firms is always well under 1 per cent of the total number. In absolute terms, to take some examples, only 57 firms out of a total of over 300 000 in France in 1988 and only 70 firms out of more than 200 000 in Great Britain in 1990 had more than 1 000 employees. The average sizes of firms in the ten countries all fell within the range 4–17 employees per firm (except for Belgium with an average of 50).[1]

The economic significance of small firms, however, should not be over-stated. The large proportion of small firms is responsible in all countries for a much smaller proportion of both employment (Table 8.3) and output (Table 8.4), while the minute proportion of large firms makes a much larger relative contribution to employment and output. Broadly speaking, the 50–90 per cent of firms with 5 employees or less account in no country for more than around one-third of employment and one-quarter of output, while the small proportion of firms employing 500 or more account, in round terms, for about 10–30 per cent of both employment and output.

An analysis of the nationality of the top 100 largest contractors (as measured by turnover) within Europe in 1990 shows that France and the United Kingdom accounted for almost half of the total (46 out of 100) with the next 20 companies coming equally from Germany and Spain (see Table 8.5). In sum, two-thirds of the top 100 contractors come from four countries. The remaining third is spread across eight countries, the leaders being Sweden, Italy and the Netherlands. In this group, however, it is notable that Sweden – one of the smaller countries – provides a disproportionate share of the leading contractors, including two from the top 20.

The size of these firms is determined in part by their success in winning contracts outside their domestic markets. Indeed the only sense in which there may be said to be a European construction industry, rather than a set of national industries, is that some of the largest firms do compete across national boundaries, although competition is then around the world and not simply, or even mainly, within Europe (see section 8.4). Further analysis of the top 20 firms – identified in Table 8.6 – shows that 'exports' accounted for a major part of the turnover of many individual firms, varying from 9 to 51 per cent. A word of caution is required in the interpretation of those figures, for some of the contractors concerned are part of diversified groups engaging in a range of activities including engineering, the manufacturing

Table 8.5   *Nationality of Europe's Top 100 Contractors Ranked by Turnover, 1990–91*

Country	Top 20 turnover £1 529mn or more	21–50 Turnover £579–1 522mn	51–100 Turnover £283–561mn	Total
France*	7	6	7	20
UK	8	6	12	26
Sweden	2	2	4	8
Germany	2	3	5	10
Italy	1	1	5	7
Spain		5	5	10
Netherlands		4	3	7
Finland		3	2	5
Switzerland			4	4
Norway			1	1
Denmark			1	1
Belgium			1	1

Note: *France is ranked first because it has the largest company.

Source: *Building*, 22 November 1991, 39–53.

and distribution of building materials and other products and even the provision of shipping services (as in the case of P&O in the UK). Nonetheless, it is clear that for some companies foreign construction work, as such, is a major part of their total construction activity (Fleming, 1988). So the structure of each country's construction industry is also determined in part by the success of its contractors in penetrating non-domestic markets. This will be considered in section 8.4.

8.2.2   Contracting practices

While there are similarities in the nature of demand faced by the industry in each country as well as in the nature of construction work itself, both of which help to determine a similar market structure in each country, there are differences in industrial practices which constitute not only another influence on the structure and organization of the industry but also an important determinant of both the scope for, and the effectiveness of, international competition.

In this context, it is important to consider the requirements of the construction process as a whole from initial conception, specification and design

Table 8.6 The Top 20 European Contractors, 1990

Rank	Company	Country	Turnover £mn	% increase in turnover 1989–90	Exports as % of turnover	Profit £mn	Number of employees 000s
1	Bouygues	France	5 931	21	23	65	79.5
2	SGE	France	4 080	11	41	47	68.3
3	BICC	UK	3 890	3	44	183	44.4
4	Tarmac	UK	3 695	5	14	190	34.9
5	Trafalgar House	UK	3 452	7	45	155	28.9
6	Skanska	Sweden	3 363	17	11	225	31.7
7	Philipp Holzmann	Germany	3 272	18	47	37	36.8
8	SAE	France	2 813	4	31	26	26.4
9	Dumez	France	2 740	0	NA	NA	NA
10	Italstat	Italy	2 411	9	NA	NA	23.1
11	Spie Batignolles	France	2 353	–3	28	26	36.2
12	Beazer	UK	2 305	17	51	105	22.3
13	GTM Entrepose	France	2 283	16	25	16	37.5
14	AMEC	UK	2 218	11	16	63	30.4
15	Hochtief	Germany	2 118	10	38	58	26.0
16	NCC	Sweden	2 111	9	9	68	18.7
17	Wimpey	UK	1 905	–8	24	43	16.3
18	P&O	UK	1 788	13	NA	15	NA
19	Cegelec	France	1 596	12	39	44	27.1
20	Laing	UK	1 529	12	NA	20	12.9

Source: *Building*, 22 November 1991, p. 44.

through to construction on site. The construction industry, as such, is defined as that part concerned with construction on site. Site work, however, must generally be preceded by design work carried out by architects and/or professional engineers (civil, structural, electrical, mechanical) working to meet the varied requirements of individual clients. Conceptually the processes are distinct but in practice they can overlap and, in the limit, may be performed within one firm. There are also significant differences in the way the design and construction process is organized in each country. These too have an important impact on the scope for effective competition across national boundaries.

On the construction side, there are important differences in contracting practices in each country. The most important difference is between 'main contracting' and 'trades contracting'. In main contracting a design is produced by architects and/or engineers and a contract is then let to a main contractor who takes responsibility for the execution of the work. This contractor may sublet parts, or even all, of the work to other contractors but responsibility continues to reside with him. The more of the contract that is sublet, the more the work of the main contractor becomes simply contract management. This system is one that is commonly used in the United Kingdom, Belgium, the Netherlands, Italy, Greece, Portugal and Spain. In contrast, under the trades contracting system separate contracts are let by the client to individual trades contractors. This can mean perhaps as many as 20–30 independent contracts on even a simple building project. The management function for the project as a whole then has to be performed by the designer, or a management agent employed for the purpose, who has to take responsibility for the coordination of trades, cost and professional control. This method is used pre-eminently in France and Germany.

The system of subcontracting to specialist contractors, whether by a main contractor or directly by clients, is another reason for the proliferation of small firms in all countries. It may be seen as a market response to the demands of the construction process whereby specialization by function (trade) rather than by type of work (structure) has proved an effective way of meeting market requirements. Specialization by trade facilitates a greater continuity of work for a firm than would specialization by type of structure, as each project normally requires inputs by a variety of trades. It has also been shown to help to maintain a higher level of productivity (see Fleming, 1988, p. 219).

National differences in contracting confront contractors used to one tradition with an obstacle when they are competing in another country where a different national tradition applies. Specialist contractors, who naturally tend to be smaller than general contractors, will tend to be at a disadvantage in competing in countries where the trades contracting system applies, except for highly specialized work. Larger general contractors may be better placed to compete where main contracting applies, but they then have to contend, of course, with the differences in construction techniques and regulatory and other legal requirements in different countries, not to mention language difficulties and cultural differences in the way business is conducted.

8.2.3 Conditions of entry and competition

The conditions of entry to the industry are generally regarded as easy. The main advantages possessed by established firms relate to size, experience and reputation. They are in a position to tender or negotiate large contracts, or contracts where special experience and expertise is required, and to establish a claim to be placed on select lists of contractors who may be invited to tender for particular contracts. The majority of contracts, however, are small and require no special expertise beyond conventional trade skills. The system of contracting by trade, both under the main contracting and trades contracting systems, provides considerable market opportunities for the small firm and new entrants.

The factors that may put potential entrants at a competitive disadvantage in other industries do not apply in the construction sector. Economies of scale are of little importance as a potential barrier because the site-based nature of construction work, where each site is necessarily a temporary place of work, coupled with the individuality of most projects, means that the conditions necessary for the existence of many technical scale economies – continuity of production of standard products using specialized equipment and production techniques – do not apply. Further, the following factors ensure that capital requirements are generally low relative to the value of work undertaken. First, most construction work remains a labour-intensive activity requiring the use of a multiplicity of traditional craft skills. The requirement for mechanical equipment is confined, in the main, to earth-moving plant, cranes, hoists and other devices for lifting and moving materials, and concrete mixing plant. Beyond the use of powered hand tools, the craft processes, which predominate in construction, have remained largely immune to mechanization. Secondly, the importance of capital requirements is reduced still further in practice by the existence of plant hire facilities which reduce the need for contractors to own much plant of their own, particularly plant for which ownership by contractors would involve low capacity utilization. Finally, although the value of individual contracts may be large relative to the financial capacity of a single contractor, the significance of this is reduced both by the system of contracting or subcontracting parts of a project by trade and, especially, by systems of progress payments as the work proceeds as well as trade credit from suppliers. No contractor is required to finance the construction of a project through to completion. In addition, contracts may be priced in such a way as to ensure relatively higher progress payments in the early stages of a project so that working capital requirements may be reduced still further. In summary, the requirements for fixed and working capital are low for the vast majority of contracts and firms and thus do not constitute a significant barrier to entry. This is not to say, of course, that firms can enter and compete for contracts of any size, type and complexity, but the large number of small-scale projects and the prevalence of specialization by trade provide substantial market opportunities for the new entrant.

The scope for gaining competitive advantages by vertical integration or patent protection is also severely restricted or non-existent. Materials account for a major part of total costs, but they are drawn from a wide range of extractive and manufacturing industries: no one material predominates. It is generally impracticable for contractors to meet their own needs for materials. Likewise for materials producers, forward integration into construction provides little advantage because no one contractor is able to provide an adequate outlet. This is not to say that contractors do not diversify into materials supply and materials suppliers do not diversify into construction, but in general vertical integration is of little importance in construction and certainly not as a competitive strategy concerned with strengthening competitive positions in contracting. Patent protection in a long-established assembly industry like construction in which traditional craft processes continue to play an important part is also of no general significance as a barrier to entry. Similarly the nature of demand means that firms in construction are not able to raise barriers to entry artificially by marketing strategies such as product differentiation and advertising, which are so important for branded manufactured products.

So construction is an industry where the conditions of easy entry apply. It is also an industry of easy exit. Not only are capital requirements low, as argued above, but capital is easily transferable in use to other jobs and there is a well-developed second-hand market for capital equipment. Entry does not involve sunk costs and, in the absence of restrictions on entry arising from legal impediments, the industry may be regarded as a good case of a 'contestable' market (Baumol *et al.*, 1982).

Constraints on entry arising from legal impediments, however, do arise and vary considerably from one country to another. In a European context they may play a significant role in limiting transnational competition. In the United Kingdom there are no licensing requirements or other restrictions in the way of entry to the industry. This is not the case in mainland Europe (NEDC, 1990). For example, West Germany (the former Federal Republic) has an especially rigid structure. To set up in business a person must be a *Meister* (master craftsman), which requires a number of years' experience after qualifying as a skilled worker and passing subsequent examinations. Playing an independent part in this are 69 chambers of commerce and 42 chambers of trade with which all German companies must register, and who undertake many quasi-official functions including coordination of training (NEDC, 1990). Membership of chambers of commerce is local, so companies must re-register if they wish to work outside their area. In France it is a legal requirement to take out a ten-year liability insurance on a completed building, which means that the insurance industry has an important influence in practice. Bureaux of control act on behalf of the insurance industry for technical approval of architects' and engineers' drawings and subsequent inspections during construction. Contractors are required to be certified as competent by the OPQCB (l'Organisme Professionelle de Qualifications et de Classifications du Bâtiment et des activités annexes) for the size and type of work for which insurance is requested and usually also through a trade association. In the Netherlands and Denmark a similar system to that in Germany operates. Belgium and Luxembourg have similar systems to the French. In Spain there is an official register of firms which gives pre-qualification for public sector contracts.

8.3 Building economy

8.3.1 Price determination

The large number of firms in the industry in all countries and the absence of any barriers to entry beyond those imposed by limitations of experience and the controls operated by regulation and certification, provide essential competitive conditions. However, the fact that contractors cannot work before receipt of a contract and that each contract is unique means that special importance attaches to the way in which contractors are selected to undertake a contract and the way in which the price is set. It is in this area that the problem of non-competitive practices and, in particular, collusive tendering, arises.

The normal procedure is to seek competitive tenders. But it does not follow that the contractor submitting the lowest tender will provide the best value for money in practice because the prices quoted by different contractors may differ for a variety of reasons (Stone, 1983):

(a) because of differences in efficiency and therefore in costs;
(b) because some firms will be more anxious for the contract than others, perhaps because they are short of work, or for purposes of prestige or goodwill, and hence they will consider it worthwhile to accept only a small contribution to their overheads and profits from the job in question;

(c)   because some firms will have achieved a better understanding of the
        technical nature of the job than others and are prepared to reflect this in
        their tender price;
(d)   because some firms aim at lower standards of work than others;
        and
(e)   because some firms will have found ways of ensuring a high final
        settlement price, even on a low tender price.

Firms quoting low tender prices for one or more of the first three reasons are
likely to provide better value for money than those quoting low prices for
one of the last two reasons.

There are various ways by which a client can choose a contractor and let a
contract. The client's objective, of course, is to select a contractor able to
carry out the project at the lowest cost consistent with other objectives of
speed and quality. The problem is to select a contractor able to meet all of
these objectives. In principle, competitive tendering is a device which enables clients to select the most efficient contractor from among those willing
to undertake their particular project. However, while the system of 'open'
competitive tendering – under which a project is advertised and tenders
invited from all contractors interested in submitting a bid – may ostensibly
be best designed to obtain the lowest price, it is not best suited to achieving
clients' other objectives of speed and quality. Indeed, even the objective of
lowest cost may not be ensured because of the possibility of business failure
on the part of contractors who win contracts on the basis of unrealistically
low tender prices. Naturally, a client is not necessarily constrained to accept
the lowest tender and in practice throughout Europe tenders other than the
lowest are accepted. But the client is then faced with the problem of applying criteria other than price in exercising choice and, in the case of public
sector contracts, of satisfying the needs of public accountability for the
expenditure of public money.

The major alternative to open competition is to restrict competition to a
select list of contractors who are regarded as competent to carry out the
work and meet the required criteria. In the United Kingdom official commit-
tees have extolled the virtues of selective competition and it is in widespread
use (see Fleming, 1988). It is also widely used in other countries. An important prerequisite for the greatest value to be obtained from selective competition, however, is that all firms able to undertake particular contracts should
have an equal chance of being placed on a select list and invited to tender.
The market process of open competition is replaced by an administrative
mechanism of prior selection and it is not clear that the procedures adopted
by those compiling select lists are necessarily adequate and flexible enough
to ensure that some firms are not unfairly disadvantaged. The danger is that

up-and-coming firms may not be able to establish a track record and prove their worth because they are not able to gain a place on a select list in the first place; they are therefore caught in a vicious circle. Where standing lists of contractors are maintained, rather than *ad hoc* lists drawn up for specific contracts the equally important danger is that some firms are not considered for promotion or relegation to higher or lower categories on the list or removed altogether. A final reservation is that the restriction of competition to a small group of firms facilitates collusion amongst them. This is especially true where standing lists are maintained. Certainly in the United Kingdom a number of cases of collusive tendering, especially among specialist firms on select lists, have been detected by the competition authorities. There is no reason to doubt that the same opportunities for collusion are not grasped by contractors in other countries especially where the competition laws are less strict or less effectively applied. In some countries organized collaboration between contracting firms may even be countenanced, as in Belgium apparently, under the 'Charpo' system (Male and Stocks, 1991). Here, although open tendering procedures are used, the final price of the lowest-price bid includes a sum decided by the contractors themselves, to avoid 'suicidally low prices' being submitted.

For some contracts no competition between contractors may take place at all. Instead a contract is let by negotiation between the contractor and the client and his professional advisers. This can be beneficial when the building itself or the site conditions make it especially difficult to provide a sufficiently firm basis for the estimation of costs, and thus prices, in advance and hence provide a reasonable basis for competition. Indeed the work may be such as to make it advantageous to appoint a contractor at an early stage of the design process to work closely with the designer in the development of the design in order to achieve an optimum solution in the light of practical construction considerations. But in these cases it then becomes important to adopt a remuneration system for the contractor which encourages efficiency and economy in both design and construction.

The simplest form of contract in these circumstances allows for the reimbursement of costs together with a fee to cover overheads and contractor's profit with the fee being calculated as a percentage of the costs of the work – generally referred to as a 'cost plus' contract – the bid being in terms of the fee. This form, however, provides a direct incentive to inefficiency since the higher the cost of the work the greater the fee. A good discussion has been provided by Stone (1983). An alternative is to substitute a fixed fee for management in place of the percentage fee. This removes the incentive for inefficiency but provides little or no positive incentive for efficiency. A third form of cost reimbursement contract is the 'value cost' contract under which the fee is fixed in relation to the estimated cost of the works but the fee percentage is increased as the saving in actual, as compared with estimated, costs rises and reduced as any excess over estimated cost increases. This form of contract provides a direct incentive to the contractor to keep costs down. But the difficulty with all cost reimbursement contracts, as Stone notes, is the necessity either for complete confidence by the client in the integrity of the contractor or for careful scrutiny of accounts. However, detailed scrutiny may easily absorb any savings this type of contract may bring.

8.3.2   *The design and construction process*
In the context of international competition for construction contracts, there is a further dimension to the price determination problem which is important. This relates to differences in the functions traditionally performed in different countries by contractors on the one hand and design professionals on the other. In the United Kingdom where design professionals are employed independently by the client (as opposed to those working within construction firms) there is a clear division between the design phase and the production (construction) phase. The price set by a contractor for undertaking the work is therefore closely dependent, among other things, on his ability to make an appraisal of exactly what a particular design will demand in terms of construction effort and, in particular, the ease or difficulty of construction. This in turn depends not only on the thoroughness and quality of the design itself but also on the information made available to the contractor at the tender stage.

In the United Kingdom, a quantity surveyor will be employed by the client for most building projects to draw up a bill of quantities on the basis of the design drawings and specification. This provides details of all the operations required on site as well as the quantities of materials needed to realize a particular building design. The bill of quantities then becomes a standard document on which all contractors tendering for the contract are able to base their bids. In mainland Europe, however, different practices prevail. There is no direct equivalent of the quantity surveyor and a bill of quantities will often not form part of tender documentation. In these circumstances contractors themselves must determine the requirements of the design on the basis of drawings and specifications. Naturally, this introduces a further source of variation in the prices likely to be submitted, and an additional difficulty in appraising bids because of differences in the interpretation of the documents made by different contractors. This is all the more likely when detailed production drawings are not available – as is often the case – at the tender stage. A further aspect of the problem is that in some countries, France for example, positive encouragement may be given to contractors to submit variations to the design or specifications at the time of their bid. Naturally, contractors brought up in one tradition find it difficult to adapt and compete successfully in these circumstances, quite apart from the influence of other technical and cultural differences.

The system of subcontracting also poses important questions for the management of the whole construction process on site. The different management demands of the two systems may tend to constrain competition inasmuch as the domestic practices in one country do not provide the appropriate background in experience and training, and thus the expertise, for effective competition in another country where functions differ.

The issue of price determination goes deeper than the mechanisms used for placing contracts, determining contract prices and contract management. Economy in resource use demands not only efficiency on the part of contractors and an effective method of price determination and contractor selection but also a system that achieves economy in design. In manufacturing industry the functions of design and production are closely integrated. In construction, as noted above, these functions are largely separate. This division between the design and production stages is a factor of great potential importance because it precludes any interaction of design and production considerations except in so far as production aspects may be taken into account by the designer. Consequently, much depends on the training and experience of the designer. Experience is of course limited to that obtained on particular contracts, but as these are unique and involve only transient relationships with particular contractors, there is little opportunity for feedback from construction to design and a joint solution of problems.

Again in a European context, the training received by design professionals and the functions performed differ. Given the variety of practices found throughout Europe, one can do no more here than highlight some of the differences by way of example. Germany and France provide good contrasts. In Germany (the former Federal Republic) standards of technical training are high and the professional team in construction is generally regarded as better qualified technically than teams in the United Kingdom. The architect, engineer and site manager all come through the same basic educational system (Biggs *et al.*, 1990). West German architects traditionally have a wider responsibility than their UK counterparts. Their role embraces design and drawing to production level detail, cost budgeting, tender documentation and coordination of trades contractors. It is said, however, that a possible consequence of this is a weakness in conceptual creativity (Biggs *et al.*, 1990). France, on the other hand, presents a very different picture. The French architect is regarded as being less broadly based than his or her UK equivalent, both in education and functions (Meikle and Hillebrandt, 1989). The architect's education is still strongly influenced by the *beaux arts* tradition, and includes less technical and management input than in the UK. The role of the architect is to undertake the design of the building in broad terms; the detailed and working drawings are normally produced by the contractor or a *bureau d'Études techniques* (BET).[3] This is in marked contrast to the situation in the UK or Germany. At the same time, the design–production divide is reinforced in France by architects being precluded from working for a contractor (the same being true in the UK until recently – see Button and Fleming, 1992a) or other commercial organization, including BETs.

It has been pointed out that 'although the functions to be carried out in the execution of a French construction project are broadly similar to those on a British project ... the manner in which they are carried out, and who does what, are often very different' (Meikle and Hillebrandt, 1989). The French industry does not have the more or less clear-cut traditional distinctions of professional consultants and contractors. For example a BET – which will be staffed largely by architects and engineers and will undertake all kinds of design and technical studies but may well be owned by contractors – has a very important role in many projects.

In the context of building economy, the system of remuneration for design services is important. This too varies from country to country. It is common for remuneration to be based on *ad valorem* fee scales where the fee is calculated as a percentage of the contract value, with such rules being enforced either by professional self-regulation or legally by the State. Such systems provide no incentive for economy in design. In the UK, a mandatory fee scale has been replaced by a recommended scale so that, in principle, fee competition can now take place (Button and Fleming, 1992a). In Germany an agreed scale of fees is legally enforceable as part of HOAI (*Honorarordnung für Architekten und Ingenieure*) – a national ordinance which fixes the payment to architects and engineers for all construction work. In France there is no fee competition for public sector work – percentage fees having been laid down in a 1973 law – but in the private sector there is no mandatory fee scale (advisory scales are published but are said to be often negotiated downwards).

Finally, another way of overcoming the problem of the design – production divide may be considered. This is to let contracts to firms which undertake both design and construction. Such all-in design and build services – often referred to as 'package deals' or 'turnkey' projects – have grown in importance. They are generally provided by contractors rather than design professionals. Indeed until recently it was not possible for architects in the UK to offer design and construction services or to accept employment in a construction firm and retain their professional status (Button and Fleming, 1992a) and it still remains impossible in other countries. The main reservation about the design-build solution is that the quality of design may suffer – the builder subordinating design to production.

8.4   International contracting

The largest contractors have for long carried out construction contracts in other countries, not only in Europe but around the world. Apart from reasons associated with the scale of the project, this has often been because of colonial and trading links. Indeed for some contractors, British and French for example, these historic links still exercise a notable influence on the pattern of overseas work today. In the case of the United Kingdom, for example, around half or more of the value of overseas contracts in the years 1986–90 was in the Americas; only 4–11 per cent was in Europe (of which 3–7 per cent was in the European Community) while Africa constitutes the most important overseas market area for France. Special expertise is also important. Dutch contractors, for example, have an international reputation for specialized hydraulic, marine and offshore construction work.

Taking the European market as a whole, differences in national contracting practices and in the roles and functions performed by both contractors and design professionals coupled with the differences in legal requirements relating to licensing and certification, building regulations, planning controls and the like, naturally present obstacles to international competition. The principal steps being taken to remove these obstacles as part of the creation of the Single European Market are considered in the next section. The advent of the single market will naturally increase opportunities, although existing EC regulations have already increased the openness of competitive bidding (see Section 8.5.1). Here the focus is on the current extent of international competition in the European market and on the competitive success of European contractors both within Europe and around the world.

Already, work overseas constitutes a major part of the turnover of top European contractors. 'Exports' as a percentage of turnover exceeded 40 per cent for several contractors among the top 20 European contractors in the period 1989–90 (see Table 8.6).

Comprehensive figures on the degree of market penetration obtained by non-European contractors within Europe and the degree of intra-market competition between European contractors themselves are not available. However, a good indication of the nature and extent of the competition may be obtained from data collected in surveys of the top 250 international contractors. In the context of construction, it should be noted that the data go somewhat wider in covering contracting more generally (for example, process plant construction) but construction, as officially defined, would constitute a major part of the total.

The data show that Europe is the biggest single market, accounting for a quarter of the total, followed closely by North America and the Middle East, and then Africa and Latin America. European contractors gained 40 per cent of the total contracts by value; they shared the European and African mar-

kets equally with non-European contractors but were relatively more successful in North America. Details are given in Table 8.7. These data provide
a snapshot at a single point of time. Over a longer time scale the size of
different markets around the world changes quite markedly. The Middle East
was a more important market in the 1970s and early 1980s than now. Likewise, the competitive success of different contractors can vary markedly;
Korean contractors, for example, were significant competitors during the
1970s.

*Table 8.7   Overseas Contracts Won by European and Non-European
Contractors by Region, 1990**

Market	European contractors' share	Non-European contractors' share	Total
	(%)	(%)	(%)
Middle East	6.2	10.3	16.5
Asia	5.1	17.4	22.5
Africa	6.1	6.5	12.7
Europe	12.6	12.7	25.3
N. America	10.8	7.3	18.0
Latin America	2.3	2.5	4.8
Total	43.2	56.8	100.0

Notes: *Shares of the top 250 international contractors. Components may not sum to the
totals shown due to rounding errors.

Source: *Engineering News Record*, 22 July 1991.

8.4.1   The European market

In 1990 European contracts represented one-quarter of the total value of
foreign contracts won by the top 250 international contractors. Within this
market, American contractors provide the dominant source of competition,
27 firms winning a share of more than 40 per cent. The remaining 60 per
cent was shared, in the main, by contractors from within Europe. Leaders in
this group were contractors from Italy – 25 Italian contractors gained a 13.9
per cent share of the market. The other leading competitors came from
Germany, Great Britain and France. Details are given in Table 8.8.

It is notable how far competitive success is not matched directly with size
of firm within Europe. Italy, for example, which heads the field in terms of
intra-European competition, is ranked equal sixth in terms of size of firm

*Table 8.8   The European Market – Contracts Won by Nationality of
              Contractor, 1990*

Contractor nationality	Number of firms	Market share
American	27	43.8
Italian	25	13.9
West German	12	9.9
British	10	9.8
French	9	8.4
Dutch	5	4.5
Other	45	9.7

Source: As for Table 8 7.

(see Table 8.5), while Sweden, which has two firms in the top 20 European
contractors by size, does not rank quite so high in terms of success in the
international market.

8.4.2   European contractors in the world market
In a world context, out of the leading 250 international contractors gaining
overseas construction contracts in 1990, 108 were European in origin. Within
this group, Italian contractors had the greatest success with 38 firms winning

*Table 8.9   European Contractors' Share of Contracts Won by the Top 250
              International Contractors, 1990*

Contractor nationality	Number of firms	Share of total contracts by value (%)
Italian	38	11.1
British	14	10.4
French	10	8.6
West German	13	7.6
Dutch	5	2.5
Yugoslavian	8	0.6
Other	20	2.4
Total	108	43.2

Source: As for Table 8.7.

an 11 per cent market share, followed closely by 14 British contractors with a 10 per cent share. Full details are given in Table 8.9

Needless to say, the determinants of success in the world market are multifarious and beyond the scope of this chapter. However, it is worth pointing out that they extend beyond considerations of size, managerial efficiency, expertise and technical competence to embrace other factors. A useful review has been provided by the OECD (1992). For work in developing countries it is suggested that the provision of project financing may be critical, contractors often needing to put together a financing package for the client through arrangements with banks or their own governments. Countries with large progressive banking sectors or where there is close coordination of the financial and construction sectors (as in France and Japan) have an advantage. The attitude of foreign governments to tied aid is also an important factor. Finally, the ability to provide a total services package is said to be becoming a more important competitive factor in the international construction market, with clients now looking to firms to provide a complete construction package including design, engineering, construction and management services as well as project financing.

8.5   The Single European Market
The advent of the Single European Market at the end of 1992 will have no major impact on the organization and structure of the construction industry in each member state, the nature of the construction market or the competitive conditions that prevail. For one thing, legislative progress towards satisfying the requirements of the Single European Market has been taking place over a number of years but, more importantly as far as construction is concerned, the non-transportability of the product – the localized nature of production on individual sites – means that most construction work must inevitably continue to be carried out by national industries. The aim of creating a single market requires that artificial restrictions on, and barriers to, competition should be removed. As far as construction is concerned, the essential requirements are that the construction team – design professionals and contractors – should be free to move to locate in other countries, that all should have an equal opportunity of competing for the contracts available and that other artificial impediments to competition should be removed as far as possible. Here the action which has been taken to meet these objectives is reviewed.

Most of the EC legislation affecting the construction industry is in the form of 'Directives', rather than 'Regulations' or 'Decisions'. This means that although member States are required to conform with Directives, they are only required to do so in terms of achieving defined objectives, the precise way of doing so being left to the discretion of each member country.

As far as construction is concerned, the main areas affected are public procurement, construction materials and other aspects of harmonization relating to design, insurance and liability for building defects, and measures to ensure freedom of movement, as in the mutual recognition of qualifications.

8.5.1   EC public works contracts

Building and civil engineering works are a major part – almost one-third – of all public procurement in the EC, most of which should be open to all member states and awarded by competitive tender. A directive regarding public works has been in existence for several years. The current directive, dating from 1989, contains provisions relating to the advertising of contracts and guidelines for open, restricted and negotiated tendering. The directive is aimed at overcoming restrictive practices that have operated such as procedures for admittance to select lists of contractors, the acceptance only of domestic standards, requirements for licensed offices in member states and the use of high proportions of local labour and materials. The same principles are being applied to procurement in the Community's utilities sector – water, energy and transport. This will also open up market opportunities for construction contractors.

In addition a compliance directive provides for the payment of damages to contractors unfairly treated by member states. It allows the EC Commission to intervene in the award of a contract and, if necessary, to suspend the award.

8.5.2   Construction materials

This chapter is concerned with the provision of construction services rather than the construction materials sector, but work on harmonization in this area will not only open up market opportunities for construction materials producers, it will also have a wider impact in the construction sector. The Construction Products Directive was required to be implemented across the EC by 27 June 1991 (though there has been delay in implementation in some countries; in the UK implementing regulations came into force in December 1991). It will ensure that products comply with EC standards and that no member state will be able to obstruct the use of such materials. Further, under a public supply directive, contracting authorities will be required to specify products that meet agreed conforming standards.

8.5.3   Design services

Again, detailed consideration of the design professions is outside the scope of this chapter but EC provisions regarding the free movement of persons and freedom of establishment is a key element in the establishment of the Single European Market and is particularly important with regard to the professions. Sectoral and general directives are in place regarding freedom of establishment of construction professions in other member states and the mutual recognition of qualifications. These are important not only for the professions themselves but also in helping to facilitate entry by contractors through association with the architectural and engineering professions involved. For further discussion and details, see Button and Fleming (1992b, 1992c). Another general directive, adopted in June 1992, will extend recognition to non-degree-level qualifications.

8.5.4 *Other aspects of harmonization*
Other important aspects of harmonization relate to design codes and insurance and liability for defects. Work is being pursued to replace national design codes with Eurocodes. Once again, the intention is to remove artificial barriers between member states which exist through the proliferation of differing requirements in individual national codes. It seems, however, that it will take many years to achieve this objective. Finally, work is in progress to ensure a common approach to the question of liabilities, guarantees and insurance for construction defects. This is a particularly important issue for the construction sector, where defects can be extremely dangerous and costly and may not be evident for many years, and where liability may impinge on designers as well as contractors. As yet no directive has been issued in this area.

8.6 Prospects
The actions that have been taken, and the work that is being done, relating to the creation of the Single European Market will undoubtedly open up many market opportunities within Europe. As far as construction is concerned, no sudden or major impact is to be anticipated. In this sector of the economy, as in others, the passage of the year 1992 will certainly not constitute a 'Big Bang'. In construction there will remain a set of national industries, each satisfying the predominant part of its own domestic market requirements. Despite harmonization and the removal of impediments to competition, significant transnational penetration of construction markets will not take place. The main arena for competition will naturally remain those contracts which are large and/or where special expertise is required. It is in this field that competition will intensify but, as now, the competition will not be confined to European contractors.

Apart from international contracting, the main impact of the Single European Market on construction will be through the establishment by firms of a presence in other countries to take advantage more readily of local market opportunities. But, as emphasized above, the problems of language and the barriers of geography and varying local conditions and customs and the like will inevitably remain and are not easily overcome. The main entry routes are likely to be through the takeover of domestic firms or the formation of joint ventures or consortia to gain access to local knowledge and skills, rather than entry *de novo*.

Notes

1. The figure for Belgium is so out of line with those for other countries as to suggest that the data may be deficient.
2. The system of architectural education was reformed in 1968 when the Ecole Nationale des Beaux Arts was closed down and 22 new schools were set up in Paris and the provinces.
3. These are multidisciplinary offices providing design and other technical services. They may be led by an engineer but the larger offices are often subsidiaries of contractors. They have no direct equivalent in the UK.

References

Baumol, W.J., Panzar, J.C. and Willig, R.D. (1982), *Contestable Markets and the Theory of Industry Structure*, New York: Harcourt Brace Jovanovich.

Biggs, W.D., Betts, M. and Cottle, M.J. (1990), *The West German Construction Industry*, London: Construction Industry Research and Information Association.

Button, K. and Fleming, M. (1992a), 'The Effects of Regulatory Reform on the Architectural Profession in the United Kingdom', *International Review of Law and Economics*, **12**, 95–116.

Button, K. and Fleming, M. (1992b), 'The Professions in the Single European Market: A Case Study of Architects in the UK', *Journal of Common Market Studies*, **30**, 403–18.

Button, K. and Fleming, M. (1992c), 'The Changing Regulatory Regime Confronting the Professions in Europe', *Antitrust Bulletin*, **37**, 429–52.

Fleming, M. (1988), 'Construction', in Peter Johnson, *The Structure of British Industry*, 2nd ed., London: Unwin Hyman.

Males, S. and Stocks, R. (eds) (1991), *Competitive Advantage in Construction*, Oxford: Butterworth Heinemann.

Meikle, J.L. and Hillebrandt, P.M. (1989), *The French Construction Industry*, London: Construction Industry Research and Information Association.

NEDC (1990), *Gateway to Europe*, London: National Economic Development Office.

OECD (1992), *Globalisation of Industrial Activities*, Paris: OECD.

Stone, P.A. (1983), *Building Economy*, Oxford: Pergamon Press.

Further reading

Chapman, N.S.F. and Grandjean, C. (1991), *The Construction Industry and the European Community*, Oxford: BSP Professional Books.

Commission of the European Communities, *Panorama of EC Industries*, Luxembourg: Office for Official Publications of the European Communities [annual].

Fleming, M. (1988), 'Construction', in Peter Johnson (ed.), *The Structure of British Industry*, 2nd edn, London: Unwin Hyman.

Male, S. and Stocks, R. (eds) (1991), *Competitive Advantage in Construction*, Oxford: Butterworth Heinemann.

OECD (1992), *Globalisation of Industrial Activities*, Paris: OECD.

Rainbird, H. and Syben, G. (eds) (1991), *Restructuring a Traditional Industry, Construction and Skills in Europe*, New York and Oxford: Berg.

Seymour, Howard (1987), *The Multinational Construction Industry*, London: Croom Helm.

Stone, P.A. (1983), *Building Economy*, Oxford: Pergamon Press.

Strassman, W.P. and Wells, J. (eds) (1988), *The Global Construction Industry: Strategies for Entry, Growth and Survival*, London: Unwin Hyman.

Key statistical sources include
Building: annual survey of contractors.
Engineering News Record: annual survey of top international contractors.
Eurostat, *National Accounts ESA, Detailed Tables by Branch*, Luxembourg: Office for Official Publications of the European Communities.
Eurostat, *Structure and Activity of Industry, Data by Size of Enterprise*, Luxembourg: Office for Official Publications of the European Communities.
OECD, *National Accounts, Detailed Tables Vol. II*, Paris: OECD.
United Nations, *Annual Bulletin of Housing and Building Statistics for Europe*, Geneva: United Nations.

9 Air transport

Peter Johnson

9.1 Introduction

Historically the air transport industry in Europe has been characterized by a high degree of government intervention and control. Most of Europe's major airlines are wholly or partly state owned. For many years, national regulatory bodies have had the responsibility of vetting proposed fare changes and of controlling capacity and entry. They have also been required to assess the financial fitness of existing or would-be airlines. Air services between countries in Europe have been the subject of bilateral agreement on pricing and capacity between the governments involved. This pattern of regulation reflected the long-established perception, not just in Europe but throughout the world, that traffic rights are valuable national assets to be traded for reciprocal traffic rights or even rights in other areas. Such a perception was enshrined in the 1944 Chicago Convention (Balfour, 1990). In Europe itself, air transport was given special treatment by the Treaty of Rome: it was specifically excluded from the general provisions of transport policy and until 1986 there was some doubt about whether the Treaty's competition provisions, particularly Article 85 – which deals with agreements or practices between firms which affect intra-Community trade – applied to the industry.[1] Given this background of government regulation, the introduction of a common air transport policy in Europe raises particularly difficult challenges, some of which are outlined later in this chapter.

Scheduled passenger air transport within Europe – the primary interest of this chapter – has grown significantly in recent years. Table 9.1 provides some relevant data. As this table shows, there are severe restrictions on data availability. For example adequate passenger kilometre statistics for road travel are available only for four countries and the air figures exclude charter operations. However, the broad trends are probably correctly identified. Not surprisingly, all transport modes have grown in importance over the 1980s, with major expansion occurring in scheduled air, and cars and taxis. By far the most rapid growth has been in domestic air services. But it is important to recognize that although air transport is growing in relative significance, it still only constitutes a small proportion of passenger kilometres travelled. For the four EC countries for which adequate road and rail data are published (see Table 9.1), intra-European scheduled traffic of the main airlines of these countries is equivalent to less than 2 per cent of the passenger

Table 9.1   Passenger Traffic in the European Community: % Increase in Passenger Kilometres 1980–90, by Mode

Mode	% Increase
Rail[1]	14
Road[2]	
Passengers, cars and taxis	31
Buses and coaches	15
Scheduled Air[3]	
Domestic	65
Intra-European	31

Notes:
1. The EC 12.
2. Denmark, France, the Netherlands, the United Kingdom.
3. Eleven member airlines of the Association of European Airlines: SAS, plus ten others registered in the EC.

Sources: *Annual Bulletin of Transport Statistics in Europe*, UN, 1992; *Yearbook* of the Association of European Airlines, various years; *Traffic Commercial Air Carriers*, International Civil Aviation Organization, various years.

kilometres travelled by road (and to about 20 per cent of rail passenger kilometres).[2]

Not surprisingly the UK, France and Germany are the main origin and destination countries for intra-European traffic. For example, these countries provide the origin airport for well over half the number of passengers leaving an EC country (CEC, 1991b, pp. 25–45). The dominance of these three countries is also shown in routes, as Table 9.2 demonstrates.

The growth in air traffic in Europe has varied significantly across routes. For example between 1985 and 1990, the busiest trunk routes – those with more than 500 000 passengers – grew by 4.4 per cent, while those in the 100–500 000 range grew by 12 per cent and the still thinner routes by 18 per cent (AEA, 1991, p. 4).

Air transport has not grown smoothly in Europe. Not surprisingly, given the evidence on income elasticities (see section 9.2.2), the industry is sensitive to fluctuations in the general level of economic activity. The airlines also suffered badly from the Gulf War in 1990–91: during the six weeks of conflict, European traffic fell by a quarter compared with the previous year's level (AEA, 1991, p. 11). This fall was not matched by a corresponding reduction in capacity. As a result capacity utilization, measured here in terms

Table 9.2   *International European Routes Served by Members of the Association of European Airlines, 1991*

To/from	Number of routes
Germany	308
France	193
UK	186
Italy	165
Spain	151
Scandinavia	117
Belgium	70
Portugal	65
Netherlands	63
Greece	52
Ireland	36
Luxembourg	26

Source: AEA (1992).

of a load factor which expresses revenue passenger kilometres as a percentage of available passenger kilometres, fell significantly.

Passenger services account for more than 85 per cent of European airlines' total revenue (CEC, 1991b, pp. 25–45).

9.2   Costs and demand

9.2.1   Costs
Some idea of the breakdown of costs for European airlines may be obtained from Table 9.3, which provides data for the three leading European airlines. The data cover *all* the activities of the airlines; separate figures are not published for their European activities. Differences in the relative importance of the various cost categories reflect differences in the route structures and aircraft fleets, and international differences in (for example) labour costs. The figures are also sensitive to the precise way in which the airlines allocate their costs across categories.

Many of the costs referred to in the table may be referred to as *capacity costs*. Once the airline has decided on its fleet and schedules, these costs do not vary very much with the passenger numbers carried by the airline. The main categories of capacity cost are expenses arising from flight operations, maintenance and overhaul, depreciation and amortization, and landing charges unrelated to passenger numbers. If it is assumed that half of user charges and

Table 9.3 Operating Expenses: Three Major European Airlines

Expenses category	%[1] of total operating expenses		
	British[2] Airways	Lufthansa[3]	Air France[4]
Flight operations, of which	22.1	22.9	27.4
Flight crew salaries and expenses	5.8	5.7	6.0
Aircraft fuel and oil	13.5	10.7	13.4
Maintenance and overhaul	9.8	14.9	11.0
Depreciation and amortization	4.0	7.7	9.0
User charges and station expenses, of which	17.0	17.9	20.9
Landing and associated airport charges	6.0	4.3	5.4
Station expenses	8.1	11.1	13.4
Passenger services	15.0	11.3	12.7
Ticketing, sales, promotion	17.6	18.1	16.1
General and administrative	10.7	7.1	3.0
Other operating expenses	3.8	–	–
Total[5]	100.0	100.0	100.0

Notes:
1. The percentages are calculated using data based on the reporting currencies.
2. Year ending 31.3.1991.
3. Year ending 31.12.1990.
4. Year ending 31.12.1989.
5. The columns may not sum to 100.0 because of rounding errors.

Source: International Civil Aviation Organization, *Financial Data: Commercial Air Carriers*, 1989 and 1990, Digests of Statistics Nos 374 and 386 (Series F-Nos 43 and 44). Reproduced with the permission of ICAO.

station expenses may properly be classed as capacity costs, then the latter account for between 44 and 59 per cent of the total operating costs of the three airlines. Those costs which vary with passenger numbers (passenger services, ticketing, sales, promotion and, say, the remainder of user charges and station expenses) may be referred to as *traffic costs*, and account for a further 38 to 41 per cent. Administrative costs account for the rest.

Many of the charges that an airline has to pay lie outside its direct control. However, the larger airlines may be able to exercise some buying power in certain markets; and they may lobby effectively over charges that are controlled by government. And of course even if input prices lie outside the control of airlines, the efficiency with which they are utilized does not.

Before the more general relationship between airline size and costs is examined, it is worth noting the following. First, costs per seat mile will, for a given load factor, decline with sector length at least up to the aircraft design range, since many costs do not increase proportionately, or in some cases at all, with distance. For example, manufacturer's data for the British Aerospace ATP200 suggests that costs per seat mile – for a 60 per cent load factor – fall by about a third as the sector increases from 200 to 700 miles (Johnson, 1988). Secondly the marginal costs of carrying an additional passenger on a flight are very small (up to capacity limits). Finally as the number of passengers travelling on a given sector grows, so the costs per seat mile will tend to fall because of economies of density. The airline may be able to take advantage of larger aircraft. Capacity costs do not rise proportionately with aircraft size: not only are there economies of increased dimensions, but some costs, for example crew and equipment costs, may be largely invariant with respect to aircraft size. Furthermore, the fixed costs at each terminal will be spread over more passengers, and the airline can take fuller advantage of massed reserves, and any economies of scale in servicing aircraft. However, it is unlikely that the economies from higher throughput on a single sector are limitless: congestion and the strains on the structural integrity of ever larger aircraft are two factors likely to impose ultimate constraints on cost reductions.

There is some conflicting evidence on the level at which economies of density are exhausted. Keeler (1991, p. 126) has argued that for the US at least, recent results are consistent with very few such economies on the average trunk route. Whether or not a natural monopoly exists on a given route will depend on demand as well as on cost conditions. Most airlines do not of course operate on a single sector, but have an intricate web of routes. In these cases the relationship between the overall size of an airline and unit costs, both measured with reference to some generalized unit such as available seat kilometres, becomes much more complex and will depend in part on the precise network operated by the airline.

The existence of network economies is one factor underlying the development of 'hub and spoke' operations. In such operations, flights are funnelled through major 'hub' airports in strategic locations and in this way easy transfer between flights is facilitated. Of course separate airlines may be able to develop integrated hub and spoke operations through contracting. However, passengers usually have a clear preference – for obvious reasons – for dealing with one airline only. The available (American) evidence (see Caves *et al.*, 1984) suggests that while the trunk airlines may be able to achieve some economies of density by utilizing a given network more intensively (by adding flights or seats on existing flights)[3] there is little support for the presence of airline economies of scale (unit costs falling as flights to airports not previously served are added).[4] If the evidence is correct and is applicable in Europe, then the move towards larger size that some of the bigger EC airlines (comparable in size to some US trunks) are seeking (see section 9.4.2) needs to be scrutinized very carefully. Any justification for merger activity which is derived from the argument that increased economies of scale will result, may be questionable. Recent moves towards merger and other forms of cooperative arrangement may of course have motivations other than cost savings.

9.2.2 Demand

An individual wishing to travel from A to B will compare the relative costs of undertaking the journey by different modes (or by different combinations of modes). 'Costs' here include not only fares and, where appropriate, additional expenditure on meals and accommodation, but also the cost of time and any discomfort incurred. Such discomfort will be affected, *inter alia*, by load factors; most passengers prefer to have empty seats beside them.

The schedules of the different modes, and their perceived reliability, will play a part in determining the costs of time. In this context it should be noted that not all time spent travelling will be wasted.

Air fares tend to be more expensive than the direct costs of surface modes of travel. However, the time saving from air transport tends to rise with the distance travelled, as do the ancillary expenses of surface travel (meals, accommodation). It is hardly surprising therefore to find that as the length of trip increases, so air travel takes an increasing share. This is shown – for business travel – in Figure 9.1. At around 500–600 km, air transport has about the same market share in business travel as the private car and rail. The leisure traveller's cost of time will typically be lower than the business person's and this will tend to move the 'equal market shares' point, to the right.

The evidence on price elasticities in air transport is rather sparse. However a study of leisure air travel by UK residents taking independent holidays in Europe (Witt and Martin, 1985) suggests wide variations across routes and, perhaps surprisingly, absolute values which are mostly less than one. The latter result reflects a variety of influences including the relatively low price sensitivity of the higher-income groups who tend to use air rather than surface transport for their visits. The same study showed most income elasticities to be greater than one, thus classifying leisure air travel as a luxury.

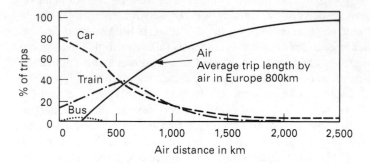

Source: Airbus Industrie data, quoted in AEA (1992), p. 19.

Figure 9.1   Modal Split for Business Trips

Business travel is of course a derived demand, and so its price elasticity is determined *inter alia* by the price elasticity of demand for the final product or service; the relative importance of expenditure on air travel in total costs; and the availability of suitable substitutes (e.g. surface travel, telephone calls and transmission, correspondence). A study of a domestic trunk route in the UK (TRRL, 1981) which is dominated by business traffic suggests absolute elasticity values of less than 0.3. Studies of US routes, reported in Johnson (1988), highlight the way in which such values tend to rise as distance falls and as the availability of other modes increases.

9.3   The structure of the industry

9.3.1   An overview
Table 9.4 provides some summary data on the scheduled activities of those member airlines of the Association of European Airlines (AEA) which are registered in the EC. It should be noted that there are a number of EC airlines, for example British Midland, which are not members of the AEA, and that SAS is a joint Norwegian, Danish and Swedish venture. (Only Denmark is currently in the EC.) Nevertheless the figures provide a broadly accurate representation of the overall picture. Well over a quarter of a million people are directly employed in the airlines listed in Table 9.4. Indirect employment in infrastructure and support industries will add significantly to this total: for example more than 100 000 are employed in the EC's major airports (CEC, 1991b, pp. 25–56).

Table 9.4 Some European Airlines: Key Statistics, 1990

Airline	Total scheduled traffic RPKs(m)[1]	% of total	European scheduled traffic[2] RPKs(m)	% of total	Domestic scheduled traffic RPKs(m)	% of total	Revenue load factor[3] Total	Employment	% of total
Aer Lingus	4 191	1.6	1 731	3.3	70	0.3	71.3	7 059	2.5
Air France	36 653	14.0	6 081	11.5	7 630	27.3	69.2	39 810	14.2
Alitalia	19 126	7.3	4 834	9.2	1 984	7.1	64.6	19 730	7.0
British Airways	66 795	25.5	10 218	19.3	3 961	14.1	71.7	53 615	19.1
Iberia	22 112	8.4	6 587	12.5	4 772	17.0	69.3	28 843	10.3
KLM	26 390	10.1	2 754	5.2	8	–	70.3	26 434	9.4
Lufthansa	41 903	16.0	7 808	14.8	2 852	10.2	64.8	47 619	17.0
Luxair	253	0.1	253	0.5	–	–	59.1	1 096	0.4
Olympic	7 764	3.0	2 691	5.1	1 175	4.2	63.8	11 906	4.2
Sabena	7 572	2.9	1 654	3.1	–	–	64.4	7 505	2.7
SAS	16 516	6.3	5 772	10.9	3 276	11.7	64.7	19 550	7.0
TAP	6 836	2.6	2 446	4.6	768	2.7	70.3	10 493	3.7
UTA	6 101	2.3	–	–	1 502	5.4	67.7	6 946	2.4
All airlines	262 212	100.0	52 829	100.0	27 998	100.0	67.0	280 606	100.0
% Total RPKs	100		20		11				

Notes:
1. Revenue passenger kilometres.
2. Includes all routes originating and terminating in Europe.
3. Revenue passenger kilometres/available passenger kilometres x 100.

Source: AEA (1991).

Domestic operations account for 11 per cent of total revenue passenger kilometres (RPKs) and intra-European traffic which covers international flights in the whole of Europe, not just the EC, for a further 20 per cent. These percentages vary from airline to airline: for example 21 per cent of Air France's RPKs are in the domestic market, whereas the corresponding figure for Lufthansa is 7 per cent. Similar differences exist on the intra-European side, although, in all cases, such traffic is much less important than international traffic (mostly long-haul) to points outside Europe. However it is worth noting (Encaoua, 1991, p. 113) that the relative importance of European routes is much greater for the southern carriers (Alitalia, Iberia, TAP and Olympic Airways). These airlines are also under considerable pressure from the charter airlines. Given these factors, it is hardly surprising that the governments of the countries concerned have been the most strongly opposed to further liberalization.

Three airlines (Air France, British Airways and Lufthansa) accounted for 55 per cent of total RPKs. In Europe, their share was rather less – 46 per cent – reflecting the relatively greater importance of long-haul intercontinental flights in their route structure. (The Spanish airline Iberia has a rather larger share of intra-European RPKs than Air France.) Air France dominates domestic traffic (27 per cent of the total). Four other airlines each account for over 10 per cent of this traffic.

9.3.2   Competition between the airlines

The summary figures on total traffic shares in the first column of figures in Table 9.4 are helpful in providing an indication of the relative sizes of the different airlines. In so far as overall size reflects the scale of the route *network* offered by an airline, the figures also offer a measure of the overall competitive position of an airline, since the comprehensiveness of the route structure offered is likely to be an important determinant of an airline's attractiveness to customers.

The data do not, however, show the significance of the airlines on particular routes. As indicated in section 9.1, competition on routes between EC countries has a long history of regulation. Bilateral agreements between the countries involved have restricted entry and controlled prices and capacity. Most routes in Europe have traditionally been served by one or two carriers: Pryke (1991, p. 232) shows that of the 750 non-stop short-haul flights in Europe in 1989, 71 per cent had only one carrier, and a further 24 per cent had only two.[5] Of Pryke's densest routes (those with 75 flights per week or more) only half have three or more airlines. These routes are mostly international ones; domestic routes are overwhelmingly monopolies or duopolies. But it should be noted that on many single airline routes, it would not be economically viable to have more than one or two operators, so it would be a mistake always to equate what is, in *structural* terms, a monopoly or duopoly with a market in which the incumbents are able to exercise market *power*. On the long-haul routes out of Europe the major airlines compete indirectly with each other, and on some of these routes a more relaxed regulatory regime operates. On some of the intercontinental routes competition is very intense: for example, eight airlines operate direct flights between London and New York. Entry on to domestic routes has often been subject to tight control. (It is the Commission's intention to open up such routes to foreign competition, at least from airlines registered in the EC: see section 9.6).

In the mid-1980s Belgium, the UK, the Netherlands and Ireland antici-pated the development of EC policy and adopted a more relaxed regulatory regime, permitting new entrants to operate on key routes and freeing con-trols on capacity. Even here, however, not more than three airlines serve even the densest routes. Contestability theory (see for example Baumol, 1982) suggests that the number of incumbent firms may offer little guide to the effectiveness of the *threat* of *potential* entry. There has been much debate on how contestable a deregulated airline market is. The view among some economists in the early 1980s was that the US deregulated market was highly contestable, with investment in aircraft constituting 'capital on wings' (Baumol and Willig, 1986). This view has since been modified as it has become apparent that incumbent airlines may be protected in a variety of ways, for example through control over scarce runway slots, the use of biased computer reservation systems and marketing programmes such as 'frequent flyer' promotions. It is worth noting too that most of the newer airlines that emerged in the post-deregulation period in the US have now disappeared (Pryke, 1991, p. 221). There is also evidence to suggest that concentration and fares on particular routes are positively correlated (Kahn, 1988), and that domination of a hub may lead to higher fares to and from that hub (Keeler, 1991, p. 158). Of course, such evidence is still consistent with potential entry exercising *some* moderating influence on an incum-bent's behaviour (Morrison and Winston, 1986). For Europe, even in a completely deregulated environment, the very considerable constraint on runway slots would be likely to blunt the force of potential competition.

Table 9.4 excludes non-scheduled operations. Most of the charter airlines are concentrated in the UK (CEC, 1991b, pp. 25–45). Some are of a signifi-cant size: for example Britannia Airways flew more RPKs (14 115 million in 1991) on non-scheduled operations than six of the airlines listed in Table 9.4 did on scheduled services. Apart from Aer Lingus, the AEA airlines in Table 9.4 obtained only a very small proportion of their business from charter operations, although many have an ownership stake in a charter airline. The Commission estimates that non-scheduled airlines are responsible for about 65 per cent of all air transportation within the Community. (CEC, 1991a, p.

16). Over the years this non-scheduled traffic has exercised some competitive constraint on scheduled services – indeed it has in part arisen *because* of a lack of competition in the latter – although it has largely been restricted to the North Atlantic and to holiday routes, especially to Spain. Charter services have operated under a much freer regulatory environment than their scheduled counterparts (Abbott and Thompson, 1991; Button and Swann, 1989).

Any analysis of behaviour on European routes must acknowledge the interdependence of the different activities identified in Table 9.4. On the demand side, the domestic intra-European and other international services feed each other. On the supply side interdependencies also exist. There are many costs – for example in relation to ticketing and reservations – that are joint to the different markets, and an airline may be able to achieve some economies in activities that are not specific to particular markets.

How do the main EC scheduled airlines compare in world terms? Six of the world's top 20 airlines are EC based. British Airways is the largest *international* airline, but its RPKs still only represent 54 per cent of those provided by American Airlines, the world's largest airline.

9.3.3   Load factors
The load factor in Table 9.4 is one possible measure of efficiency (although an airline may be able to raise its profitability by reducing its load factor and raising prices). It is perhaps significant that the three airlines most involved to date in liberalization (Aer Lingus, British Airways and KLM) have the highest load factors.

9.3.4   Ownership
Most of the major airlines in the EC are wholly or partly state owned and are therefore likely to be subject to government control, and to be eligible for public funding. Aer Lingus (Ireland), Air France (France), Iberia (Spain), Olympic (Greece) and TAP (Portugal) are effectively state enterprises, although the mechanism for public ownership varies from country to country. The state also has a significant holding in Alitalia (Italy), Lufthansa (Germany), Sabena (Belgium) and SAS. Of the major European airlines, only British Airways is wholly within the private sector, having been privatized in 1987. More privatizations are likely: the German government is keen to sell its 59 per cent stake in Lufthansa, and Greece intends to sell its 49 per cent shareholding in Olympic (*The Economist*, 1992). Many of the major airlines have ownership stakes in other EC and non-EC airlines. For example a recent EC report (CEC, 1991b, pp. 25–51) shows that Air France has an equity share in twelve airlines, and KLM in seven.

9.3.5 Infrastructure

Air transport depends critically on two key elements of infrastructure: air traffic control (ATC) and airports. The scale of such infrastructure and the efficiency with which it is operated inevitably influence the activities of the airlines and *their* efficiency. The AEA estimated that in 1991, delays directly attributable to infrastructure factors led to 54 000 lost aircraft hours, equivalent to the workload of a fleet of 20 short-haul jets (AEA, 1992, p. 16). Infrastructure provision may also have implications for the structure of the industry: for example if runway capacity is fully utilized, new entry is possible only if incumbent airlines reduce their activities.

ATC in Europe is currently highly fragmented. In 1991 there were 44 control centres (Transport Committee, 1991a, p. xx). Many of these centres use different equipment and software: in a recent review of a rather larger number of European ATCs conducted on behalf of the air transport authorities (quoted in AEA, 1992, p. 17), there were 31 separate systems, with computer hardware from 18 suppliers, running 20 operating systems using 70 different programming languages. Three-quarters of the centres, according to the review, had 'significant' or 'major' system deficiencies. These differences between ATC centres inevitably make for inefficiencies and hence a loss of capacity: one estimate suggests that capacity could be increased by 30 per cent if coordination difficulties were resolved (Transport Committee, 1991b, p. 111). The cost penalty of ATC fragmentation in 1988 was put at $4 190 million by the AEA (AEA, 1990, p. 7). Even if allowance is made for the fact that the AEA has a vested interest in reducing the losses from poor ATC, the penalty is still likely to be very substantial.

In 1992 transport ministers agreed to work towards a more integrated ATC system in Europe. Integration of national systems is, however, different from having the kind of single system that would maximize efficiency; but such a system would present considerable political problems in respect of the exercise of national sovereignty.

The most heavily utilized airports in Europe are listed in Table 9.5. London dominates the scene, accounting for nearly 28 per cent of passengers. London handles 18 of the top 30 intra-EC scheduled routes (Transport Committee, 1991b, p. 21). Numerous European airports face, or are likely to face, capacity problems unless remedial action is taken (*ibid.*, p. 181). These airports include London, Frankfurt, Düsseldorf, Milan, Brussels and Madrid. Such problems arise because of physical limits on either terminal or runway throughputs. The measurement of such limits is complex and depends on institutional as well as technical influences. Size of aircraft and the pattern of arrivals and departures over time also play an important role.

One issue relating to airport operation that has attracted considerable attention in recent years is the process by which runway slots are allocated.

Table 9.5   Top Ten EC Airports, 1990

		Million passengers embarked/disembarked
1.	London (total)	63.6
	Heathrow	42.6
	Gatwick	21.0
2.	Paris (total)	46.8
	Orly	24.3
	De Gaulle	22.5
3.	Frankfurt	28.7
4.	Madrid	15.9
5.	Rome	15.5*
6.	Amsterdam	14.9
7.	Copenhagen	11.8
8.	Düsseldorf	11.6
9.	Palma (Majorca)	11.3
10.	Athens	10.1
Total		230.2

Note: *1989.

Source: *Airport Traffic, 1990* (ICAO Digest of Statistics 383).

Slot allocation procedures become particularly important where airlines are competing for similar departure/arrival times. Times that enable business people to make a round day trip are likely to be particularly attractive.

At present the allocation system is largely based on 'grandfather' rights – an airline that is using a slot has an automatic continuing entitlement to it, even if it does not use it on the *same* route. The exercise of grandfather rights at congested airports make access by new entrants very difficult and stifles potential competition.

One possible answer to the problem is to develop a mechanism for slot auctioning between airlines. This procedure, which has been tried at a number of congested airports in the US, could be seen as a move towards a market-based mechanism for allocating the available capacity and eliminating unsatisfied demand for slots. However, such a mechanism raises a number of difficulties. One preliminary issue concerns the *ownership* of the slot. Does it belong to the airport or the airline? The airlines' views on this issue are predictable: for example, British Midland has argued that a slot 'represents a tangible symbol of our investment in [the] service and what we are selling is that' (Transport Committee, 1991a, p. xvii). Even if it is assumed that the airline owns the slots and can therefore trade them, American experience with a slot 'market' suggests that such a mechanism is unlikely to have a significant competition-enhancing effect at congested airports. Current EC proposals for slot allocation recognize the existence of grandfather rights, and the current scheduling procedures have also been exempted from the competition provisions of Article 85 of the Treaty of Rome. However, the Commission is seeking greater 'transparency' in allocation procedures, and the development of a pool of unused or underutilized slots, half of which would be available to new entrants. The proposals also allow, where necessary, for some limited reallocation of slots from incumbent airlines to new entrants. Not surprisingly, they are unpopular with the airlines that might have to give up slots.

So far the Council of Ministers has postponed consideration of the proposals. But even if the changes suggested by the Commission were implemented they would be unlikely to have more than a marginal effect on competition. A much more radical approach might involve the auctioning of runway slots *by the airports*, in much the same way as (for example) TV franchises are sold in the UK. The period for which runway slots might be allocated by this means would reflect appropriate business time horizons, and the fact that an airline may need some time to build up its market.

9.4 Aspects of behaviour

9.4.1 Pricing

Sawers (1987, p. 59) argues convincingly that the lack of competition on European routes has led to high fares. He shows that in 1983 the average fare per passenger mile, even allowing for variations in input prices, was nearly double that for comparable routes in the US. He also argues that the availability of discount fares is more restricted in Europe. Sawers's evidence relates largely to Europe *as a whole* (although he does cite fares on individual routes to support his case). The picture is likely to vary from route to route depending *inter alia* on the extent of charter competition and the strength of competition from surface transport.

Section 9.6.2 examines the likely effect of deregulation on fares. Downward pressure is almost certain, although the intensity of this pressure will depend on how protected the existing airlines are from potential new entrants. Where significant entry *is* possible, price increases are likely to be moderated and more discount fares introduced. Where airlines are unable to achieve price coordination through regulatory agencies, the cost structure of airline operations – high fixed costs, low marginal costs – is likely to lead to more discounting when demand is slack.

9.4.2 Merger activity

In recent years there have been a number of attempts by the larger European airlines to strengthen their position through merger or other links. For example in 1991 BA and KLM explored the possibility of a merger but discussions foundered on how ownership should be split between the British and the Dutch. In the same year BA also entered discussions with Sabena (the Belgian airline) with a view to obtaining an ownership stake. Again these came to nothing. Air France now has an 85 per cent share in the international French airline UTA and effectively controls the domestic airline, Air Inter. The three airlines make up Group Air France. Air France is also seeking a stake in Sabena. Air France and Lufthansa have signed a cooperation agreement. Some European airlines have also sought to link up with US airlines: for example in July 1992, British Airways announced its intention to buy into USAir, the fifth largest US airline, and KLM has a 20 per cent interest in North West. These moves are designed to give the airlines involved a stronger market base in an increasingly global industry, and in particular to strengthen their hub operations at key airports and to increase the scale of their networks. Both are likely to play a key role in determining the overall attractiveness of an airline's services. It is less clear what the welfare gains will be.

9.4.3 Restricting competition

Airlines may utilize a variety of approaches to limit new or increased competition. They may increase frequencies to make a new entrant unprofitable. They may also place restrictions on 'interlining', which allows passengers on different airlines serving the same route to exchange tickets. For example, in 1987 when the (now defunct) Air Europe lowered its fares to and from Germany by 15 per cent, Lufthansa cancelled their acceptance of Air Europe's documents (Air Europe eventually received a ruling that such retaliation was illegal and Lufthansa then reinstated their acceptance). The regulatory authorities are now becoming more vigilant on these issues: Aer Lingus was recently fined by the Commission for cutting off an interlining agreement with British Midland Airways on the Heathrow–Dublin route.

There are some areas in which cooperation between airlines may benefit customers. Computerized reservation systems, for example, may provide fuller information and hence greater choice, provided no one airline is allowed to dominate such systems. The two systems operated by EC airlines, Galileo and Amadeus, are jointly owned by a number of airlines, so are less open to abuse.

9.5 Performance

Performance may be measured in a wide variety of ways. In air transport it is common to present an array of different measures, each of which gives only a partial picture and requires careful interpretation (Forsyth *et al.*, 1986). These caveats must be borne in mind in the following discussion, which focuses on costs, productivity and profitability.

One of the measures sometimes used is cost per available (or revenue) passenger (or tonne). Such a measure can provide some guide to efficiency, but the mix of the outputs makes comparison across airlines difficult. For example the leisure–business split will influence overall unit costs since leisure travel tends to be of lower quality. Again, airlines operating on lengthier routes will tend, *ceteris paribus*, to have lower unit costs. It is also the case that some costs vary significantly across national boundaries. However, it is unlikely that these factors alone can explain the very considerable differences in unit cost that exist between airlines. For example, Encaoua (1991) has shown that in 1986 the cost (in cents) per available tonne kilometre on European routes varied across airlines registered in the EC from 62.0 for Iberia to 98.8 for KLM. (The unweighted mean for the eight EC-registered airlines examined by Encaoua was 80.2.) Nearly 20 cents of the difference between Iberia and KLM was due to variations in indirect costs.

Sawers (1987) has compared costs per seat on European routes with those of airlines offering similar services in the US, and found that in 1983 the former was over 60 per cent higher (after allowance is made for differences in input prices in the two continents). Sawers argues that these figures reflect lower efficiency in Europe, and that the biggest differences in efficiency are in labour-intensive activities such as maintenance and marketing. Interestingly, the unit cost of *all* the operations of European airlines was only 20 per cent higher than that of all the operations of US airlines, suggesting that outside Europe competitive forces may ensure a greater convergence of costs. Encaoua's finding – that cost per available tonne kilometre is two to three times higher on European than on the North Atlantic routes – offers some support for this proposition.

Productivity may be variously measured. One common yardstick is labour productivity measured for example in terms of available, or revenue, tonne kilometres per employee. These two measures show a virtually continuous increase in Europe over the period 1985–91: see figure 9.2. This figure, which relates only to AEA members, does however show a dip in revenue tonne kilometres per employee in 1991, reflecting the fall in capacity utilization resulting from the combined effects of the Gulf War and the recession.

These measures have many limitations. Although ostensibly measures of labour productivity, they are affected by factors other than labour's performance, notably capital investment, technology and institutional factors. They

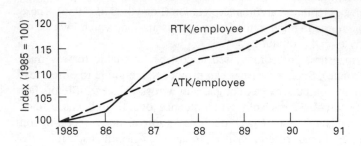

Source: AEA (1992), p. 13.

Figure 9.2   Labour Productivity Trends (AEA Members)

are also dependent on the extent to which the airline buys in services (e.g. baggage handling) from other businesses, and on route structure. These factors contribute to the significant variations in labour productivity across European airlines (Windle, 1991). A better measure of productivity, which takes into account the contribution of capital, is total factor productivity (TFP). Interestingly, Windle (1991) shows that the labour productivity measures suggest much wider differentials in productivity across airlines than the TFP indicators. Windle's study suggests that TFP in the US airlines is 19 per cent ahead of the European airlines. However it also shows that this advantage does not fully feed through into a unit cost advantage because of the higher input costs – particularly labour – faced by US airlines. The overall unit cost advantage of these airlines over their European counterparts is estimated at 7 per cent. (Higher traffic density in the US serves to keep this advantage higher than it might otherwise be.) The advantage is considerably lower than that implied by Sawers (1987); differences in methodology, in the airlines included in the comparisons, and in the time periods chosen explain the difference. Data on TFP trends by airlines are limited although Encaoua has looked at what has happened on European routes for five airlines over the period 1981–86. His results suggest wide variations in productivity growth but some convergence of performance over the period. British Airways and KLM, the two airlines most involved in liberalization, showed the highest growth over the whole period.

Profitability varies significantly across airlines. For example the increase in British Airways' profitability in 1991 stands in marked contrast to the substantial losses incurred by some of its European counterparts, such as

KLM, Iberia and Aer Lingus. Overall, the 1990s have seen a plunge in profitability, as Figure 9.3 shows. The operating ratio given in the figure expresses operating revenues as a percentage of operating costs, including interest payments. The effects of the recession in the early 1980s and 1990s are easily apparent.

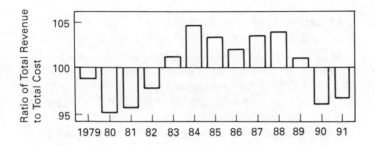

Notes: Operating ratios are for total international activities; after interest. AEA members only. 1991 figures are estimates.
Source: AEA (1992), p. 12.

Figure 9.3   Operating Ratios

Sawers (1987, p. 57ff.) has argued that profit margins appear to be higher on international intra-European services than on any other international routes. His figures are subject to some limitations, not least the fact that any calculations of profits on European routes require costs to be allocated to those routes, but these limitations are unlikely to explain the fact that in 1984, for example, the profit margin after interest payments, as a percentage of costs on European routes, was over six times that earned by US domestic and national airlines, and four times that obtained by the US majors. Encaoua (1991) has shown that in 1985–86 there was a very substantial difference in the profitability per revenue tonne kilometre (RTK) or per RPK on European and North Atlantic routes: with some airlines the former is ten times higher than the latter. He also shows that there are marked variations in profitability across European carriers. SAS, for example, made 3.3 US cents per RPK on its European routes while British Airways made half that figure.

9.6 Policy

9.6.1   *The policy framework*

The EC's air transport policy covers four main areas: liberalization; harmonization (e.g. over slot allocation procedures at airports, consumer protection and safety); infrastructure (mainly in relation to the provision of runway and air traffic control capacity); and external relations with non-EC countries. The focus here is on liberalization although clearly the various strands of policy are related.

The policy on liberalization has evolved in stages. The first stage was introduced at the beginning of 1988.[6] The second stage came into force towards the end of 1990. The third and final stage was agreed in June 1992 and mostly came into effect on 1 January 1993. (Council Regulation (EEC) 2407/92, 2408/92, 2409/92.) This 'gradualist' approach – which reflects political realities – contrasts with that adopted towards US deregulation, which was largely achieved in one major step.

The underlying objective of the policy has recently been set out by the senior official involved, Frederik Sørensen (1991). According to Sørensen, the aim is to achieve a market structure that will 'sustain competition'. Such a structure is characterized, *inter alia*, by a sufficient number of actual or potential competitors and by freedom for airlines to determine their prices and capacity on different routes according to their own judgement, but in a context where the authorities may still intervene to stop (for example) anti-competitive practices. In this way, it is argued, flexibility and choice are generated (CEC, 1991a, p. 4).

To achieve this objective, controls on entry, pricing and capacity have been progressively dismantled. On entry, policy has developed on two fronts. The first relates to the issuing or confirming of operating licences for air carriers. Here a common set of licensing criteria which apply throughout the Community and which determine the requirements for technical and economic fitness have been developed.[7] A crucial aspect of these criteria is that they do not incorporate any protection for existing carriers. Under the new scheme, a licensed airline is in principle able to operate anywhere in the Community. The second issue on entry relates to licensing on particular routes. The ultimate goal here is to open up all routes to potential competition from any airline registered in the EC, subject to certain restrictions – for example where the route involved has a low volume of traffic. The most significant element in this development is the provision of full 'fifth freedom' rights under which airlines are free to offer services between *any* two countries in the EC, and of cabotage rights, which permit a foreign airline to operate on the *domestic* routes of a member state.

On pricing, the Commission's intention is that airlines should ultimately be free to determine their own fares, subject to certain conditions. For example airlines may be required to withdraw fares which are deemed excessively 'high' relative to costs, or which result in widespread losses for the airlines concerned. The rules on capacity abolish the restrictions that have existed on many routes, except where there are serious congestion and/or environmental problems. The rules also allow the Commission to 'stabilize' capacity for a limited period where 'serious financial damage' to scheduled airlines may result.

Although the implications of the policy changes are potentially far-reaching, their full implementation clearly depends on the commitment by the member states to the underlying principle of achieving competitive market outcomes. In the majority of member states the leading airline is government owned and receives political and financial backing as the 'flagship' airline. In these circumstances it is less likely that a country will be willing to see its airline overwhelmed by competition in either domestic or international markets. Furthermore, the policies leave plenty of scope for interpretation, and the Council of Ministers' meeting in June 1992 built in a number of 'safeguards' which may blunt the cutting edge of competition (Council of the European Communities, 1992).

The lack of enthusiasm for full liberalization by some countries is shown in the decision by the Council of Ministers to delay the starting date for the introduction of full cabotage rights; instead the Council approved a transitional period until April 1997 in which such rights are reduced. In this period, an airline may fly between two points in a country other than the one in which it is registered, provided one of these points is the destination/origin airport for a flight from/to the country of registration. Thus British Airways may fly London–Paris–Bordeaux, but not simply Paris–Bordeaux. Such 'consecutive cabotage' – on which the foreign airline's use of its capacity is to be restricted in any case to 50 per cent (of its seasonal capacity) during the transitional period, thereby greatly reducing the likelihood of profitability – is clearly a considerable restriction and demonstrates some of the political difficulties in the path of full liberalization. (The four-year delay was itself a compromise; six countries wanted a six-year period.)

Two other potential obstacles to full liberalization should be mentioned. First, under certain conditions state aid is still to be permitted, a reflection of the political reality that many airlines, including Air France, Sabena and Iberia, are in receipt of substantial government funding without which they would be unable to survive. (Such aid has led British Airways to claim, with some justification, that competition is distorted as a result.) Secondly, if 'grandfather' rights to runway slots are retained and the present capacity difficulties over runways and air traffic control are not alleviated, the scope for entry will be heavily restricted.

9.6.2   The effects of the new policies

It is too early to say what the long-run shape and effects of the new policies will be. However, it may be helpful to consider what lessons can be learned from studies of the effects of deregulation in the US and of the bilateral liberalization that has already occurred on certain routes in Europe.

The US experience   In the US there can be little doubt that deregulation has led to an overall reduction in fares. For example Keeler (1991, p. 138) shows that between 1976, the last year of full regulation, and 1987, the real yield (cents per mile) on unrestricted fares fell from 4.4 to 3.2. (The yield on all fare types fell from 4.8 to 3.3 cents per mile.) Of course it may not be possible to attribute the whole of these reductions to deregulation; other price-reducing influences – for example increases in efficiency – may have been at work. Yet even if such influences had an impact they are unlikely to explain the full extent of the fall. The effect on fares has varied across fare types and sectors: Morrison and Winston (1986, pp. 16–17) show that in general, deregulation had a downward effect on discount fares and an upward impact on unrestricted fares, although there were some variations across routes they studied. Meyer and Oster (1987, pp. 112–13) found that the unrestricted fare fell by an average of 9 per cent on very high-density routes, but on average rose by 3 and 6 per cent respectively on medium- and low-density routes (see also Bailey, 1986). Keeler (1991, p. 140) has, however, pointed out that the results for the medium- and low-density routes must be interpreted in the light of two factors. First, the unrestricted fare has become much less significant since deregulation (over 90 per cent of passengers on the major carriers now travel on some form of discount); and secondly, the use of data from the last years of regulation as a yardstick is misleading as fares in those years had already been significantly reduced following a major fares investigation by the Civil Aeronautics Board. Comparisons with earlier yardstick years would show a fall in the unrestricted fares even on the lower density routes.

On service, the evidence suggests that overall, deregulation led to higher frequencies on most routes, although there may also have been some overcrowding. There is little evidence to suggest that safety has been adversely affected by deregulation (Keeler, 1991, p. 145).

Caves *et al.* (1987, p. 186) show that efficiency in the US airline industry increased significantly as a result of deregulation: their results suggest that by 1983 US airlines' unit costs had fallen by 10 per cent. Bailey (1986) also provides clear evidence of cost savings. Nevertheless, expansion of the industry meant that growth in efficiency did not lead to a fall in employment, which may even have risen. For example, Meyer and Oster (1987, p. 105) suggest that if regulation had continued employment would have been 3.7 per cent lower. Profitability appears to have remained largely unchanged (Keeler, 1991, p. 145).

On the structural side, there has been a move – largely unrestrained by the authorities – towards mergers (Kahn, 1988). As a result a significantly higher concentration has developed in the industry. The relaxed attitude to airline mergers reflected the view early in the deregulation period that contestability in the industry was high: see section 9.3.2.

How good a guide is the experience of US deregulation to the likely impact of air transport liberalization in Europe? There are a number of important respects in which both the policies themselves and the context in which they are being implemented differ. On the policy front, the EC has been rather more cautious in its approach, and sees a continuing important role for intervention by the authorities (Sørensen, 1991). As indicated above, a number of 'safeguards' have been built into the policies. As far as the industry itself is concerned there are important differences between the US and European situations which make comparisons hazardous. First, it is clear from the discussion in the previous sections that the political framework may make a policy of liberalization more difficult to implement. The US airlines were and still are privately owned, whereas the main European carriers are state owned and may have less flexibility and face less pressure to respond to market forces. As has been shown, they may be supported by state aid. The EC market also crosses numerous national boundaries, with each country having its own policy agenda. Secondly, it may be argued that the European industry has long faced sources of competition that have not existed (or at least not to the same extent) in the US, and so US scale gains cannot be expected in the EC. For example, in Europe charter services have historically been much more important and *already* exercise a competitive influence on the scheduled airlines on some routes, particularly the longer-haul leisure routes (Abbot and Thompson, 1991). This is not however true for routes dominated by business traffic. A further possible source of greater competitive pressure in Europe is surface transport, which is likely to become even more attractive with increased air traffic congestion and the development of high-speed railway networks (CEC, 1991b). Thirdly, gains from a liberalization policy may be relatively small because greater congestion in Europe may restrict the scope for new entry where it matters. It is also true that there is a much smaller proportion of very dense routes capable of sustaining new entry: Pryke (1991) shows that routes with more than 200 flights per week represent 12 per cent of all US flights, but only 3 per cent of European traffic. Given the differences between the US and European situations, there are differences of view on the likely overall impact of the European liberalization programme. Pryke (1991) has argued that the net benefits or liberalization are likely to be smaller than those from deregulation in the US. He shows that monopoly and duopoly routes are relatively more important in Europe and argues that the established airlines will be relatively more adept at countering the threat of any significant entry. He also suggests that bilateral agreements have *already* led to the kind of hub and spoke arrangements that have generated important welfare gains in the US in recent years. It is not possible here to analyse Pryke's arguments in any detail, but it is perhaps worth noting that some routes where there are only one or two operators would not be *viable* with more; on such routes the scope for market exploitation may be very limited, even where entry is unrestricted.

Barrett (1991) has taken a rather different stance. His argument is that in Europe, fares have a higher initial margin over competitive levels compared with the US position before deregulation (although the evidence he presents does not directly address this comparison). Barrett also argues that Europe is able to learn from the US experience in the formulation of policy and is better equipped to deal with abuses of market power.

These authors differ on the likely *scale* of the benefits from European liberalization; neither denies that there will be *some* gains. Much will depend on how the package finally evolves and on the extent to which the major airlines can dominate any freer market that develops through mergers and other links, and through the maintenance of grandfather rights.

The effects of bilateral liberalization in Europe   Abbott and Thompson (1991) present data on the behaviour of average prices on seven European routes on which liberalization has already occurred and on four that remained subject to traditional regulation throughout the period studied. Their findings are characterized by some diversity and the limitations of the study must be taken into account. However, there are marked differences between the two groups of routes in the behaviour of real leisure prices: on six of the seven liberalized routes prices fell – in some cases significantly – whereas on all the regulated sectors, prices rose. The fall in prices on the liberalized routes was on average much greater where entry had occurred. Interestingly, entry was more likely on routes where there was substantial leisure traffic. No clear pattern emerges from their analysis of business prices.

9.7   Conclusion

The airline industry in Europe is facing potentially fundamental changes in the policy and commercial environment in which it is required to operate. For many of Europe's airlines, long accustomed to state protection, the challenge of much stronger competition from both new and established airlines would require major rethinking of business strategies. Yet the airlines involved in the bilateral liberalization programmes have shown that adaptation is possible. How far such adaptation goes will be dependent on the extent to which national governments accept the spirit of the new policies and on the capacity of the infrastructure to allow expansion and change.

Notes

1. These doubts were largely eliminated following the European Court's decision in the Nouvelles Frontières case (*Ministère Public* v. *Lucas Asjes*, 1986, 3CMLR, p. 173).
2. These percentages must be treated very cautiously. The air figures exclude charter traffic. Data on charter traffic *in* Europe are not readily available. It should be noted that the intra-European data included in Table 9.1 cover flights to all parts of Europe, and not just those in the EC.
3. With no change in load factor, stage length or the number of airports served. It should be noted that when Caves *et al.* (1987) examined *variable* rather than total costs they were unable to reject the hypothesis that economies of density were constant for the trunk airlines.
4. With no change in load factor, stage lengths or density. The evidence also suggests constant economies of scale for the smaller local airlines.
5. According to Pryke (1991) short-haul flights account for 94 per cent of all European flights. Domestic flights are included, as are some non-EC countries, in Pryke's analysis.
6. The genesis of the current policy does in fact go back to 1983: Mason and Gray (1991).
7. The Council of Ministers has agreed that common criteria should be in place by 1 July 1992 (CEC, 1991a).

References

Abbott, K. and Thompson, D. (1991), 'Deregulating European Aviation', *International Journal of Industrial Organization*, 9, 125–40.

AEA (Association of European Airlines) (1990), *Yearbook May 1990*, Brussels: AEA.

AEA (1991), *Yearbook May 1991*, Brussels: AEA.

AEA (1992), *Yearbook May 1992*, Brussels: AEA.

Bailey, E. (1986), 'Price and Productivity Change following Deregulation: the US Experience', *Economic Journal*, 96, 1–17.

Balfour, J. (1990), 'Air Transport and the EEC', *European Access*, 2, (April), 13–15.

Banister, D. and Button, K. (eds) (1991), *Transport in a Free Market Economy*, London: Macmillan.

Barrett, S. (1991), 'Discussion', in Banister and Button (1991), pp. 242–48.

Baumol, W.J. (1982), 'Contestable Markets: an Uprising in the Theory of Industrial Structure', *American Economic Review*, 72, 1–15.

Baumol, W.J. and Willig, R.D. (1986), 'Contestability: Developments since the Book', in D.J. Morris, P.J.N. Sinclair, M.D.E. Slater and J.S. Vickers (eds), *Strategic Behaviour and Industrial Competition*, Oxford: Oxford University Press, pp. 9–36.

Button, K. and Swann, D. (1989), 'European Community Airlines – Deregulation and its Problems', *Journal of Common Market Studies*, 27, 259–82.

Caves, D.W., Christensen, L.R. and Tretheway, M.W. (1984), 'Economies of Density versus Economies of Scale: Why Trunk and Local Service Airline Costs Differ', *Rand Journal of Economics*, 15, 471–89.

Caves, D.W., Christensen, L.R., Tretheway, M.W. and Winde, R.J. (1987), 'An Assessment of the Efficiency Effects of US Airline Deregulation via an International Comparison', in E.E. Bailey (ed.), *Public Regulation: New Perspectives on Institutions and Policies*, Cambridge, Mass.: MIT Press.

CEC (Commission of the European Communities) (1991a), *Completion of the Civil Aviation Policy in the European Communities: Towards Single Market Conditions* (September, COM(91) 275 Final), Brussels: CEC.

CEC (1991b), *Panorama of EC Industry 1991–92*, Luxembourg: CEC.

Council of the European Communities (1992), *Press Release 7281/92* (Presses 123–9), Luxembourg: Council of the European Communities.

The Economist (1992), 'Who Dares Merges', 15 February, 93.

Encaoua, D. (1991), 'Liberalizing European Airlines: Cost and Factor Productivity Evidence', *International Journal of Industrial Organization*, **9**, 109–24.

Forsyth, P.J., Hill, R.D. and Trengove, C.D. (1986), 'Measuring Airline Efficiency', *Fiscal Studies*, **7**, 61–81.

Johnson, P.S. (1988), 'Domestic Air Transport', in P.S. Johnson (ed.), *The Structure of British Industry*, London: Allen & Unwin, pp. 281–307.

Kahn, A. (1988), 'Surprises from Deregulation', *American Economic Review (Papers and Proceedings)*, **78**, 320–22.

Keeler, T.E. (1991), 'Airline Deregulation and Market Performance: the Economic Basis for Regulatory Reform and Lessons from US experience', in Banister and Button (1991), pp. 121–70.

Mason, K. and Gray, R. (1991), 'The Liberalisation of Civil Aviation in the European Community – an Overview', *European Research*, July, 11–15.

Meyer, J.R. and Oster Jr, C.V. (1987), *Deregulation and the Future of Intercity Passenger Travel*, Cambridge, Mass.: MIT Press.

Morrison, S. and Winston, C. (1986), *The Economic Effects of Airline Deregulation*. Washington, DC: Brookings Institution.

Pryke, R. (1991), 'American Deregulation and European Liberalisation', in Banister and Button (1991), pp. 220–41.

Sawers, D. (1987), *Competition in the Air* (Institute of Economic Affairs Research Monograph 41), London: Institute of Economic Affairs.

Sørensen, F. (1991), 'The Changing Aviation Scene in Europe', in Banister and Button (1991), pp. 177–85.

Transport Committee (1991a), *First Report: Developments in European Community Air Transport Policy, Vol. I, Report, Minutes of Proceedings and Appendices, HC 147–1, Session 1991–92*, London: HMSO.

Transport Committee (1991b), *First Report: Developments in European Community Air Transport Policy, Vol. II, Minutes of Evidence, HC 147–1, Session 1991–92*, London: HMSO.

TRRL (1981), *Rail and Air Travel between London and Scotland: Analysis of Competition using Box-Jenkins Methods* (TRRL Laboratory Report 1978), Crowthorne: TRRL.

Windle, R.J. (1991), 'The World's Airlines', *Journal of Transport Economics and Policy*, **25**, 31–49.

Witt, S.F. and Martin, C.A. (1985), 'Forecasting Future Trends in European Tourist Demand', *Tourist Review*, **4**, 12–19.

Further reading

Banister, D. and Button, K. (eds) (1991), *Transport in a Free Market Economy*, London: Macmillan.

Button, K. and Swann, D. (1989), 'European Community Airlines – Deregulation and its Problems', *Journal of Common Market Studies*, **27**, 259–82.

Commission of the European Communities (1991), *Completion of the Civil Aviation Policy in the European Communities: Towards Single Market Conditions* (September, COM(91) 275 Final), Brussels: CEC.

Commission of the European Communities (1991), *Panorama of EC Industry 1991–92*, Luxembourg: CEC.

Organization for Economic Cooperation and Development (1988), *Deregulation and Airline Competition*, Paris: OECD.

Sawers, D. (1987), *Competition in the Air*, London: Institute of Economic Affairs.

Association of European Airlines *Yearbooks* and *Statistical Appendices*, Brussels: AEA.
International Civil Aviation Organization regular *Digests of Statistics* including *Traffic: Commercial Air Carriers; Financial Data; Commercial Air Carriers; On-Flight Origin and Destination*; and *Airport Traffic*.

10 Tourism

Barry Thomas

10.1 Introduction

Tourism is the world's largest industry. In 1990 it employed over 101 million people (6.3 per cent of the global workforce), had gross sales of over US$2 trillion, and accounted for 5.5 per cent of the world's GNP.[1] Within this industry Europe is dominant: it has almost two-thirds of international tourist arrivals and about half of international tourist receipts. Table 10.1 shows that European countries account for eight of the world's top ten destinations (these countries accounting for about 45 per cent of the world total), seven out of the top ten earners (the seven accounting for about 41 per cent of the world total), and seven of the top ten spenders (40 per cent).

This chapter examines the tourism industry in Europe. After a brief discussion of the nature of tourism the principal trends in tourism and the differences in the size of the industry across different European countries are examined.[2] The chapter then considers aspects of the structure, conduct and performance of the industry, and finally discusses some issues in tourism policy. The chapter concentrates on certain parts of the industry such as hotels and tour operators. Space does not permit coverage of all the different kinds of business activity involved in tourism and there are therefore some significant omissions, the most notable being transport.

10.1.1 What is tourism?

The tourism industry is difficult to define exactly because the 'product' comprises a range of outputs and activities. There is however a fair measure of agreement that one convenient and sensible definition, in Wanhill's (1988, p. 2) words, is the 'temporary movement of people to destinations outside their normal places of work and residence and the activities undertaken during the time spent at those destinations'. This type of definition, which has been used by many writers,[3] will be adopted in this chapter. By convention, 'temporary' means less than one year, and it is customary to draw a distinction between different types of 'visitor': 'tourists' are those who stay at least one night in the place visited, and 'excursionists' or 'day-visitors' are those who do not stay overnight. Tourism embraces several purposes of visit – including holidays, business, visiting friends and a variety of purposes such as study visits, and visits for religious or health reasons.[4]

Table 10.1   The World's Top Destinations, Earners and Spenders, 1990

	International arrivals		International tourism receipts			International tourism expenditures		
		Millions*	% Share of world total		Millions US$*	% Share of world total		Billions US$**	% Share of world total
1.	France	51	11.6	USA	41	15.9	USA	39	16.1
2.	USA	40	8.9	France	20	7.9	Germany	30	12.4
3.	Spain	34	7.7	Italy	20	7.8	Japan	25	10.4
4.	Italy	27	6.0	Spain	19	7.3	UK	19	7.9
5.	Hungary	21	4.6	UK	15	5.9	Italy	14	5.7
6.	Austria	19	4.3	Austria	13	5.1	France	12	5.2
7.	UK	18	4.1	Germany	11	4.2	Canada	8	3.5
8.	Germany	17	3.9	Switzerland	7	2.7	Austria	8	3.1
9.	Canada	15	3.4	Canada	6	2.4	Netherlands	7	3.1
10.	Switzerland	13	3.0	Mexico	5	2.1	Sweden	6	2.5

Note:
* Rounded to nearest million.
** Rounded to nearest billion.

Source: WTO, Yearbook of Tourism Statistics (1992).

231

It is evident that the tourism industry is very diverse. Supplies of accommodation, transport, retail services, insurance and other financial services (such as foreign exchange), leisure services (such as sports facilities or theme parks), 'attractions' (such as museums, ancient monuments or opera houses), conference facilities, catering services, study centres, 'events' (such as major exhibitions or sports competitions), and the supply of many other goods and services may all contribute to the tourism industry.

The rationale for grouping together this seemingly vast array of activities under the label of a single 'industry' is that they do have some things in common. First, they involve some transfer of income from the area of residence into the area in which it is spent and thus tourism acts as a mechanism for the geographical redistribution of spending power. Secondly, the main activities which make up tourism – transport, accommodation and entertainment (widely defined) – are often complementary and this is why they are packaged together in the provision of inclusive tours.[5] Thirdly, although the two main forms of tourism – holidays and business activities – may be regarded as distinct activities there may be some substitutability on the supply side. For example, hotel rooms or aircraft seats may be used to meet either business or holiday demand. Finally the identity of the 'tourism' industry is real enough for suppliers, who frequently form industrial or professional associations, and for governments who treat it, albeit weakly, as a policy concern.[6]

The tourism product has been heavily dependent on natural resources such as climate, attractive scenery, ski runs and sandy beaches. This is still the case though the dependence is changing as urban tourism (especially for business, conferences and cultural attractions) becomes more important and as newer forms of tourism emerge such as 'health-care tourism', 'heritage tourism' and special events (such as World Fairs or the Olympics). An important consequence of the dependence on natural resources is that when 'capacity' is reached there is little scope for increasing it. To the extent that there are common property rights in such resources, externalities in the form of damage will be unchecked without government intervention.

10.1.2   Trends in European tourism

Europe's share in the world industry   It has already been noted that Europe is dominant in world tourism. There are several reasons for this. Incomes in Europe are high by world standards and there is a generalized system of paid holidays and flexible frontier controls. More than half of the population takes a holiday every year (and increasingly there is a trend towards taking more than one holiday a year). In addition Europe is well endowed with attractive natural and historical resources. Finally, many European governments have actively encouraged the development of the tourism industry.

The tourism industry in Europe has experienced strong growth but the rate of growth is now slowing and it is losing some of its global market share as measured by international arrivals and receipts. In terms of arrivals, after reaching a peak of well over 70 per cent in the late 1960s and early 1970s Europe's share declined to less than two-thirds by 1990, as Table 10.2 shows. In terms of world receipts Europe's share has also declined, though it still stands at well over half.

Table 10.2   Europe's Share of World International Tourist Arrivals and Receipts (%)

	1950	1960	1970	1980	1990	2000[1]
Arrivals						
Europe[2]	67	73	71	69	64	53
Africa	2	1	2	3	3	5
Americas	30	24	23	19	20	20
Asia-Oceania	2	2	5	10	13	22
World[3]	100	100	100	100	100	100
Receipts						
Europe[2]	42	57	62	60	55	39
Africa	4	3	2	3	2	3
Americas	51	36	27	25	26	28
Asia-Oceania	3	5	8	12	17	31
World[3]	100	100	100	100	100	100

Notes:
1. Projected.
2. Includes Eastern Europe.
3. Figures may not add exactly because of rounding.

Source: Adapted from WTO (1991).

Europe, then, while still dominant in world tourism seems to be on the downward part of a long-run cycle of market shares. It was increasing its share in the 1950s and 1960s. The Americas had already peaked earlier and after experiencing a declining market share throughout the 1950s and 1960s their share since the 1970s seems to have stabilized at about 20 per cent of arrivals and 25–30 per cent of receipts. The loss of Europe's share, which is likely to continue, is associated with a rise in the share of Asia-Oceania, which is also likely to continue. The location of the global tourism industry thus shifts as destinations fail to attract a permanent flow of repeat business and as new destinations are developed.

Differences across Europe in the growth and size of tourism   Tourism tends to be more important in southern European countries, which specialize in 'sun, sand and sea' type holidays, than in northern countries which rely more on urban tourism. The (unweighted) average figure for tourism as a percentage of GNP in 1988 was 5.4 per cent for 11 EC countries (Luxembourg excluded). The countries with above-average figures were Greece, Spain, France, Portugal and Ireland, and those with below-average figures were Belgium, Denmark, Germany, Italy, the Netherlands, and the UK.[7] Italy and Ireland are the only countries that do not conform to the general pattern.

This split between countries corresponds fairly closely to that shown in Figure 10.1. Although Western Europe as a whole has a credit balance with the rest of the world – that is, international tourism receipts exceed tourism expenditures[8] – it is evident that the southern European countries shown on the left-hand side of Figure 10.1 tend to be net recipients, and the northern European countries, on the right, the main generators of tourist traffic. The position of Germany, whose expenditures exceeded receipts by almost US$ 20 billion in 1990, is particularly striking.

In terms of absolute size, as measured by international arrivals and receipts, the pre-eminence of France (with some 50 000 arrivals in 1990 and receipts of almost US$22 billion) is shown in Figure 10.2.

This cross-section picture (Figure 10.2a) might seem to suggest a non-linear relationship between receipts and the number of visitors: as visitors increase so do receipts, but at a diminishing rate (Figure 10.2b). But a more plausible interpretation might be that there is a rough division between two clusters: on the one hand are those countries specializing in mass tourism where sun is a key element and cheap accommodation is important, that is those with less than average receipts per arrival; and on the other hand those countries with higher than average receipts per arrival, where urban tourism – with concomitant higher spending on accommodation, entertainment and other items – is more significant (Figure 10.2c). Such a division is clearly only an approximation, and it is interesting to note that the Alpine countries, Austria and Switzerland, belong to the high-spending group.

All European countries have experienced substantial growth in tourism, as Figure 10.3 shows. Portugal has had a remarkable performance, with both international arrivals and receipts growing at 11.5 per cent per annum, but the main feature of Figure 10.3 is the evident dispersion in growth rates. No obvious general pattern is apparent apart from the fact that for all countries except Greece and Portugal, receipts, in current prices, have grown faster

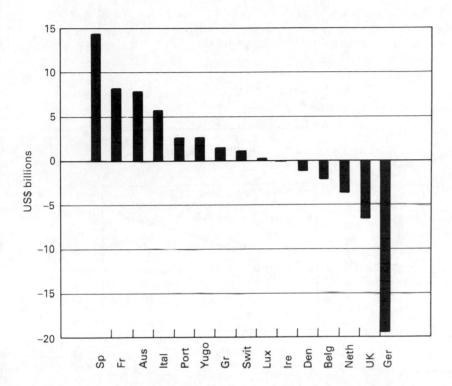

Source: Based on WTO (1991).

Figure 10.1   Net Receipts from International Tourism, 1990

than arrivals. Arrivals have typically grown by 2–5 per cent per annum and receipts by 5–10 per cent. This reflects the moves 'upmarket' as well as inflation.

The main source of international arrivals is Europe itself: there are substantial cross-border movements. In 1989 (WTO, 1990) intra-European tourists accounted for 85 per cent of arrivals and the rest were from the Americas (8 per cent, but declining), Africa (2 per cent), East Asia and the Pacific (3 per cent) and the Middle East (2 per cent).

The figures for international tourism quoted in this section do not of course take account of substantial domestic tourism. Some estimates (for

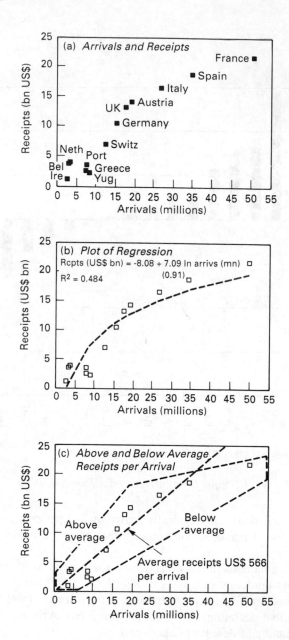

Source: Based on WTO (1991).

Figure 10.2   International Arrivals and Receipts, 1990

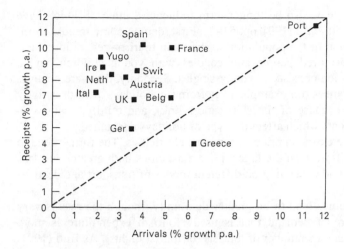

Source: Based on WTO, 1991.

Figure 10.3   *International Arrivals and Receipts: Annual Percentage*
               Increase, 1980–90

example Williams and Shaw, 1991, p. 30) put this between five and ten times
higher than international tourism.

10.1.3   Demand

The demand for tourism is frequently measured by the number of tourist
arrivals in a destination, or by expenditure. This views the demand for a
package of tourism products – travel, accommodation, entertainment, catering and other services – as a single purchase.[9] (This is the stance adopted here,
though for some purposes it is useful to examine the demand for individual
products.) The different elements in the purchase are generally regarded as
complements, though they are substitutes for each other in so far as each
competes for a share of the tourist's budget for the trip. Most international
tourist trips (about 70 per cent) are for holiday purposes and it is only for
these trips, unlike most business trips, that individuals are free to choose all
aspects of the package.

    Several variables influence demand. Not surprisingly, the voluminous lit-
erature shows that incomes and relative prices (and/or exchange rates) are
relevant.[10] The price variables are particularly important in determining the
demand for competing destinations. Other variables have been shown to be
significant in econometric investigations. Transportation costs, promotional
activity, and short-run factors such as the weather, and political disturbances
like the Gulf War of 1991 or bouts of terrorist activity, can all have an

influence. There may also be longer-term influences, three of which have been noted by Witt *et al.* (1991 pp. 51–2). First, demographic trends: an increasing proportion of the population in the main tourism-generating countries consists of retired people and couples with young children, and a declining proportion consists of young singles. Secondly, there are changes in holiday preferences (for example away from sun holidays towards activity holidays, partly because of the skin cancer link), and thirdly, changes in holiday entitlements which affect the type of holidays demanded.

Much evidence exists on price and income elasticities. The former tend to be much less uniform than the latter: price elasticities both greater and less than unity are found depending on different modes of transport and destinations.

Income elasticities tend to be greater than unity, though the results vary with the measure of demand that is used. Tourism expenditure is more income elastic than the number of tourists (or tourist nights). As Bull (1991, p. 37) notes, this is because 'consumers whose incomes rise may still be constrained by time to the same length of tourist trip, but substitute a higher-priced one. Similarly, once a tourist trip particularly a vacation becomes an established part of a household's expenditure, a fall in income might mean cheaper vacations rather than fewer.'

Income elasticities also vary with different forms of tourism. Business tourism and visiting friends and relatives are less income elastic (usually less than unity) than holiday tourism, and main holidays tend to be less income elastic than additional ones. Holidays appear to be luxuries with many elasticities (for trips from the USA and from the UK to Europe) reported in the range 2 to 5 (see Martin and Witt, 1988) though there is much variation.[11] For some products such as long-distance coach travel and boarding house accommodation negative elasticities are reported, which suggests that these are inferior goods.

In general, however, income elasticities are high. The demand for tourism will thus continue to grow as real incomes rise though there are likely to be ceilings. One ceiling arises from the availability of time for travel which, for the employed population, will be bounded by annual vacation time. A second ceiling is financial. Typically necessities such as housing, heating, food and essential clothing absorb half or more of all post-tax household incomes, and some observers (EIU, 1988, p. 146) believe that no more than 15 per cent of national post-tax incomes could ever be devoted to travel.

10.2   Market structure

The tourism industry comprises a diverse set of organizations and activities though all have a single focus – serving the tourist. There are many chains of transactions from the tourist to the ultimate producers of the basic services such as transport, accommodation and the running of tourist attractions.

These chains may be direct (e.g. a tourist may book a room or an air ticket directly from a hotel or airline) or through a series of retailers and whole-salers.[12] Several types of organization may be involved, as the following list (which draws on Holloway, 1989, p. 54) shows:

Producers
    carriers (air, sea, road and rail transport operators);
    accommodation (hotels/motels, guest houses, self-catering apartments, camp sites, etc.);
    attractions (theme parks, galleries, ancient monuments, leisure centres, catering services, the management of natural attractions, etc.).
Intermediate organizations
    tour operators and brokers;
    travel agents.
Support services
    private sector (travel insurance and financial services, guiding services, marketing support services, etc.);
    public sector (national and regional tourist organizations, visa and pass-port offices, public ports, etc.).

There is considerable variation in the pattern of ownership (public and private sector) and in the extent of vertical and horizontal integration.

This complex pattern of diverse activities means that it is not always meaningful to talk of the structure of the tourism industry as a whole. This section will examine separately some of the elements listed above. Accom-modation, tour operators and travel agents have been selected on the ground that their business is exclusively confined to tourism. Some of the other organizations listed serve many product markets: for transport operators, galleries, restaurants, and insurance companies for example tourists are not the only consumers they serve.

10.2.1 Accommodation
The supply of accommodation can be divided into hotels and non-hotels.

Hotels There is a high degree of geographical concentration in many Euro-pean countries, especially those offering sun, sand and sea holidays. In Greece for example in 1985 17 per cent of hotel beds were in Greater Athens, 15 per cent in Rhodes and 14 per cent in Crete (Leontidou, 1991, p. 96); in Portugal, Lisbon has approximately one-quarter of all tourist accom-modation, and dominates the upmarket sector, having 43 per cent of all five-star hotel rooms (Lewis and Williams, 1991, p. 115). In France and the UK there is some geographical concentration on the capital cities, but this con-centration is less marked in Germany and Italy.

Table 10.3   Hotel Supply, 1991

	France	Germany	Italy	Spain	UK	Total
Total rooms (000s)	518	335	920	359	500	2 632
Number of quoted companies with hotels	12	11	11	14	60	108
Number of plc hotels	1 064	172	89	72	1 363	2 760
Number of plc rooms (000s)	94	36	17	12	119	278
Plc market share (% of total rooms)	18	10	2	3	24	11

Note: plc = public limited company

Source: EIU (1991a, p. 26).

In terms of economic concentration there is some polarization with international hotel chains at one end, accounting for just over 10 per cent of the total rooms (see Table 10.3), but much fragmentation at the other end with a preponderance of small family businesses. This pattern seems common throughout much of Europe though there are some variations in the level of concentration, as Table 10.3 shows. For the five countries shown the levels of concentration reflect different stages in the development of the economies. The UK has the most developed service economy and has the highest concentration in the hotel industry. (In this respect it seems to be following the USA, which has the most explicit service economy and the most concentrated hotel industry.) Even in the UK, however, the largest chain, operated by Forte, had less than 6 per cent of the market share of rooms in 1991, and most chains in the UK had less than 1 per cent.

The concentrated segment of the hotel industry is almost entirely confined to the better-quality hotels: most of those graded three star or higher belong to chains or consortia (Witt *et al.*, 1991, p. 25).

The grouping of hotels into chains is not necessarily an indication of ownership. Consortia of independent hotels and of franchising are growing in importance. Ownership of the largest hotels is by a mixture of firms whose principal interests are leisure and catering, breweries and airlines, as well as hotel specialists.

Wholesalers are of growing significance and are likely to become even more prominent in the hotel sector. They act as intermediaries for potential hotel customers in booking rooms and include travel agents, tour operators and large business corporations who negotiate with the hotel to provide a block of rights to rooms.

Non-hotel accommodation   There has been rapid growth in this sector. By its very nature it is difficult to judge the size of this form of accommodation, but throughout Europe it may account for as much as 60 per cent of all bed spaces. Self-catering is the dominant form: this includes camp sites, apartments, villas, timeshare 'second homes', and other forms. The camp-site sector is dominant in some regions – in the Netherlands for example there are about 3 000 camp sites, which provide 93 per cent of all land-based tourist accommodation (Pinder, 1991, p. 227). The concept of owning 'second homes' which can be rented has also become a significant sector. The most important development here is timeshare, which continues to grow faster than the overall leisure market (EIU, 1991b) though this development has been associated with much adverse publicity because of controversial sales techniques, environmental effects and other policy issues (see Goodall and Stabler, 1992). The owning of second homes which are sometimes rented is seen in some countries, for example Spain, as a degree of unfair competition for established businesses (Valenzeula, 1991, p. 47).

A further type of non-hotel accommodation is the holiday centre. These centres have developed from the old holiday camps which were once prominent in Britain and which catered for lower socioeconomic groups by providing all-in catering and entertainment and chalet-style accommodation. In the last decade they have moved upmarket, abandoning their old image. The concept has been a success in the Netherlands (home of Center Parcs) and France (notably the Club Méditerranée) but still generally on a modest scale.

In many countries, especially Greece and Portugal, non-hotel accommodation is predominantly used by nationals rather than by foreign visitors.

10.2.2 Tour operators

Tour operators provide an integrated product of transport, accommodation and other amenities and services (such as assistance during the stay, excursions and entertainment). They became prominent in the 1960s with the evolution of air transport, particularly charter services, but the product has changed somewhat and the almost exclusive reliance on air transport and hotel accommodation has now given way to more provision of self-catering accommodation (such as villas, apartments and camp sites) and self-drive packages.

Operators' contact with the consumer may be direct or via a travel agent. Practice varies. In the UK for example the travel agent is the main outlet for operators' packages: about 90 per cent of packages were sold through agents in the 1980s (CEC, 1985, p. 39). In Italy the tour operator and travel agent are in direct competition, as the latter organizes its own holidays. In other countries there is neither dependence nor competition: the agents deal with made-to-measure holidays for people who do not want standard packages.

Operators are most important in the main tourist-generating countries of northern Europe, especially Germany and the UK. They are typically aimed at a mass market though some smaller niche players are now catering for specialized tastes. There is a high degree of concentration in both Germany and the UK, which in the latter case has been increased by a spate of mergers in the 1980s. The leading operator in the UK, Thomsons, had a 40 per cent market share by 1989 and the five-firm concentration ratio was 72 per cent (based on EIU, 1989).

The major tour operators are concerned only with outbound visitors though the general growth in the 1980s of Europe as a destination from other regions of the world provided some business for inbound tour operators and this form of business is likely to grow. The most spectacular example of this is Eurodisney at Marne-la-Vallée outside Paris. The park is planned to have, by the early years of the next century, over 18 000 rooms on site and a large proportion of these will be managed by Eurodisney itself. So 'there may be a need to enter the tour business directly to help maximise occupancies' (EIU, 1991c, p. 61).

10.2.3 Travel agents

Retail travel agents are an important outlet for the products of airlines, tour operators and hotels. In addition to providing information and booking services they often supply other services such as insurance and travel exchange. Unlike retailers in most other sectors of the economy, the travel agents appear to take few risks: they do not buy and resell hotel accommodation, holiday packages or travel seats, but simply reserve the package when a client has decided to buy. This has allowed very easy entry and as a consequence there have been many small operators. But the number of operators is now falling rapidly,[13] partly because of technological innovations that favour large operators. Concentration is rising: in 1988 large multiples (Lunn Poly, Pickfords, Thomas Cook, Hogg Robinson, A.T. Mays and W.H. Smith) accounted for 26 per cent of all agencies in the UK, whereas in 1982 they accounted for only 16 per cent (see Holloway, 1989). These large companies in turn belong to larger groups (for instance Thomas Cook is owned by LTU, Germany's third biggest tour operator, and Lunn Poly by Thomson International). A similar pattern of concentration exists in other countries. In Germany, for instance, Touristik Union International (TUI) is dominant.

10.3 Market conduct and performance

10.3.1 Costs, prices and competition

Unlike most other products, the provision of many tourism products usually entails the consumer (tourist) travelling to the point of production. The producer's 'plant', as Bull (1991 p. 83) notes, 'therefore has to exist and operate in many cases regardless of the number of tourists provided for, or "product units supplied" ... [and thus] a major feature of tourism supply is the heavy preponderance of fixed costs'. So there is a strong concern to operate at full capacity. An important performance target for the hotel industry, for example, is the occupancy rate,[14] and high load factors are important for the transport industry.

Tour operators, who buy both accommodation and transport, have usually based their business on high volumes. Their large scale provides some monopsony power, which allows them to achieve low prices, a factor that has sometimes caused resentment in host countries.[15]

The pricing of hotel rooms tends to be based on a 'going rate' for each category of room, but given the perishability of the product and the fluctuations in demand there is considerable price discrimination in order to increase occupancy rates. Differing elasticities of demand, for example on weekdays and weekends, permit different prices. There is a growing tendency towards negotiating discounts for frequent or major customers: the largest discounts are given to tour operators providing the greatest number of clients but large business corporations can increasingly obtain substantial discounts.

Tour operators set prices on the basis of the cost of components of the package, plus commission paid to travel agents, plus a profit margin. The components of the package, for example the particular characteristic of the location and the hotels, influence quality and are significant determinants of price. Sinclair *et al.* (1990) found, on the basis of applying the hedonic price model to package holidays in southern Spain, that large size of hotels and a central location within resorts have a negative effect on price, whereas a children's swimming pool and a night club have a positive effect.[16]

Some of the large tour operators can use differential pricing in various separable sub-markets in order to maximize profits, and those which have interests in hotels or activities in different countries can arrange internal prices to reduce tax liabilities in different countries.

The tour operators' market has been fiercely competitive, especially in the UK. The dominant position of Thomson has not given it dominant market power. Smaller operators have used joint bargaining power under the banner of the Association of Independent Tour Operators to offer competitive prices, but most importantly there has been a price war for market share between the market leaders.

The price war in the UK partly has its roots in the declining rate of growth of the inclusive tour market. This slowdown was to some extent attributable to changes in consumer preferences. Consumers are 'becoming tired of the increasingly commercialised "sun and sand" resorts' (EIU, 1989, p. 64).[17] The decline has also been induced by the limited capacity of airports.

Since profit margins are sensitive to the capacity utilization rate (Gray, 1982) it is not surprising that there have been attempts to boost this rate in the face of a slowing growth rate of output. This has led to low prices; often considerable discounts are offered, especially for late sales. In the UK tour operators used to dictate prices to travel agents,[18] though now they do not

Table 10.4   Cost Breakdown of a Typical Package Holiday Sold by a UK Tour Operator, 1989

	%
Travel agent's commission	10.2
Airline costs	38.2
Administration and marketing	7.3
Transfers	1.8
Hotel costs	41.8
Tour operator's profit	0.7
Total	100.0

Source: Thomson Holidays (quoted in EIU, 1989).

put any restrictions on them and agents are free to discount. This has kept profit margins low. Table 10.4 shows the slim profit margin for a package tour. The net profit margins of the top 30 air travel organizers in the UK fell steadily from 3.9 per cent in 1983 to a loss of 0.9 per cent in 1987, since when there has been some recovery (EIU, 1989, p. 59),[19] but this has been partly because quantity reductions have played a more important role than price reductions (Tourism Society, 1990, p. 23). Capacity has been reduced to a level that can be sold without price reductions.

10.3.2   Market entry and segmentation
Some parts of the tourism industry such as small hotels or bed and breakfast accommodation are easy to enter. These establishments may lack facilities such as bars, swimming pools and private bathrooms and have to compete instead on price (often relying on unpaid family labour to cut margins) or by offering a distinctive product. Large hotels are a more difficult field to enter (other than by acquisition) given the significance of fixed costs, though it is important to note that economies of scale are often derived from common services such as marketing (including branding), finance, training, purchasing and computerized technology, and these can be reaped by groups of independent hotels. The increasing concentration in hotels is therefore not only in terms of larger individual hotels but also in the growing importance of hotel chains.

The increasing relevance of economies of scale and the growth of hotel chains has meant that branding has become a prominent feature of hotels since the 1980s. It is likely to remain dominant though the proliferation of brands may not continue, and even in the case of the larger hotels there are growing departures from the original brand specifications. This is partly because the pattern of hotel demand is specific to a given location – the same hotel configuration can attract different demand in different locations[20] – and partly because replication of external specifications and architecture is usually only possible in newly built brand developments in the mid- and economy segments of the market: for example the chain of Travelodges in the UK. At the more expensive end of the market most of the expansion has come from the acquisition of small chains and independent hotels and so there is less possibility of maintaining a uniform brand.

Segmentation of the market seems to be increasing. In the accommodation market different suppliers are typically aiming at different market segments. Larger hotels are directed at upper income groups: many now provide a package of on-site services (such as conference facilities, leisure facilities, restaurants and bars) and off-site services (such as car hire, transport to and from airports, organized tours and theatre tickets). There is also some specialization amongst some of these hotels and some even have 'hotels-within-hotels' to accommodate the interests of different groups such as family tourists and business travellers. The large chains have used different brands with different standards of service, and prices, in order to attract different segments of the market.

Lower down the market there has been a marked growth especially in France and the UK of the 'budget' hotel concept, first developed in the USA, which offers consistent low-risk accommodation on peripheral sites often with minimal restaurant facilities and low service levels but good quality standards.

The two barriers to entry to the tourism market which have not so far been discussed are the presence of exclusive dealing agreements, and technology. The first is exemplified in the tour operators' market. Such operators have tended to be based in the country of visitor origin. They have not been very mobile because there are high start-up costs in cross-border investment (especially language problems like printing brochures in various languages) and few advantages. These difficulties were highlighted by the attempt by Intasun of the UK to set up a tour operation in West Germany in 1986. The project was aborted in 1988, a major reason being the difficulties of competing with well-established German operators. Particularly damaging for Intasun was the contractual arrangement between the German market leader TUI (which had 3.5 million passengers of an annual 16 million) and 2 600 travel agents which prevented their selling any other operator's product.

New technology is a factor which favours larger organizations because of the size of the investment required. In the case of hotels, travel agents and tour operators, computer reservation systems are now common for larger players who are also at the forefront of other developments (such as vision data systems which can provide video images of destinations and accommodation, touch screen ordering, self check-in and check-out at hotels, in-room entertainment and so on). By comparison smaller travel agents are still limited to traditional viewdata systems, which essentially present static information such as timetables.

10.3.3   Responses to seasonality

The demand for tourism is marked by some strongly seasonal factors.[21] The most specialized destinations such as beaches and mountains are usually most affected. The main countries with a single peak are the Mediterranean countries of Greece, Spain, Portugal and Italy. Austria, Switzerland, and to a lesser extent Norway, have a double peak associated with a winter sports and a summer walking/touring season. The countries with the lowest seasonal peaks are Germany, the Netherlands and the UK, which are affected less by climate and where urban cultural and business tourism play a greater role.

A strongly seasonal demand causes obvious problems for resource use and there are several strategies for handling these (see Witt *et al.*, 1991, pp. 41–2), all of which have been used in Europe. First, changing the product mix has been evident, for example in the behaviour of summer resorts such as Brighton in the UK in attracting off-season conference trade, or in the provision of all-weather leisure and accommodation facilities such as the development of Center Parcs in northern Europe. A second strategy is market diversification, as in the successful attempts to attract retired people from northern Europe to winter in Spain.[22] Thirdly, pricing policies have been used to fill in the trough between peaks, for example by the provision of cheap 'winter break' holidays at many of the major hotel chains. Finally, state encouragement or measures to stagger holidays and alleviate the seasonality problem can be adopted and this has formed an important part of discussions on EC tourism policy.

10.4   Tourism policy

Tourism is a large and high-profile industry which generates positive and negative externalities: the benefit and costs for society as a whole can greatly exceed the private benefits and costs. These externalities are market failures which lead to promotion and regulation as the twin strands of tourism policy, and there is often some tension between the two.

The benefits of tourism are thought to be economic, social and environmental. The economic arguments are, first, that tourism makes a contribution to wealth and job creation.[23] The role of tourism in regional development has received particular recognition, especially in countries where the less developed regions with lower incomes have experienced less industrialization and thus have a stock of unspoilt natural amenities which are attractive to tourists. A second kind of economic benefit is the contribution that the tourism industry can make to a country's balance of payments. A strong tourism industry not only brings revenues from overseas tourists but also is a source of savings if residents holiday at home rather than abroad. The social advantages of tourism can be seen in national terms, such as the fact that the industry 'provides and helps to support facilities for residents, including provision for arts, entertainment, leisure facilities and catering' (Tourism Society, 1990, p. viii). Social advantages can also be seen, perhaps more importantly, at the supranational level. The European Community has consistently taken the line that 'as a genuine integrating force, tourism represents *the best* way of improving reciprocal knowledge between the peoples of Europe and of helping them to discover and forge common cultural links' (Eurostat, 1990, p. 4; emphasis added). Environmental benefits are said to accrue because a successful tourism industry depends on the quality of the built and natural environment, so residents benefit from a strong industry.

These various benefits can be accompanied by costs where the number of visitors is large relative to the capacity of an area.[24] Damage to the natural, cultural and built environment can occur. Part of the problem stems from the fact that tourism is geographically concentrated, for example along coastlines or in certain cities or heritage sites, so the pressure of visitors in particular localities can become intense. There are many examples of environmental problems which have occurred in the absence of controls. In southern Italy as a result of 'the burgeoning of second homes around the coasts, many stretches have been ruined' (King, 1991, p. 80), and in cities such as Florence and Rome the irreplaceable artistic heritage is being damaged by tourists who have been dubbed the 'new barbarians'.[25] The Algarve in Portugal has suffered environmental pollution problems (Lewis and Williams, 1991, p. 110), damage has been caused by the development of new ski runs in France (Tuppen, 1991, p. 110), and in Germany many lake fronts are no longer accessible to the public because of tourism developments (Schnell, 1991, p. 221). It is easy to multiply these examples. There are also problems of pressure on resources such as road space leading to traffic congestion; land prices (which provides one-off gains for local landowners, but can cause difficulties for locals who are not in the tourism industry); labour markets (which lead, in parts of Spain for example, to difficulties in recruiting farm workers in the hinterland of tourist areas); and on the supply of water (which causes problems, on the Costa del Sol for example, for fruit and vegetable growers). In addition, and possibly most important of all, tourism can lead to the disruption of communities and cultural traditions which have existed for centuries.

There is a lack of precise quantitative studies providing estimates of the damage caused by tourism, unlike say the numerous estimates of employment generated by tourism, but the significance of these problems is not in doubt, nor the need for regulation.

Tourism policy is formulated and implemented at local, national and EC levels. Policies tend to be similar across different countries. Most European countries have used public expenditure for the promotion of the tourism industry. In some cases, such as Spain in the 1950s, this has been a major national strategy of economic development. In other cases it has been more modest, as in the UK, where some financial aid has been offered for investment in England, but not on a sustained basis.[26] Most countries have a network of quasi-governmental national and regional tourist organizations, supported by public and private funds. These are involved in the general promotion of tourism (especially the provision of information and accommodation booking services through local offices),[27] and in the proper management of tourism.

These roles of promotion and regulation/management can sometimes conflict. In the UK, for example, the British Tourist Authority was set up in 1969 together with three national tourist boards for England, Scotland and Wales, and a series of regional boards. But the partnership of private and public interests in these boards highlights the issue of the appropriate balance between serving commercial interests and the needs of economic development and protecting the environment. The latter seems to be increasingly recognized, and more emphasis is now given to 'managing' visitors.

Direct regulation of tourism has tended to be more prominent in northern European countries (usually as part of a system of general planning controls on new developments, such as local authority planning controls in the UK or land use regulations in the Netherlands. In part this may reflect the size of the industry: where it is larger, say as a percentage of GDP, the balance is more likely to tip in favour of promotion rather than regulation.

At the EC level policy has been weak. There has been a general recognition of the importance of tourism and the case for developing a policy,[28] but specific community-wide initiatives have been limited. The EC Year of Tourism in 1990 (declared by a Council decision of 21 December 1988) was an initiative which had some significant purposes – to encourage the inflow of non-EC visitors, to explore alternatives to mass tourism, to encourage the staggering of holidays, and to facilitate the movement of travellers – but there has been little direct action. For the most part EC policy has been confined to documents, resolutions and some directives, but these have tended to be confined to such issues as standarized hotel grading schemes, fire safety regulations, directives on harmonizing legislation on package travel, easing of border crossing controls, and cooperation between member states on the marketing of 'Europe' as a product.[29] For the most part the EC has not been involved in regulating the structure or conduct of the tourism suppliers or consumers,[30] but has been limited to rather general matters, particularly those concerned with consumer protection and service quality. There has been some financial assistance for tourism projects but this has come through structural funds such as the regional development fund. Akehurst (1992, p. 223) after a full discussion of how far the EC had developed a tourism policy was able to form no stronger judgement than that 'there are certain signs of one emerging'.

To summarize, it is clear that the promotion of tourism often leads to quicker environmental degradation. This makes an area less attractive, and there is some truth in the aphorism 'tourism destroys tourism'. As Hartley and Hooper (1992) point out, private markets where there are private property rights could solve such problems by charging prices, so excluding those who are unwilling to pay and using some of the income to maintain the market value of assets. In tourism where there is common ownership of, for example, coastal and mountain scenery, such private solutions are not suitable. The questions then arise of whether and how public bodies should implement rationing devices, such as prices, to control the flow of visitors to popular tourist sites. Such policies are under active discussion in many countries.

One way of continuing to derive economic benefits from tourism whilst limiting damage from the pressure of ever-increasing visitor numbers is to move upmarket so that a given level of visitor spending is associated with a smaller number of visitors. This strategy is being pursued by Spain which, having led the world in creating destinations for mass tourism, is now trying to take between 5 and 10 per cent of its rooms out of its stock of accommodation (*Economist*, 1991, p. 15).

10.5 Conclusion

Tourism is a large and rapidly growing industry though the rate of growth is slowing and Europe, whilst still dominant, is losing some of its global share. Although patterns of tourism have changed – for example business and urban tourism is growing in importance – the present-day industry is still similar in character to that of a few decades ago. It is simply much larger and more high profile. The industry comprises a diverse mixture of activities and organizations often with a pattern of high market concentration, but large firms coexist with a fragmented mass of very small firms. Competition is often intense and public policy has thus tended to be relatively unconcerned with microeconomic issues relating to the structural and behavioural aspects of the industry. Policy emphasis has been on the broader economic and social issues of using tourism as a vehicle for economic development, simultaneously being concerned about the environmental damage that tourism causes. Policy, particularly at the Europe-wide level, has tended to be weak. A continuing theme of policy will be to strike an appropriate balance between promoting the industry to reap economic benefits whilst finding ways of limiting or managing the industry better to preserve the quality of life and environment of the host communities.

Notes

1. These figures are taken from the *Economist* (1991) and CAB International (1991). Few would dispute their general order of magnitude though there are serious problems in measuring accurately the size of the industry: the definition of the industry is problematic; the underground economy is likely to be prominent (given that income from some activities, like those of souvenir salesmen, and some sources, such as tips, are hard to trace); tourists who receive 'free' accommodation, for example by visiting friends and relatives, or by staying in 'second homes' (for which the national accounts do not record a rental value attributable to tourism), do not have the value of their accommodation included under tourism; there is no recording of the stock of many tourist assets such as attractive scenery; and there are some striking differences in statistics from different sources. These difficulties make comparisons across countries particularly hazardous.
2. Throughout this chapter Germany refers to the old West Germany, and Yugoslavia refers to the old federal state.
3. See for example Burkart and Medlik (1981), Holloway (1989), Laws (1991).
4. Some forms of travel, for example by groups such as nomads, members of the armed forces, diplomats and refugees, are normally excluded.
5. Buckley (1987) has explored the rationale for this kind of bundling, using a transactions cost approach.
6. There have been numerous attempts to classify the tourists themselves into different types. For a review see Lowyck *et at.* (1992).
7. These figures are taken from Eurostat (1990, p. 11). Other sources of information (e.g. WTO, 1990) show that tourism is also important in Austria and Switzerland, which specialize in Alpine holidays; and for some of the smaller island economies such as Malta and Cyprus international tourism receipts are about 20 per cent of GNP.
8. North America runs a huge deficit, which fuels the rest of the world's surplus.
9. The choices involved in the demand for tourism are typically more complex than for many other goods: they involve the type of tourism (such as winter holiday, beach holiday, business and pleasure, visiting friends), the destination, travel mode, type of accommodation, attractions and purchase method (such as inclusive tour, using an agent, and so on).
10. See Sinclair (1991) and Crouch and Shaw (1992) for reviews.
11. Johnson and Ashworth (1990) have critically reviewed studies involving the UK as an origin or destination.
12. See Witt *et al.* (1991, ch. 5) for a discussion of transactional chains in tourism.
13. The total number of agents in the UK was approximately 8 000 in 1989 but this is likely to have fallen to perhaps 6 500 by the early 1990s (Economist Intelligence Unit, 1991d).
14. To the extent that hotels are successful in achieving high occupancy rates the short-run elasticity of supply of individual establishments will be low.
15. Witt *et al.* (1991, p. 67) notes that this is the case where there is a heavy dependence on tour operators, as in the specialized Spanish tourist regions of the Balearic and the Canary Islands.
16. A similar study of inclusive tour package holidays to major European cities (Clewer *et al.*, 1992) showed the relevance of the particular characteristics of the holidays.
17. More generally, experienced tourists tend to use second homes or rent flats rather than stay in hotels, prefer activities to attractions, make their own arrangement rather than use travel agents, and so on.
18. This practice was declared illegal by the Monopolies and Mergers Commission in 1986 though interestingly the MMC did not permit cash discounts, only non-cash inducements such as free insurance.
19. The low profits were a crucial factor in the Monopolies and Mergers Commission's approval of the mergers which gave Thomson a 40 per cent market share.
20. For example, of a sample of similarly specified UK Holiday Inns in different locations the most productive hotel generated 4.3 times the revenue per full-time employee than the worst (Economist Intelligence Unit, 1991e).

21. For evidence on this see Eurostat (1990) and Williams and Shaw (1991, pp. 21–3). It should be stressed that there are some important regional differences within countries which are averaged out in national data.
22. It is worth noting that diversification across market segments and destinations can enable risks to be spread but it does not entirely eliminate them in a world of low profit margins. There were for instance major collapses, notably Clarksons in the UK in 1974, after the first energy crisis.
23. Many studies have examined tourism multipliers and the impact of tourism. For a selection of some of these see Johnson and Thomas (1992a).
24. The concept of 'capacity' is very problematic in the tourism industry.
25. For a list of examples of desecration see King (1991, p. 83).
26. Under Section 4 of the Development of Tourism Act 1969 selective assistance was given to the industry, primarily for the purpose of job creation, but was withdrawn in 1989.
27. Tourist offices usually have a strong local base. A survey by Touche Ross (1991) of tourist offices throughout Europe showed that approximately 80 per cent of funds for tourist offices were provided by local governments.
28. For an early example see the Resolution of the European Parliament 16 December 1983 (*Official Journal of the European Communities*, Series C, 16/1/84, p. 281). There have subsequently been many other similar statements, see European Commission–European Parliament (1992).
29. See Akehurst (1992) for details of some of these policies.
30. Some concerns have, however, been expressed about the adverse consequences of increasing flows of tourists. See, for example, the European Parliament's resolutions on measures needed to protect the environment from potential damage caused by mass tourism (13 July 1990) and on the danger to natural and semi-natural habitats in the Alps posed by the increase in tourism (12 June 1991).

References

Akehurst, G. (1992), 'European Community Tourism Policy', in Johnson and Thomas (1992b).

Buckley, P.J. (1987), 'Tourism – a Supply Side View', *Tourism Management*, **8**, 179–80.

Bull, A. (1991), *The Economics of Travel and Tourism*, Sydney: Longman Cheshire.

Burkart, A.J. and Medlik, S. (1981), *Tourism: Past, Present and Future*, 2nd ed., London: Heinemann

CAB International (1991), *World Travel and Tourism Review*, Vol. I., Wallingford: CAB International.

Clewer, A., Pack, A. and Sinclair, M.T. (1992), 'Price Competitiveness and Inclusive Tour Holidays in European Cities', in Johnson and Thomas (1992b).

Commission of the European Communities (1985), *The Tourism Sector in the Community*, Luxembourg: Office for Official Publications of the European Community.

Crouch, G.I. and Shaw, R.N. (1992), 'International Tourism Demand: A Meta-analytical Integration of Research Findings', in Johnson and Thomas (1992b).

The Economist (1991), 'A Survey of World Travel and Tourism', 23 March, 1–26.

Economist Intelligence Unit (1988), *International Tourism Forecasts to 1999*, London: EIU.

Economist Intelligence Unit (1989), *Travel and Tourism Analyst*, **5**.

Economist Intelligence Unit (1991a), *Travel and Tourism Analyst*, **4**.

Economist Intelligence Unit (1991b), *Travel and Tourism Analyst*, **2**.

Economist Intelligence Unit (1991c), *The European Inbound Tour Operators' Market*, London: EIU.

Economist Intelligence Unit (1991d), *Technology and UK Travel Agents*, London: EIU.

Economist Intelligence Unit (1991e), *Hotel Branding*, London: EIU.

European Commission–European Parliament (1992), *Tourism in Europe*, Luxembourg: Office for Official Publications of the European Communities.

Eurostat (1990), *Tourism in Europe. Trends 1989*, Luxembourg: Office for Official Publications of the European Communities.

Goodall, B. and Stabler, M. (1992), 'Timeshare: The Policy Issues', in Johnson and Thomas (1992a).

Gray, H.P. (1982), 'The Contributions of Economics to Tourism', *Annals of Tourism Research*, **9**, (1), 105–25.

Hartley, K. and Hooper, N. (1992), 'Tourism Policy: Market Failure and Public Choice', in Johnson and Thomas (1992a).

Holloway, J.C. (1989), *The Business of Tourism*, London: Pitman.

Johnson, P. and Ashworth, J. (1990), 'Modelling Tourism Demand: A Summary Review', *Leisure Studies*, **9**, (2), 145–61.

Johnson, P. and Thomas, B. (eds) (1992a), *Perspectives on Tourism Policy*, London: Mansell.

Johnson, P. and Thomas, B. (eds) (1992b), *Choice and Demand in Tourism*, London: Mansell.

King, R. (1991), 'Italy: Multi-faceted Tourism', in Williams and Shaw (1991).

Laws, E. (1991), *Tourism Marketing*, Cheltenham: Stanley Thornes.

Leontidou, L. (1991), 'Greece: Prospects and Contradictions of Tourism in the 1980s', in Williams and Shaw (1991).

Lewis, J. and Williams, A.M. (1991), 'Portugal: Market Segmentation and Regional Specialisation', in Williams and Shaw (1991).

Lowyck, E., Van Langenhove, L. and Bollaert, L. (1992), 'Typologies of Tourist Roles', in Johnson and Thomas (1992b).

Martin, C.A. and Witt, S.F. (1988), 'Substitute Prices in Models of Tourism Demand', *Annals of Tourism Research*, **15**, (2), 255–68.

Pinder, D. (1991), 'The Netherlands: Tourist Development in a Crowded Society', in Williams and Shaw (1991).

Schnell, P. (1991), 'The Federal Republic of Germany: A Growing International Deficit?', in Williams and Shaw (1991).

Sinclair, M.T. (1991), 'The Economics of Tourism', in C.P. Cooper (ed.), *Progress in Tourism, Recreation and Hospitality Management*, Vol. III, London: Belhaven.

Sinclair, M.T., Clewer, A. and Pack, A., (1990), 'Hedonic Prices and the Marketing of Package Holidays: the Case of Tourism Resorts in Malaga', in G. Ashworth and B. Goodall (eds), *Marketing Tourism Places*, London: Routledge.

Touche Ross (1991), *Survey of Tourist Offices in European Cities*, London: Touche Ross and Co.

The Tourism Society (1990), *The Tourism Industry 1990/91*, London: The Tourism Society.

Tuppen, J. (1991), 'France: the Changing Character of an Industry', in Williams and Shaw (1991).

Valenzeula, M. (1991), 'Spain, the Phenomenon of Mass Tourism', in Williams and Shaw (1991).

Wanhill, S. (1988), 'Tourism Statistics to 2000', in *Proceedings of Current Issues in Services Research Conference*, Poole: Dorset Institute.

Williams, A.M. and Shaw, G. (eds) (1991), *Tourism and Economic Development*, 2nd edn, London: Belhaven.

Witt, S.F., Brooke, M.Z. and Buckley, P.J. (1991), *The Management of International Tourism*, London: Unwin Hyman.

World Tourism Organization (1991), *Tourism Trends Worldwide and in Europe 1950–1990*, revised ed., Madrid: WTO.

World Tourism Organization (1992), *Yearbook of Tourism Statistics*, Madrid: WTO.

Further reading

There are numerous books on tourism. Readers unfamiliar with the field will find a number of useful sources in the references to this chapter and the bibliographies contained therein. Two useful starting points are A. Bull, *The Economics of Travel and Tourism* (1991) on some basic economic analysis and A.M. Williams and G. Shaw (eds) (1991), *Tourism and Economic Development* for a good discussion of tourism in several European countries. The best statistical sources for Europe as a whole are the publications of Eurostat and the World Tourism Organization.

11 Financial services

Lynne Evans

11.1 Introduction

11.1.1 The scale of the industry

The financial services industry is a collective term for the banking and insurance industries and stock markets. The importance of financial services to the EC economy is reflected in terms of both value-added and the number of people employed in the sector: it accounts for around 8 per cent of Community GDP[1] and employs over 10 million people,[2] nearly 8 per cent of total employment in the Community. There was considerable growth in the sector during the 1980s, yet the contribution made by financial services to the EC economy is still less in terms of value than that recorded in the United States and Japan. As can be seen from the international comparisons presented in Figure 11.1, EC banking institutions are particularly important on the global scale (indeed of the world's 100 largest banks, 44 are European); stock exchange capitalization represents 43 per cent of Community GNP, modest by comparison with Japan's 139 per cent figure,[3] but not dissimilar to the US percentage (52 per cent); and the aggregate figure for the share of insurance premiums in Community GNP is perhaps indicative of relative underinsurance.

Within the EC, the latest data on the composition of the financial sector[4] reveal the predominance of banking within the financial services industry (see Figure 11.2). This predominance is not surprising: the EC has 12 member states with financial systems at various stages of development, and it is well recognized that financial systems evolve in essentially three stages (Rybczynski, 1988). They begin with *bank-oriented systems* (in which banks collect and allocate the bulk of an economy's savings); these evolve into *market-oriented systems* (in which other savings institutions also allocate new savings; and capital markets channel new savings and reallocate old savings); and the final stage of development is reached in *securitized systems* (in which savings institutions collect and allocate new savings; and capital markets dominate the reallocation of old savings). Whilst all member states have formal stock exchanges and in this sense have established appropriate capital market institutions, the very modest role played by the capital market in some countries indicates that their financial systems are yet to reach maturity.

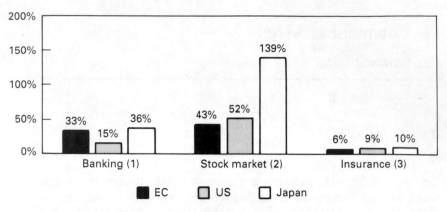

Notes:
1. Banks' share of consolidated international assets (1988).
2. Stock market capitalization as a percentage of GNP (1989).
3. Insurance premiums as a percentage of GNP (1988).

Source: CEC (1991).

Figure 11.1   Financial Markets: the EC Compared with US and Japan

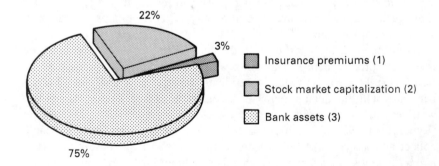

Notes:
1. Insurance premiums as a percentage of GNP (1988).
2. Stock market capitalization as a percentage of GNP (1989).
3. Bank assets as a percentage of GNP (1989).

Source: CEC (1991).

Figure 11.2   Composition of the Financial Sector, 1988–89, EC 12

In part, the different stages of financial development across the EC are reflected in the share of value-added in the financial services sector in each member state and, to a lesser extent, in the share of employment. Figure 11.3 reveals the very high share of value-added in total GDP in Luxembourg and the UK, mainly reflecting the international character of their financial markets: for example, over 90 per cent of all bonds listed on the Luxembourg stock exchange are foreign (CEC, 1990), while the market share of foreign banks is around 90 per cent (Molyneux, 1990); London is well established as the main international financial centre in Europe. Table 11.1 presents employment in the financial services industry in each member state.

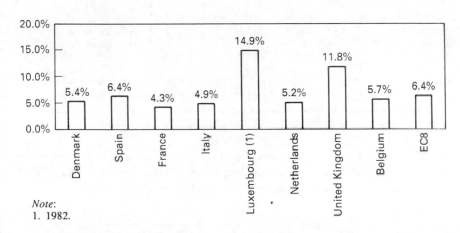

Note:
1. 1982.

Source: CEC (1990).

Figure 11.3   Share of Value-added in the Financial Services Sector in each Member State, 1985

What is clear from Table 11.1 is that the quantitative importance of employment in the financial services sector is greatest in the more evolved financial systems of northern Europe; and with the exceptions of Spain and Portugal, is relatively more important as a provider of female employment. It is also clear that, over the period 1983–89 (the latest period for which there are consistent labour force survey statistics), the financial services industry became an increasingly important employer in all member states of the EC. Both the levels of employment and the proportion of employed persons working in this sector have risen in each of the member states.[5]

This expansionary trend may be seen in the context of an industry which, from the 1970s, has embarked on an internationalization process likely to

Table 11.1   Employment in the Banking, Finance and Insurance Sector
              (000s; % of Total Employment in Each Member Country)

	1989 total		Male		Female		1983 total	
Belgium	289	(8.1)	176	(7.8)	112	(8.5)	229	(6.7)
Denmark	256	(9.8)	138	(9.7)	118	(9.9)	156	(6.5)
West Germany	2 216	(8.1)	1 198	(7.2)	1 018	(9.5)	1 813	(7.0)
Greece	169	(4.6)	103	(4.3)	66	(5.2)	122	(3.5)
Spain	646	(5.3)	458	(5.5)	188	(4.9)	N/A	
France	1 909	(8.8)	980	(7.9)	929	(10.1)	1 619	(7.6)
Ireland	89	(8.1)	50	(6.8)	39	(10.9)	81	(7.2)
Italy	855	(4.1)	531	(3.9)	324	(4.6)	636	(3.1)
Luxembourg	19	(12.5)	10	(10.3)	9	(16.5)	12	(8.3)
Netherlands	643	(10.7)	413	(10.9)	230	(10.3)	419	(8.5)
Portugal	154	(3.4)	103	(3.9)	51	(2.7)	N/A	
UK	2 823	(10.7)	1 443	(9.6)	1 380	(12.1)	1 859	(8.0)
EC 12	10 067	(7.7)	5 603	(7.0)	4 464	(8.8)	N/A	
EC 10	9 267	(8.2)	5 042	(7.4)	4 226	(9.4)	6 946	(6.5)

Source: Commission of the European Community, *Labour Force Survey* (1989).

result in a global financial industry. However, this anticipates later parts of
this chapter; at this stage it may be helpful to provide a more systematic
historical overview of the global financial services industry.

11.1.2   Historical development
The 1960s and 1970s were two decades of sustained growth in banking
activities. Important early moves were made by US banks, who expanded
significantly in the international field in the 1960s in order to capture a share
of the Eurodollar market based in London and dominated by British institutions at that time. Other European banks and the Japanese banks followed
this lead in the 1970s. The enthusiasm for the Eurocurrency market relates to
its lack of regulation. Tightly regulated domestic banks were eager to shift
their portfolio composition and strengthen their foreign activities in a climate
of slower economic growth, credit ceilings and regulatory tightness at home
(Metais, 1990, p. 173). Yet only the British and US markets had begun to
offer significant opportunities to foreign competitors. The result was that
European financial activities largely remained organized along domestic
structural and regulatory lines. Key features of these markets included
oligopolistic structures and behaviour, limitations on deposit rates, solvency
and liquidity ratios, and entry restrictions. Competition among banks occurred

mainly in the unregulated Eurocurrency markets where price competition played an essential regulatory role.

In the 1980s there was a shift in the balance of power among financial institutions: investment and merchant banks, securities dealers and brokers emerged as major players, whereas deposit banks had to reallocate part of their resources towards these new activities or retreat into their domestic market. The buzz words of the period were 'innovations', 'securitization' and 'globalization'. Competition became fiercer – through both prices and a flurry of innovations – and profits in traditional banking were forced down. It is arguable that during the 1980s the banking systems of the main industrial countries built up a financial intermediation 'over-capacity' which, in its turn, has largely fuelled the observed deregulatory process (Metais, 1990, p. 175). The strong commitment of many governments to structural deregulation was a prominent feature of financial systems in the 1980s and this has not only affected the banking sector.

More generally, the financial services sector has experienced fundamental changes in: (1) the organizational form of its firms; (2) the sectors in which they have traditionally operated: (3) competition; (4) products and services offered; and (5) methods of delivering these outputs. Taken together, these have been labelled the 'financial revolution'.[6] At a global level, this revolution has broken down the historically segmented financial institutional sectors. In many countries banks have moved into non-traditional areas like mortgage finance and insurance. Savings banks, traditionally retail-type organizations, have been encroaching on corporate and investment banking fields. Insurance companies have been moving into traditional banking areas, and vice versa. In addition, new forms of competition have emerged. New, more customer-oriented, methods of marketing and delivery have been developed, and in some sectors there are strong pressures to depersonalize the distribution of services stimulated by technical advances. The growing efficiency of financial markets has encouraged the comparative growth of credit intermediation through financial markets rather than through traditional (financial) institutional channels. This 'securitization' trend has been especially marked since 1982 in international banking and at the top end of the corporate banking market. Although this financial revolution did not have such a big impact on continental Europe as it did on the US, Japan and the UK, securitization is continuing to grow in most European domestic financial systems. Indeed, over the 1980s EC countries have been increasingly affected by the globalization trends, the technological developments and the widespread adoption of structural deregulation policies which make up the financial revolution – a process which has been accelerated by moves towards the single European market.

However, it would be wrong to think that the financial systems on continental Europe have already developed financial markets on a scale comparable with those of the so-called Anglo-Saxon countries: at the present time, continental Europe remains a largely intermediated financial system. Complete liberalization in the financial services industry (in the sense of allowing all appropriately qualified firms to operate in the markets of their choice) is clearly a long-term goal. But this must be based on the assurance of adequate regulation throughout the EC.

11.1.3 What is special about this industry?

Regulatory structure lies at the heart of the financial services industry. This industry is special, and it is special in two major respects. First, governments attach special value to it – often to control the process of channelling savings to private or government use; often to ensure solvency; and always to protect savers from fraud and misappropriation of funds. Secondly, the industry is universal – whilst not every country has a car industry, every country has a financial services industry. Taken together, these observations demonstrate why debates relating to the development of this industry so often dwell on the issue of government involvement/ownership in the industry and the optimal regulatory stance.

To better understand this, it is helpful to consider the nature of the output of this industry. The financial system performs three functions: it runs and administers the payments system; it collects new savings from those who generate but cannot directly employ them and employs them where they can earn the highest returns consistent with the savers' proclivity to assume risk; and it provides facilities for the transfer of ownership (that is, the market for corporate control). In discharging these basic functions, the financial system is dealing with risk, and a characteristic of this industry is the management and monitoring of information. Consider the banking industry. Banks are multi-product firms which practise cross-subsidization of services and maintenance of non-profitable operations (e.g. the payments mechanism). Whilst there is high substitutability between bank products, they are not perfect substitutes, a fact which is attributable to confidence and reputation. The customer acts on the basis of a bank's reputation and confides information about present and planned income and wealth. The service received is to a large extent intangible and embodied in personal relationships and common trust. Both parties, customer and bank, will find information and monitoring costs lower in the case of a long-standing relationship. As a result, customers find it difficult to compare *effective* prices; moreover, they are also unlikely to be very responsive to any changes in perceived prices. These features suggest that the comparative advantage of a bank, much more than in industry, does not lie in a particular product or production process, but in reputation, confidence and customer proximity.

In the insurance industry the central role of the diversification of risk is self-evident, both for life/non-life insurance and the reinsurance industry. What is perhaps less obvious are the ways in which the industry is involved in a number of markets – in addition to its involvement in the market for protection from risk, it is involved in the markets for savings, investment funds and fund management loss. The underlying principle of non-life insurance is the 'mutualization of risks' transferred by a wide range of insured persons or institutions; in life insurance, the principal function is the management and investment of savings. Insurance companies manage a large volume of assets, invest in other companies (industrial, commercial and financial) and are often involved in the direction of whole groups of companies. They are important for underwriting debt and in purchasing equities in the stock market; they also take up significant amounts of government debt. With regard to the distribution of premiums between life and non-life (with the exception of Luxembourg, Ireland and perhaps Italy), it appears that insurance in general and, in a more marked way, life insurance, has a positive elasticity (greater than one) in relation to the income of a country; more wealth implies more insurance (CEC, 1990).

The business of the stock markets is to gather savings and channel them towards the bodies that need them. The stock markets can be grouped into different categories, the most important of which are: capital and money markets (long- and medium-term instruments and short-term instruments, respectively); primary and secondary markets (issues of securities and subsequent dealing in these securities respectively); stock exchanges (which are regulated markets subject to specific dealing rules); and spot and forward markets (payment due immediately or at a specified date in the future). The primary customers of the industry are financial intermediaries (commercial or investment banks), but many private investors are able to invest in transferable securities through entrusting portfolio management to professionals who can spread the risk over a large number of different securities.

11.2 Market structure

11.2.1 An overview

All twelve member states of the EC have a financial services industry consisting of all three components – banking, insurance and stock markets. However, it should be emphasized that there are large variations in the degree of development of these components, especially the stock markets. Not all the member states have markets for the trading of futures and options, and in several countries these markets are of very recent origin (for

Table 11.2 Stock Markets in the European Community

Country	No of stock exchanges	Most important stock exchange	Market value of equity shares of domestic companies[1]		Volume of trading in equity shares (1989)		Recent reforms or changes	Restrictions on foreigners	Trading in futures & options	
			bn ECU	1989/88	bn EC (total)	% foreign companies			futures	options
Belgium	4	Brussels	62.9	24.8	10.6	27.5	Brokers' monopoly on trading removed. Reform period 1988–92	Only EC citizens may be members of Stock exchange		
Denmark	1	Copenhagen	33.7	46.5	12.8	n/a	Swedish financial institutions have been buying Danish brokerages in advance of 1992 to get foot hold in market	Foreign members admitted under EC regulations	launched 1988	launched 1988
Germany	8 (linked)	Frankfurt Düsseldorf	306.3 (combined German markets)	42.5	664.0	4.8			legalized 1989	legalized 1989
Greece	1	Athens	n/a	n/a	n/a	n/a	Brokers' monopoly on trading removed			
Spain	4	Madrid Barcelona	102.7 93.3	32.3 30.8	31.7 4.3	0 0	Banks and other financial institutions allowed to take shares; abolition of fixed commissions by 1992; automated trading introduced (1989)		exists but is unregulated	launched 1989
France	7	Paris	282.3	48.4	104.7	4.1	Self-regulating since 1988; brokers' monopoly on trading removed; abolition of fixed commissions (1988)	Foreign membership of Paris Stock Exchange frozen until 1992	MATIF set up 1986 as futures market for government bonds. Since then amalgamated with existing commodities markets (futures and options available)	

Country		Exchange								
Ireland	1	Dublin					Dublin Stock Exchange has been absorbed by London Stock Exchange but is administered separately		opened 1989	opened 1989
Italy	10	Milan	136.9 (Italy)	18.6	38.2	0	Change of regulations to allow foreign companies to be listed (1989)	Stockbrokers must be Italian citizens		exists
Luxembourg	1	Luxembourg	45.8	15.9	0.1	21.0		Foreigners permitted to join Luxembourg Stock Exchange		
Netherlands	1	Amsterdam	129.4	40.5	44.8	1.0	Abolished fixed commission, 1990	Stock Exchange only open to companies established in the EC. No restrictions on ownership of Dutch shares.	opened 1987	officially opened 1978
Portugal	2	Lisbon	n/a	n/a	n/a	n/a	Programme of reforms announced 1988 – established uniform prices and common brokers	Only Portuguese citizens may be stockbrokers		
UK	1	London	682.9	12.6	411.4	30.0	'Big Bang' 1986 abolition of minimum commission rates; abolition of distinction between brokers and market makers; allowing outside companies to take over Stock Exchange member firms		founded 1982	founded 1978

Note: 1 The data in this column refer to the stock exchange(s) mentioned in the previous column, unless otherwise indicated.

Sources: CEC (1991); Hay (1990).

example in Denmark, Ireland, Spain and the Netherlands). Each member state has at least one stock exchange and in most countries there have been moves to reform the institution in recent years. For example, the brokers' monopoly on trading has been removed in Belgium, Greece and France; and fixed commissions have been abolished in Spain, France and the Netherlands. The degree of openness of the exchanges to foreign membership and the willingness of governments to allow foreign companies to be listed on the stock exchange also varies across the countries.

11.2.2   Stock markets

An overview of the stock markets across the member states is presented in Table 11.2. From the first two columns it can be seen that only in some countries is there a single stock exchange but in those countries where there are a number of stock exchanges there is a tendency for one to predominate (see for example Belgium, France and Italy). The last four columns of Table 11.2 characterize each country's recent developments in the stock markets. Much of this relates to deregulatory changes and the development of trading in futures and options.

Unfortunately, no homogeneous data are available on the value of debentures in circulation in the member states. The only comparable available data concern the value of bonds and debentures quoted on the different main stock exchanges of the Community. Table 11.2 (columns 3 and 4) presents the latest comparable data together with information on the development of the money markets in comparison with the previous year. The stock exchanges of London, Germany and Paris are predominant, but it is also interesting to note the high increases recorded by some of the other stock exchanges: Copenhagen (46.5 per cent) and Amsterdam (40.5 per cent). These growth rates contribute to an overall growth rate in the EC 10 countries of 26.7 per cent, which is much higher than the increase recorded in either Tokyo (9.2 per cent) or New York (20.2 per cent) (CEC, 1991, pp. 26–10). A more general indicator of stock exchange business is the volume of transactions in transferable securities. The figures given in Table 11.2 (columns 5 and 6) indicate that by far the most active stock exchanges are those of Germany and London; with a clear preponderance of domestic firms in the German market, and a large presence of foreign firms in the London and Brussels markets (30 per cent and 27.5 per cent respectively).

11.2.3   Insurance industry

The insurance industry is a large and important part of the Community's financial sector. Insurance premiums account for around 6 per cent of GDP (CEC, 1990, 1991), the highest percentage being recorded in Ireland (10.9 per cent), and the lowest in Greece (1.2 per cent). Following 20 years of growth, the share accounted for by the EC insurance market diminished during the 1980s, while those of the US and Japan increased. By far the largest market in the EC is that in Germany whilst the southern European and Irish markets are relatively small. However, small does not necessarily imply underdeveloped; Ireland is a notable exception with one of the smallest markets yet one of the highest per capita expenditures on insurance. Columns 2, 3 and 4 of Table 11.3 present comparative data on insurance penetration in the twelve member states. Simply defined, 'insurance penetration' is the total premiums collected by insurers (other than the State) as a percentage of GDP: this gives an indication of the importance of the insurance business within each economy. It is a rather crude indicator as it is markedly influenced by the volume and extent of public insurance. Nevertheless, it appears that in Ireland, the UK and the Netherlands the insurance business is important, whereas in Italy, Portugal and Greece it is not. Also, there is no marked shift in rankings when one looks at the subdivision of insurance penetration indicators into life and non-life business. More generally, life insurance penetration seems to be primarily influenced by the strength of public pension schemes; while habits and legal requirements influence non-life insurance penetration.

Turning to the structure of the industry; it is unambiguously the case that the insurance industry is highly concentrated. In the EC, the ten leading companies in life insurance account for nearly 30 per cent of all the business, and the top 20 nearly 40 per cent. For non-life insurance, the market shares of the 10 and 20 largest companies are, respectively, 18 per cent and 27 per cent (CEC, 1990, pp. 26–32). Taking into account groups of insurers, the degree of concentration will inevitably be greater. Comparable data on concentration within each member state does not seem to exist, but from the information presented in Table 11.3 it can be seen that there are some examples of very high concentration: for example in Ireland the life insurance business is dominated by just one firm (43 per cent); and in Portugal and Greece the market is dominated by nationalized companies (state-owned banks) which control 87 per cent and over 70 per cent, respectively, of the insurance business. One of the least concentrated insurance markets is in Germany, where the top 15 firms account for less than 20 per cent of the non-life market; with a corresponding figure of 26 per cent for the life market.

Some member states have a high percentage of foreign-owned establishments – Belgium, Greece, Ireland, Portugal and the UK – but this gives little indication of the importance of the business concerned: for example in Greece foreign ownership accounts for 39 per cent of the establishments yet their market share is just 9 per cent.

Table 11.3   EC Insurance Industry

Country*	Total no. of companies (1986)	Insurance penetration			Regulatory intensity	Foreign ownership
		life (1987)	non-life (1987)	total (1987)		(% market share)
Belgium	282	1.6	3.4	4.9	1.45	41 (36)
Denmark (segregation of life and non-life business. One dominant life firm holds 40% of the market; one dominant non-life firm holds 17% of the market)	233	1.7	3.1	4.8	1.66	23 (n.a.)
Germany (segregation of life and non-life business)	771	2.5	3.4	6.0	2.36	14 (4)
Greece (state-owned banks control over 70% of life and non-life markets)	141	0.4	0.8	1.2	1.92	39 (9)
Spain (relatively unconcentrated; largest life company has 10% of market; largest non-life company has 15% of market)	521	1.6	2.2	3.7	1.75	6 (7)
France (segregation of life and non-life business. Large portion of market is state controlled)	548	2.2	3.4	5.6	1.5	29 (small)
Ireland (segregation of life and non-life business. One of smallest markets, but one of highest per capita expenditure. Life market dominated by one firm – 43% of market)	67	6.4	4.5	10.9	1.75	66 (50)
Italy (relatively underdeveloped market – approximately $1/3$ expenditure per capita of that in UK)	214	0.6	2.1	2.7	2.0	Insurance can only be offered by companies authorized and established in Italy
Luxembourg (one firm has 50% of market share)	81	0.7	2.3	2.9	1.48	n/a
Netherlands (segregated life and non-life business)	694	3.0	3.8	6.8	1.28	25 (8)

Country*	Total no. of companies (1986)	Insurance penetration			Regulatory intensity	Foreign ownership
		life (1987)	non-life (1987)	total (1987)		(% market share)
Portugal (market dominated by nationalized companies – 87% market share; very low per capita expenditure)	51	0.3	2.3	2.6	1.96	50 (n.a.)
UK (UK insurance companies offer widest range of products in Europe. Many non-life lines are tailor-made to suit individual requirements. On life side, investment-linked products have become much more popular. Non-life industry much more concentrated than life. Non-life top 15 firms have nearly 80% of market; life top 15 firms have about 60% of market)	835	5.0	5.8	7.7	1.4	44 (8)

Note: *Annotated with information on market concentration.

Sources: CEC (1990); Molyneux (1990).

One key feature of the industry is that it is subject to high levels of regulation, which is intended to ensure the solvency of insurance companies in order to strengthen the safety of the financial system and to provide adequate consumer protection. A judgemental indicator of the regulatory intensity of this industry in each member state is given in column 5 of Table 11.3. At one end of the spectrum are Germany and Italy with high scores on 'regulatory intensity'; the UK and the Netherlands are at the low end of this scale.

11.2.4   Banking

The most extensively studied financial services industry is banking. This reflects both its predominance within the sector and the fundamental nature of banking services. Competitive forces and regulations have produced a variety of bank structures in Europe as elsewhere. Yet even in those member states where universal banking is allowed (for example Germany), specialized financial institutions exist and perform well. Similarly, the absence of regional restrictions in national markets has not led to the disappearance of local or regional banks. Across the EC national, regional and local banks coexist.

The study of market structure in banking involves examination of size, numbers and comparative significance of banks. However, differences in the

Table 11.4 EC Banking Industry

Country	Significant factors	No. institutions in banking system (1988)	Banks' assets[3] (bn ECU) (1989)	Sector ownership (% of aggregate total assets, 1988)[1]				Market domination Concentration Ratios[2] (% of total market, 1988)	
				Private	Public	Foreign	Mutual[4]	Assets (3 firm)	Deposits (3 firm)
Belgium	Before 1934 Belgian banks were 'universal'; bank ownership of shares in industry banned since 1935	120	239	37.0	16.8	35.2	11.0	57.1	59.0
Denmark	Many banks started making losses in late 1980s, prompting merger activity. Recent moves to strengthen supervision may disadvantage Danish banks when EC markets fully liberalized	165	147	69.5	1.3	–	29.2	36.7 (Big 3)	45.3
Germany	German banks are 'universal' banks dealing in credit deposits, payment transactions, but also investment banking and securities. Long-standing arrangement whereby commercial banks hold major shareholdings in industrial companies which, in the past, has brought large parts of German industry under bank control	4390	1579	32.0	49.5	1.8	16.7	21.2 (Big 6)	19.1

Country	Notes								
Greece	Foreign banks (except EC banks) may not hold more than 40% of share capital of a Greek bank	41	39	11.0	83.7	5.3	–	– (1 state-controlled)	49.7
Spain	Spanish government has been reducing the level of its regulation of banks and encouraging bank mergers in anticipation of opening of markets through liberalization programme. Savings banks (which allocate 50% of annual surplus to social security functions) have been growing faster than commercial banks	491	386	49.0	2.3	11.0	37.7	21.9	24.3
France	Major financial institutions nationalized in stages after 1945; but since mid-1980s some have been returned to private ownership. 1984 Banking Law removed distinctions between categories of banks to encourage competition	1999	728	24.2	42.2	13.5	20.2	42.3	45.5
Ireland	Government has been attempting to encourage financial services companies to set up in Ireland – through tax advantages	47	25	61.7	4.0	21.4	12.9	71.0 (Big 2)	–
Italy	Central Bank is encouraging mergers amongst the joint stock banks and cooperative banks	1100	542	12.3	67.9	3.0	16.8	35.2 (Big 4)	41.6

Country	Significant factors	No. institutions in banking system (1988)	Banks' assets[3] (bn ECU) (1989)	Sector ownership (% of aggregate total assets, 1988)[1]				Market domination Concentration Ratios[2] (% of total market, 1988)	
				Private	Public	Foreign	Mutual[4]	Assets (3 firm)	Deposits (3 firm)
Luxembourg	Low rates of taxation and strict banking secrecy laws have contributed to making Luxembourg a significant financial centre. Most banks are known to be foreign banks	143	239	n/a	n/a	90.0	n/a	16.7	16.5
Netherlands	From beginning of 1990, no restrictions on Dutch banks investing in insurance companies, and vice versa. Savings banks gradually being reduced through merger	169	343	61.2	8.1	13.0	17.7	71.3	83.9 (Big 2)
Portugal	Since 1987, programme of reprivatizing the banks (and large industrial companies) nationalized in 1975	27	35	6.8	87.1	4.2	1.9	49.7 (1 public sector credit institution)	49.6
UK	1987 Act further strengthened regulation	784	1449	31.8	1.0	53.3	14.0	26.5 (Big 4)	21.6

Notes:

1. Figures for Denmark and Greece relate to % of total deposits and total credit respectively.
2. Note in parentheses indicates a particular characteristic of market domination.
3. Figures for Denmark and Italy are estimated values.
4. Mutual institutions include savings banks, building societies, cooperative banks and credit unions, together with their central organizations.

Sources: CEC (1991); Gardener and Molyneux (1990); Hay (1990); Molyneux (1990).

use of the term 'bank' lead to some difficulties with comparison. The establishment data presented in Table 11.4 refer to the total number of banks in the market and include not just authorized commercial banks but also savings banks, cooperative banks and mortgage credit institutions. On this measure, by far the largest banking sector is in Germany, which has over 4 000 bank institutions; France has almost 2 000 establishments; and Greece, Ireland and Portugal each have small sectors with less than 50 institutions each. When size is measured by banks' assets, Germany and the UK are outstanding with around 1 500 billion ECU bank assets in each of their banking sectors; whereas Greece, Ireland and Portugal each have less than 50 billion ECU bank assets.

Despite differences relating to establishment, every banking system in the EC has a group of dominant or 'core' banks which are recognized by both the authorities and the general public; for example the Big 3 in Denmark and the single state-controlled bank in Greece (see columns 8 and 9). Concentration measures show that of the three largest banking markets (Germany, France and the UK), France has the most concentrated (over 40 per cent); yet Ireland and the Netherlands have higher concentration ratios (over 70 per cent). In his overview of the European banking scene, Dietrich (1991) finds that the largest banks are in the largest economies: France, the UK, Italy and Germany. However, there is no apparent tendency among the larger banks (defined as those with over \$10 billion assets) to cluster in the largest economies: for example, Belgium, Denmark and Spain all have several banks with over \$10 billion assets, despite their widely differing levels of income and population. Indeed few generalities regarding relations between bank size, average bank operating characteristics and countries and levels of economic activity can be made from Dietrich's analysis. His tentative conclusion is that the extent of bank intermediation in various European countries does not seem to be importantly related to economic conditions. It seems that each banking system has its own distinguishing features, which traditions and public policy environments have created.[7]

A key distinction relates to the significance of the public sector, which accounts for more than 50 per cent of total assets in Greece, Italy and Portugal;[8] yet less than 2.5 per cent in Denmark, Spain and the UK (see column 5 of Table 11.4). Importantly, the public sector declined in virtually every Community banking market over the 1980s – the notable exception is Italy, where this sector increased its share by 7.5 per cent (between 1983 and 1988).

Another distinction is the difference in the relative importance of foreign banks within each country's banking sector (column 6). Foreign banks dominate in the UK system and also control a large proportion of banking sector assets in Belgium, Luxembourg and Ireland. Luxembourg is a particular outlier in this respect: some 90 per cent of its banking assets are accounted for by foreign banks. Foreign bank penetration is particularly low in Germany, Greece and Italy. In recent years foreign bank presence has increased in nearly all the EC's banking markets, reflecting the trend towards greater internationalization of this sector.

Another distinction worth noting is the relative importance of the mutual sector, which includes cooperative banks, building societies and credit unions. As can be seen from column 7, its significance ranges from nearly 38 per cent in Spain to zero per cent in Greece. Mutual sector presence is also low in Portugal and Belgium.

Some explanation for these distinctions can be gleaned from an appreciation of the various characteristics that distinguish continental banking systems from the Anglo-Saxon. Revell (1987) identifies common elements of continental banking systems. These include:

1. the presence of various credit institutions, typically publicly owned, providing funds for specific sectors such as industry, agriculture and property;
2. the increased importance of savings banks, cooperative (popular) banks and cooperative credit associations;
3. a long history of commercial bank participation in the ownership and management of industrial enterprises;
4. the importance of banks and other institutions organized on a local or regional basis, typically servicing small enterprises in both industry and agriculture.

These common elements help to explain the relative proliferation of bank credit institutions in continental European banking systems and some relatively high public sector involvement (particularly in Germany, France and Italy).

11.2.5   Barriers to entry and contestability

The most recent structural trend in the EC financial services sector, most noticeable in Germany and the UK, has been the integration of banking, mortgage finance and insurance services. Cooperation and acquisition amongst financial institutions is a response to the obvious incentive to spread overhead costs by producing several services. Highly diversified yet integrated conglomerates avoid marketing individual products separately; rather, they differentiate their products by packaging financial services for target customers. In addition they reduce the aggregate costs of information gathering and reduce their own exposure to the risk of consumer shifts across the highly substitutable products of this sector.

These presumed advantages of integration of the sector lead to questions about economies of scale and the extent to which the industry is contestable. The relatively high levels of concentration in banking and insurance tend to suggest that there may be economies of scale in the provision of financial services. However, evidence for both the insurance and the banking industry does not unambiguously endorse this. For example in an EC-commissioned study of the insurance industry, Aaronovitch and Samson (1985, p. 194) concluded that the existence of scale economies remains uncertain; and many studies of economies of scale in banking imply that such economies, if they exist at all, are very small. Some argue that economies of scope are more important. These exist when a single firm can produce a given level of output of each product line more cheaply than a combination of separate firms. However, it must be recognized that economies of scale and scope are two properties of the productive process which are difficult to distinguish, particularly in empirical tests (see Bailey and Friedlander, 1982) and especially in the financial services industry (see Gilbert, 1984, p. 617).

With regard to contestability, especially important in these industries are the potential barriers to entry in relation to: regulation; capital requirements; and degrees of reversibility regarding sunk costs. Until recently these factors were thought to be equally relevant; but now the position is looking rather different. The thrust of Community policy is to dismantle regulatory barriers to entry; and the processing and delivery of new financial products (typical of the securitization and internationalization moves within the industry) do not require the same type of fixed capital as the traditional bank products. Technological advances may also facilitate a move towards heavy reliance on extensive hardware, sophisticated software and telecoms equipment rather than extensive heavily staffed branch networks. The balance of costs could fall either way, but the costs of hardware and telecommunications are declining all the time. If 'hit and run' strategies continue to be unattractive, financial services markets are imperfectly contestable. A closer look reveals that a deregulation process in itself represents a barrier to entry – entry into a market in transition is risky. But there can be no firm conclusion on this issue: what is clear is that the EC's policy on regulatory change implicitly accepts that these markets are essentially contestable – that is, that both entry and exit are relatively costless in the absence of regulatory inhibitions to either.

11.3   Market behaviour

Customer confidence and the reputation of a financial institution tend to be such important factors in the financial sector that customers are likely to be relatively price insensitive. Moreover, the multi-product nature of the business, together with the characteristic long-standing relationships between customers and their institutions, makes it difficult for customers to compare

effective prices. Not surprisingly, significant price differences are found
even within national markets where suppliers are faced with the same regulatory barriers. Comparisons across national markets are even more marked.
For example, commercial fire and theft insurance is approximately four
times more expensive in Italy than in Belgium or the Netherlands (see Table
11.5). Such observations have led to the view that the removal of regulatory
barriers to trade is unlikely to result in a single price (Price Waterhouse,
1988).

*Table 11.5   Comparative 'Prices' of Purchases of a Range of Financial
Services in Eight EC Countries (ECU)*

	B	D	S	F	It	L	NL	UK
Banking services								
Commercial loans*	45	50	56	44	51	50	68	69
Consumer credit	12	46	27	40	43	14	26	43
Credit cards	94	84	66	37	99	46	75	61
Mortgages*	4.8	5.8	8.0	6.5	3.5	n/a	3.4	2.9
Travellers cheques	7.3	5.0	7.0	7.5	6.6	5.0	7.2	5.0
Current accounts	0	117	2	10	240	8	0	112
*Insurance services**								
Term insurance*	3.8	2.3	2.9	2.9	3.9	3.6	2.0	1.5
House insurance*	1.2	1.4	1.4	2.0	2.5	2.2	1.6	2.7
Motor insurance*	4.9	4.4	7.6	4.1	9.4	6.7	3.5	3.2
Commercial fire and theft*	13	20	18	36	49	12	14	18
Securities services								
Private equity transactions	14	11	17	9	10	11	22	23
Private gilts transactions	65	108	180	69	21	72	148	77
Institutional equity transactions*	17	23	35	13	20	23	17	7
Institutional gilts transactions*	215	54	90	88	107	36	46	n/a

Notes:
The London gilt market is now on a net of commission basis.
*measured in 100 ECU units.

Source: Survey results presented in Price Waterhouse (1988).

11.3.1 Price variability

Table 11.5 shows the prices of a number of the financial services examined in an EC commissioned report (Price Waterhouse, 1988). Caution must be exercised in interpreting the price comparisons; in particular many of the products represent the margin over wholesale money market rates and so the 'prices' do not represent the cost to the consumer. Nevertheless the data serve to illustrate wide variation in the price of some financial services across the main EC countries: for example, consumer credit is nearly four times as expensive in Germany as in Belgium. UK house insurance is around double the cost of that in Spain; yet UK motor insurance is roughly a third of that levied in Italy. The most dramatic variation in the securities services relates to the cost of private gilts transactions, where the Spanish price is almost nine times that in Italy.

11.3.2 Innovation

As noted previously, competition within the financial sector has tended to take the form of product innovation. Financial firms have broadened and improved the quality of their services and hence their customer bases. Through market segmentation, product differentiation and accurate packaging they have begun to offer services in designated target markets. For the retail banking sector, the maintenance of a strong hold on the payments mechanism is a critical factor in preserving customer bases: in consequence the banks have actively sought to introduce automation to the cheque clearing and deposit collection services, and offer more sophisticated data processing. However, one should be wary of believing that there is a great deal of scope for innovation in the financial services industry. There are several character-istics which distinguish innovation in this industry from innovation in, say, manufacturing, and contribute to seriously limiting its scope.[9] These are:

1. *Exhaustibility* – product innovation is narrowly bounded in that prod-ucts are either loans (deposits), options, or payment transfers. Innovations are therefore restricted to different packaging of the product and in-creases in the size and number of transactions.
2. Financial innovations serve to *circumvent regulation* or to catch up when regulation is relaxed. One of the best known examples can be found in the growth of the Euromarkets or securitization. If and when there is a perfectly liberalized financial market in the EC, then a transitory explo-sive bout of innovation may result, with innovation tapering off to zero.
3. Unlike some innovations in industry, innovations in finance are *public goods*, so the innovator receives no monopoly right for their exploita-tion. Commercialization of the new product means revealing the idea to competitors, and no patent protection prevents market entry by competi-

tors. As a result, the overall incentive to innovate is reduced, with reputation placed at risk.

Nevertheless, competitive pressure is such that few financial firms can resist the introduction of innovations, once these have been made by others. As a result the main impact of such innovations may be to drive down profits within the sector as a whole.

11.4   Performance

The EC financial sector is an important and powerful force on the world stage; by far the most powerful international industry is EC banking, which accounts for 33.3 per cent of total consolidated international assets, while Japanese banks accounted for 36.4 per cent and US banks 14.5 per cent (see Figure 11.1). Data on profits in this sector are particularly sensitive to the type of statistical source used. Nevertheless, there is some justification for using operating expenses to gross income as a measure of profitability which is suitable for international comparisons.[10] Table 11.6 shows that banks in Luxembourg appear to be the most profitable in the EC, whereas those in Belgium and the UK are the least profitable. A word of warning is in order when interpreting profitability data in this industry: low profitability may be a result of a particularly strict regulatory environment and have little to do with operating efficiency.

Table 11.6   Gross Income as a Multiple of Operating Expenses for Commercial Banks (1980–85 averages)

Country	Multiple
Belgium	1.20
Denmark	n/a
Germany	1.53
Greece	n/a
Spain	1.52
France	1.47
Ireland	n/a
Italy	1.52
Luxembourg	3.33
Netherlands	1.56
Portugal	1.64
UK	1.44

Source: Gardener and Molyneux (1990), p. 38.

11.5 Public policy

11.5.1 Regulation

Regulation of the financial services industry is universal: one of the reasons for this relates to the strong premise that consumers of financial services need to be protected, but a desire to ensure the solvency of financial institutions is also relevant. Put more generally, regulation seeks both to reduce the risks of institutional failure and to ameliorate the consequences of any failures that may occur. Systems of regulation differ significantly; for example, in Italy a 1936 Act combines severe restrictions on bank activity (to reduce risk) with a guarantee of Central Bank assistance if a bank gets into trouble – so bank failure is virtually prohibited: this Act is reinforced by voluntary deposit insurance. The result is a system which severely restricts competition. In the US the authorities combine a compulsory deposit insurance (to protect depositors up to $100 000) with a liberal approach to competition. The result is fairly frequent bank failures. Most European authorities select an intermediate position, which involves some risk, some guarantee fund on deposit insurance (to protect small depositors) and a significant though not unrestricted amount of competition.

The systems of regulation that have evolved in the EC, whilst differing from country to country, have some commonality. Importantly, they share a common basis of three assumptions: (1) a closed, essentially contestable, financial system; (2) each agent operates predominantly in one market; and (3) each agent pursues a limited and constant range of activities. Yet in recent years innovation and internationalization have wrecked these assumptions. In particular, internationalization means that the consequences of insolvency are no longer confined to the citizens of the host country and it seems unlikely that tax payers' funds can be used to bail out institutions to the benefit of citizens of other countries. What should be appreciated here is that the pressures to change regulatory structures are in part independent of the single market programme. Many of the pressures for financial deregulation in the Community have come from such changes in internationalization alongside a recognition of the underdevelopment of domestic capital markets in some of the continental member states. Such underdevelopment implies a relative absence of market-determined financial prices, with a consequent propensity for resource misallocation.

11.5.2 EC initiatives

Thus some momentum for reform within financial systems has taken place within nations. However, more encompassing have been the changes instituted by the European Commission. As long ago as 1966 the EC reported on the reasons for weaknesses in the European capital markets (the Segre Report); these weaknesses included 'monopoly, structural deformation and high liquidity preferences' (quoted in Bisignano, 1991, p. 266 and attributed to Charles Kindleberger). Since then there has been significant integration of European capital markets; and the typically segmented institutional structure is gradually giving way to a broadening and homogenization of financial services and of the institutions which provide them.

This movement has been aided by a number of EC directives relating especially to the banking industry, but also covering stock exchange practices, insurance and fund management services. The most widely quoted is the second banking directive, which aims to establish a single banking licence valid for both establishment and freedom of banking services throughout the Community. Crucially, the EC's directives embody the principle of 'home country regulation' (as opposed to 'host country' regulation). With home country regulation, a financial institution can effectively choose which (of 12) regulatory codes it wishes to observe. The institution will opt for its preferred regulatory code, presumably that which offers it greatest freedom (for example from capital requirements).

Given this, it is often argued that home country regulation is likely to make the whole system evolve towards the most liberal regime available. This is because there is an incentive for individual regulators to move towards a more liberal regulatory stance in order to retain existing institutions and attract new foreign institutions. This argument assumes that regulatory agencies gain advantage from an expansion of the number of institutions under their jurisdiction. This is undoubtedly the case: regulatory agencies receive licence fees from their institutions, they enjoy employment benefits for their country's nationals and, perhaps not the least important, they gain international prestige. This competitive pressure on regulators is referred to as 'competition in laxity'.

Yet it is arguable whether such competition among regulators is to be welcomed. On the one hand, the institutions get the regulatory features they find most useful; yet the encouragement of more liberal regimes results in greater risks of market failure. Importantly, liberalization is not the same as deregulation; and it must be fully recognized that some new regulation may be necessary in order to ensure basic standards in the more competitive market conditions that may result from liberalization. It is in the interest of every member state to ensure that key prudential requirements are harmonized at a minimum standard, so it seems unlikely that there are serious dangers inherent in the home country principle.

Nevertheless, one should not ignore the potential of increased risk in the financial system as a whole. The combination of expanding financial services activity and intensified competition within the single market will tend to increase the level of risk in the financial markets. In practice this may require some levelling up of average prudential standards.

11.6 Conclusion

What lies in store for the financial services industry is, as yet, unclear. What is intended is relatively well defined – a Community-wide free market in financial services with little market segmentation, either geographical or institutional: what will emerge is questionable. One of the critical areas to watch is the authorities' response to potential 'exit' by a financial institution; another is the issue of government ownership of financial institutions. Increased competitive pressures would suggest failure for some financial institutions, yet there is a positive bias in the regulatory framework of European financial activity which is concerned with emergency support for ailing institutions. Given this, ailing institutions, at risk of being out-competed by new entrants, are likely to be protected by the authorities at least for some time. This will result in some over-supply of financial services; but more importantly it raises questions about whether and how the ailing institution should exit the market. One solution lies in domestic merger and takeover activity (which has implications for market concentration); yet another, not mutually exclusive, solution lies in a change of ownership (public sector or foreign financial institutions). In member states where the public sector has dominated the ownership of the financial system (e.g. Italy) governments have made moves to reduce their ownership in the run-up to 1992. However, they may yet find themselves caught up in a wave of protectionism.[11]

What is clear at this stage is that Europe has already witnessed a flurry of link-ups between banks and insurance companies and the start-up of new insurance firms by banks. Two of the most notable cases were the creation of: Deutsche Lebensversicherung in 1989, a life insurance firm, by Deutsche Bank in Germany; and the second-ranked French life insurance company jointly by Crédit Agricole (France's largest bank) and Prédica in 1985. All of this is evidence of firms positioning themselves within the industry for the post-1992 period.

Notes

1. Source: Woolcock *et al.* (1991).
2. Source: Commission of the European Communities, *Labour Force Survey* (1989).
3. The sharp drop in the Japanese stock market since 1989 coupled with Japan's modest economic growth yields a current value for Japan roughly similar to the US figure quoted here.
4. Since it is difficult to compare the volume of trading in the subsectors considered, the composition of the sector is given in terms of GNP share.
5. This expansion follows a period in which there was even more dramatic growth in at least parts of this sector, notably banking which experienced an overall growth rate of 22.5 per cent in the Community as a whole in the preceding decade (CEC, 1988, p. 62).

6. See Molyneux (1990) for an excellent overview of the 'financial revolution'.
7. These distinctions are well defined and expanded upon in Molyneux (1990) and Bisignano (1991).
8. Although nearly 50 per cent of bank assets in Germany are technically in the public sector, they cannot be regarded as under direct control of central government.
9. See Gilibert and Steinherr (1989) for more on this issue.
10. Gardener and Molyneux (1990, p. 40) attribute this suitability to the fact that 'net income measures do not take into account the difficulties associated with bad debts, taxes, different countries' accounting policies, hidden reserves and profit-smoothing techniques'.
11. See Bisignano (1991) for a discussion of questions raised by the new competitive 'banking' environment in Europe.

References

Aaronovitch, Sam and Samson, Peter (1985), *The Insurance Industry in the Countries of the EEC. Structure, Conduct and Performance*, Luxembourg: Office for the Official Publications of the European Communities.

Bailey, Elizabeth E. and Friedlander, Ann F. (1982), 'Market Structure and Multiproduct Industries', *Journal of Economic Literature*, **20**, (3), 1024–48.

Bisignano, Joseph (1991), 'European Financial Deregulation: the Pressures for Change and the Costs of Achievement', in Ian Macfarlane (ed.), *The Deregulation of Financial Intermediaries*, Sydney: Reserve Bank of Australia.

CEC (Commission of the European Communities) (1988), 'Employment in the Banking Sector Today and Some Prospects for 1992', *Social Europe*, 3/88, 62–4.

CEC (Commission of the European Communities) (1990), *Panorama of EC Industry 1990*, Brussels-Luxembourg: Commission of the European Communities.

CEC (Commission of the European Communities) (1991), *Panorama of EC Industry 1991–1992*, Brussels-Luxembourg: Commission of the European Communities.

Dietrich, J. Kimball (1991), 'Consequences of 1992 for Competition in Financial Services: Banking', in C. Wihlborg, M. Fratianni and T.D. Willett (eds), *Financial Regulation and Monetary Arrangements after 1992*, Amsterdam: North-Holland.

Gardener, Edward P.M. and Molyneux, Philip (1990), *Changes in Western European Banking*, London: Unwin Hyman.

Gilbert, R. Alton (1984), 'Bank Market Structure and Competition. A Survey', *Journal of Money, Credit and Banking*, **16**, (4), 617–45.

Gilibert, P.L. and Steinherr, A. (1989), *The Impact of Financial Market Integration on the European Banking Industry* (Cahiers BEI/EIB Papers 8), Luxembourg: European Investment Bank.

Hay, Tony (1990), *A Guide to European Financial Centres*, Cambridge: Woodhead-Faulkner.

Metais, Joel (1990), 'Towards a Restructuring of the International Financial Services Industry: Some Preliminary Empirical and Theoretical Insights', in E.P.M. Gardener (ed.), *The Future of Financial Systems and Services*, London: Macmillan.

Molyneux, Philip (1990), *Directory of European Banking and Financial Associations*, Cambridge: Woodhead-Faulkner.

Price Waterhouse (1988), *The 'Cost of Non-Europe' in Financial Services*, Vol. IX of *Research on the 'Cost of Non-Europe': Basic Findings*, Luxembourg: Commission of the European Communities.

Revell, J.R.S. (1987), *Mergers and the Role of Large Banks* (IEF Research Monograph in Banking and Finance 2), Bangor: Institute of European Finance.

Rybczynski, T. (1988), 'Financial System and Industrial Re-structuring', *National Westminster Review*, August, 3–13.

Woolcock, Stephen, Hodges, Michael and Schreiber, Kristin (1991), *Britain, Germany and 1992: The Limits of Deregulation*, London: Pinter/RIIA.

Further reading

CEC (Commission of the European Communities) (1991), *Panorama of EC Industry 1991–1992*, Brussels-Luxembourg: Commission of the European Communities.
Contemporary overviews of the financial services industry can be found in successive volumes of this EC publication.
Gardener, Edward P.M. (ed.) (1990), *The Future of Financial Systems and Services*, Basingstoke: Macmillan.
Collection of essays contemplating the future of financial services.
Gardener, Edward P.M. and Philip Molyneux (1990), *Changes in Western European Banking*, London: Unwin Hyman.
An outstanding source on European banking.
Gowland, D.H. (1991), 'Financial Policy after 1992', in D.H. Gowland and James, S. (1991), *Economic Policy after 1992*, Aldershot: Dartmouth, pp. 46–72.
Excellent introduction to financial systems post-1992.
Hay, Tony (1990), *A Guide to European Financial Centres*, Cambridge: Woodhead-Faulkner.
Authoritative guide to European financial centres.
Molyneux, Philip (1990), *Director of European Banking and Financial Associations*, Cambridge: Woodhead-Faulkner.
Authoritative guide to European financial centres.

Index